BRITAIN'S HIGHEST PEAKS

THE COMPLETE ILLUSTRATED ROUTE GUIDE

Jeremy Ashcroft

David & Charles

ACKNOWLEDGEMENTS

The preparation of this guide book would have been impossible without the unstinting assistance of many people – I am grateful to them all: Robin Ashcroft, Bob Atkins, Jack Baines, Jane Bennet, Richard Foley, John Gillham, Phil Girvin, Peter Hodgkiss, Trevor Horwood, Phil Iddon, Sheila Iddon, Geoff Langman, Harvey Lloyd, Brenda Morrison, Pia Neumann, David Ogle, Gill Page, Mike Pearson, Simon Richardson, Mike Rudd, Harry Salisbury, Graham Thompson, Paula Velarde, Vivienne Wells. Very special thanks go to Loraine Ashcroft, Harry Ashcroft and Chris Betts.

Jeremy Ashcroft, Mewith, April 1993

A DAVID & CHARLES BOOK

First published 1993
Reprinted 1994

A catalogue record for this book is available from the
British Library

ISBN 0 7153 9987 X

Typeset by Greenshires Icon, Exeter
and printed in Scotland by Bath Press Colourbooks
for David & Charles
Brunel House   Newton Abbot   Devon

CONTENTS

Approaching Broad Crag en route for Scafell Pike

INTRODUCTION	**4**
ENGLAND'S 3000FT MOUNTAINS	**7**
Scafell Pike	8
Scafell	16
Helvellyn	24
Skiddaw	37
SCOTLAND'S 4000FT MOUNTAINS	**46**
Ben Nevis	48
Ben Macdui	60
Braeriach	70
Cairn Toul	80
Cairn Gorm	89
Aonach Beag	98
Aonach Mor	106
Carn Mor Dearg	114
WALES'S 3000FT MOUNTAINS	**120**
Snowdon	121
Carnedd Llewelyn	130
Carnedd Dafydd	138
Glyder Fawr	146
Y Garn	154
Foel-fras	160
Elidir Fawr	167
Tryfan	174
Index of Peaks and Routes	183

Carn Dearg Meadhonach with Pinnacle Ridge on the right

The Glyders from Tryfan

INTRODUCTION

IN THIS BOOK YOU WILL FIND DETAILED all the main routes to the highest peaks of England, Scotland and Wales. Most of the routes are essentially mountain walks though a number of the logical lines of approach cross ground of a more precipitous nature and therefore are classified as scrambles. The information provided is based round a series of relief maps which cover each mountain separately, together with line illustrations, maps, crag diagrams, colour photographs and text. Each route is described in ascent and, where safe, descent. Link routes between adjacent peaks are also described.

The book's large format has the distinct advantage of permitting the inclusion of clear and detailed illustrations. As its size would suggest, this guide is not intended for use on the hill; the aim is rather to provide a flexible approach to route planning. Sufficient information is given to allow various combinations of ascent, descent and links between peaks to be plotted onto Ordnance Survey maps (or similar) so that a selection of routes over your own choice of peak(s), may be compiled.

PEAK SELECTION

The initial idea for this guide book was to select and detail the most significant peaks from England, Scotland and Wales which could be most accurately described as Britain's highest peaks. After much consideration I decided that peaks over 3000ft in England and Wales gave a suitable cross section while Scotland, with its 277 mountains over 3000ft, warranted a higher contour. I therefore chose the 4000ft mark, which isolated a manageable selection of fine peaks.

It is widely accepted that in England there are four 3000ft mountains with four subsidiary tops. Since the new metric mapping eight distinct 4000ft mountains with seven subsidiary tops can be identified in Scotland.* Wales, however, has traditionally claimed fourteen 3000ft peaks (fifteen since the new metric mapping). For the purposes of this book I am following Irvine Butterfield's lead by adopting the same criteria for re-classifying the Welsh 3000ft mountains and tops in his excellent book *The High Mountains of Britain and Ireland* (Diadem Books, 1986): 'To qualify as a separate mountain a "top" must have 250ft of ascent on all sides or, alternatively, must be separated from another mountain by an interval exceeding two miles.'

This gives a total of eight distinct mountains for Wales without the confusing overlap of routes had the full fifteen been detailed.

USING THIS GUIDE

This guide is designed to be used in conjunction with Ordnance Survey maps to aid in the selection of routes up and down Britain's highest peaks. The relevant maps for use on each peak are listed at the beginning of each chapter with the peak introduction. The 1:50000 Landranger series gives a good general coverage but for the more complicated approaches the 1:25000 Outdoor Leisure series is recommended. The nomenclature is derived from the latest Ordnance Survey mapping on general release. Some of the names and spellings on Ordnance Survey maps may differ from those known locally; however, for purposes of cross reference and accurate navigation it was deemed safer to be consistent with the best mapping available at the time of writing.

Near the summit of Ben Nevis with Carn Dearg in the background

Except for Sgor an Lochain Uaine on the northwest side of Cairn Toul, the same criteria applied to the Welsh peaks could be applied to all the mountains in this guide. However, it was considered that Sgor an Lochain Uaine was so close to Cairn Toul as to be part of the same mountain.

The peaks in this guide are broken down into national sections, and then into chapters in order of height. Within each chapter information is provided by a combination of illustrations, photographs and text.

ILLUSTRATIONS

Relief maps: Relief maps drawn in perspective outline the course of each route. Two maps of each peak have been drawn from different view points so that the entire course of each route can be seen.

Panoramas: Simple line drawings of valley heads to highlight the course of routes relative to major named features – some distances are given to provide a rough indication of scale.

Summit plans: Indicate final summit approaches and the location of features around the summit area.

Crag diagrams: Line illustrations generally highlighting the course of routes over ground of a confusing or difficult nature.

Detail illustrations: Simple line illustrations to identify features or structures that either are of interest or are key landmarks along the course of a route.

PHOTOGRAPHS

Colour photographs are used at two levels: first to give an overall impression of each peak so that it can be identified and second to highlight its most attractive features. The majority of these photographs were taken during spells of settled or clear weather and so can be a little misleading – such conditions being the exception rather than the rule on Britain's highest peaks.

ROUTE DESCRIPTIONS

Route title: For ease of cross reference with the maps, illustrations and photographs each route is individually named. Where there is no obvious evidence of a name one has been contrived either from the main feature it ascends or from its general compass direction.

Grades: Each route has been given a broad overall grade: easy, intermediate, strenuous or very strenuous. These relate to how an experienced mountain walker would sum up the type of terrain and the effort expended to cover it in *ideal* conditions. In addition where routes involve scrambling or become winter climbs under snow cover the standard grading system has been used:

Grade 1 scramble: simple route that has difficulties which are short and/or avoidable.

Grade 2 scramble: more sustained difficulties with greater exposure.

Grade 3 scramble: serious routes which are exposed and can involve easy rock climbing.

Grade 1 winter climb: simple snow climb up gullies or buttresses which may carry cornices.

Grade 2 winter climb: more serious route involving minor pitches on snow, ice and rock.

Time: The times listed are for *ascent only* – it is safe to assume that the descent will take a similar time, particularly if you have no prior knowledge of it. A combination of personal experience and Naismith's Rule – 3 miles per hour plus half an hour for every 1000ft of ascent (or 5km per hour plus half an hour for every 300m of ascent) – has been used to calculate the times.

Height gain: The total amount of ascent involved.

Terrain: A brief listing of the typical terrain encountered along the route.

Variation: A description of possible alternative starts, finishes or detours.

Start: Located at the most convenient road head; indicated by name and by a six-figure grid reference (the relevant maps are listed at the beginning of each chapter).

Summary: Brief outline of the route to aid selection.

Ascent: Point-to-point description so that the route can be identified on the relevant Ordnance Survey map.

Descent: Point-to-point description reversing the ascent, although the route may vary slightly to avoid dangerous ground which cannot be seen from above. **If the route has not been described in descent it cannot be recommended as such by the author.**

Steall Waterfall (An Steall), Glen Nevis

MOUNTAIN SAFETY

Mountain walking, scrambling and climbing are potentially very dangerous pursuits and no more so than when carried out amongst Britain's highest peaks. The terrain and weather conditions encountered can vary from easy angled grassland to thousand-foot cliffs and from sweltering sunshine to blizzards of Arctic proportions. It is possible to experience such ranges of terrain and conditions in one day and on one mountain, and it is therefore essential that you have the experience and equipment to deal with them.

For those new to mountaineering it is recommended that they either take a basic course, join a club or enlist the assistance of experienced friends. To start with you should build up to the peaks detailed in this book by attempting hills or mountains that are less demanding.

The potential for accidents is always present and it is important that you take every step to prepare for them. To deal with them on the hill it is important that you carry basic survival

West Wall Traverse into Deep Gill on Scafell – under snow cover most routes become considerably more difficult

and first aid equipment. Apart from normal mountaneering clothing and equipment you should carry the following:

- Map of the relevant area and compass.
- First aid kit.
- Survival bag – 8ft × 4ft (2.4m × 1.2m) 500 gauge polythene bag.
- Whistle – the International Alpine Distress Signal is six blasts followed by a pause of a minute then a repetition; the reply is three blasts.
- Torch – the International Alpine Distress Signal is six flashes followed by a pause of a minute then a repetition; the reply is three flashes.
- Emergency rations.

To help rescue services find you, should you be unable to deal with an accident yourself, you should leave information with a responsible person including the following:

- Name and home address.
- Times of departure and expected arrival.
- Planned route with grid references and basic directions.
- Any possible variations.
- Possible escape routes.
- Details of medical problems.

THE ENVIRONMENT

Britain's highest peaks are amongst the finest examples of mountain wilderness in western Europe and it is the responsibility of every mountain user that they remain so. Compared with the activities of agriculture, industry and commerce, the effect on this sensitive environment by mountaineers is small but nevertheless significant.

When embarking on a trip to the mountains we should carefully consider the environmental consequences of our activities. It should be easy enough to follow simple practices such as taking our waste home, but far harder, for example, not to disturb breeding birds (which may involve a long detour) or to use public transport instead of the more convenient car.

As regular users of the mountain environment mountaineers are in an ideal situation to monitor any abuses of it. If we genuinely wish to ensure the survival of the small amount of wilderness we have then it is important both to minimise our own impact on the environment and to campaign vigorously against its abuse by others.

ACCESS AND RIGHTS OF WAY

Although every care has been taken in the preparation of this guide book the representation of any route in no way constitutes evidence of the existence of public access or a right of way. If in any doubt, either check the Definitive Maps which are held by the appropriate County Councils and National Park Authorities or seek the landowner's permission.

The Scottish Mountaineering Trust in conjunction with the Scottish Landowners' Federation has produced a useful book, *Heading for the Scottish Hills* (ISBN 0-907521-24X), which provides names and contact addresses of landowners. It covers all the Scottish mountains dealt with in this guide. Useful addresses for the English and Welsh peaks are: **Lake District National Park**, National Park Office, Brockhole, Windermere, Cumbria LA23 1LJ and **Snowdonia National Park**, National Park Office, Penrhyndeudraeth, Gwynedd LL48 6LS.

...AND FINALLY

Please remember that mountains can be dangerous places and are ventured onto at your own risk. This book is *not* an instruction manual and neither the author nor the publishers accept any responsibility for any accident, injury, loss or damage sustained while following any of the routes or procedures described.

ENGLAND'S 3000FT MOUNTAINS

ENGLAND HAS FOUR MOUNTAINS that can claim to be separate 3000ft peaks. They all lie within the boundaries of the Lake District National Park and form three separate groupings. Scafell Pike and Scafell are part of the Scafell Massif which lies in the southern fells. Helvellyn, within the eastern fells, lies adjacent to the main Ambleside to Keswick road. Skiddaw lies north of Keswick in the northern fells.

The three distinct groupings of mountains, each with very different terrain, create a wide network of individual routes from easy walks over the grassy flanks of Skiddaw to the hardest grade of scrambling on Scafell's mighty crags.

Scafell Pike from Lord's Rake

SCAFELL PIKE
3206FT (977M)

ILL CRAG
3068FT (935M)

BROAD CRAG
3064FT (934M)

Waterfalls on the River Esk in
Upper Eskdale

SCAFELL PIKE IS ENGLAND'S HIGHEST mountain; it is suitably grand, suitably rocky and suitably inaccessible. At the very heart of the Lake District's central mountain range it lies adjacent to Esk Hause from where all the main valleys radiate. The closest valley to Scafell Pike's summit is Wasdale which lies to the northwest. Next nearest on the south and east side is Eskdale while Borrowdale and Langdale share a watershed to the north and east at Esk Hause.

Summit Hut 100yd (91m) southeast of Scafell Pike's summit cairn. The roofless remains of a simple one-room hut provide shelter and peace away from the main summit. Of similar design and proportions to Sapper's Bothy on Ben Macdui it is likely that this hut was built to accommodate surveyors during the mapping of the Scafell Massif

Scafell Pike's summit cairn
and trig point

Scafell Pike is a distinct domed peak on a high rocky ridge, it shares this main ridge with Ill Crag, Broad Crag and Great End. To the southwest along the same ridge line, but across the deep gap of Mickledore, it is linked to Scafell –

England's second-highest mountain. The length of this ridge is predominantly exposed rock. Each of the individual peaks has its own set of crags and Scafell Pike is no exception: the Wasdale face is occupied by the broken columns and narrow gullies of Pikes Crag while at a slightly lower level on the Eskdale side presiding over the marshy flats of the Great Moss is Esk Buttress.

Each of the approach routes to Scafell Pike has a special quality, none of which could be described as easy. The shortest route, directly up the moraine of Brown Tongue is an unremitting slog which has the advantage of leading to Hollow Stones, a magnificent setting right at the base of Pikes and Scafell Crags. From the north the routes either follow the Corridor Route, which traverses a rough terrace high above the upper reaches of Wasdale, or take the main ridge direct. This can be gained at a number of points, most popularly by Calf Cove; for the more adventurous a combination of Skew Gill and Cust's Gully gives a circuitous but excellent scramble. For those who

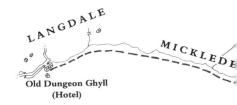

do not mind a bit of a trek there are the wilderness delights of Upper Eskdale. This northerly extension to Eskdale has not been penetrated by roads and has not suffered the agricultural tinkering apparent in other valleys.

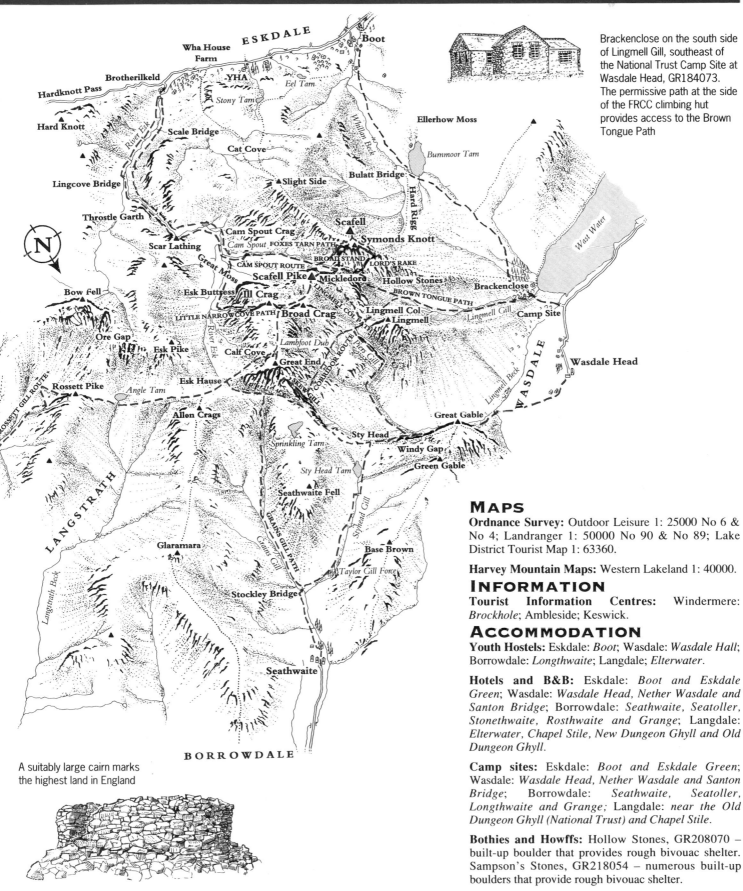

Brackenclose on the south side of Lingmell Gill, southeast of the National Trust Camp Site at Wasdale Head, GR184073. The permissive path at the side of the FRCC climbing hut provides access to the Brown Tongue Path

A suitably large cairn marks the highest land in England

MAPS

Ordnance Survey: Outdoor Leisure 1: 25000 No 6 & No 4; Landranger 1: 50000 No 90 & No 89; Lake District Tourist Map 1: 63360.

Harvey Mountain Maps: Western Lakeland 1: 40000.

INFORMATION

Tourist Information Centres: Windermere: *Brockhole*; Ambleside; Keswick.

ACCOMMODATION

Youth Hostels: Eskdale: *Boot*; Wasdale: *Wasdale Hall*; Borrowdale: *Longthwaite*; Langdale; *Elterwater*.

Hotels and B&B: Eskdale: *Boot and Eskdale Green*; Wasdale: *Wasdale Head, Nether Wasdale and Santon Bridge*; Borrowdale: *Seathwaite, Seatoller, Stonethwaite, Rosthwaite and Grange*; Langdale: *Elterwater, Chapel Stile, New Dungeon Ghyll and Old Dungeon Ghyll*.

Camp sites: Eskdale: *Boot and Eskdale Green*; Wasdale: *Wasdale Head, Nether Wasdale and Santon Bridge*; Borrowdale: *Seathwaite, Seatoller, Longthwaite and Grange*; Langdale: *near the Old Dungeon Ghyll (National Trust) and Chapel Stile*.

Bothies and Howffs: Hollow Stones, GR208070 – built-up boulder that provides rough bivouac shelter. Sampson's Stones, GR218054 – numerous built-up boulders that provide rough bivouac shelter.

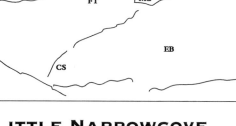

Scafell (**S**) and Scafell Pike (**SP**) from Bow Fell, **SS** Slight Side, **CS** Cam Spout, **FT** Foxes Tarn, **SK** Symonds Knott, **Md** Mickledore, **EB** Esk Buttress

LITTLE NARROWCOVE PATH

Grade: Strenuous
Time: 3 hours
Distance: 5.5 miles (8.9km)
Height Gain: 2900ft (884m)
Terrain: Long valley, boggy moss, rocky gill, scree and rocky summit
Variation: Alternative path to Cam Spout on the west side of the River Esk via Sampson's Stones.
Start: Brotherilkeld, GR212012

Summary: Remote and wild, Little Narrowcove provides a fine route to Scafell Pike. It is reached by an approach along Upper Eskdale and a traverse across the bogs of the Great Moss.

Ascent: Follow the lane towards the farm then take the narrow path alongside the River Esk. Head NE along Upper Eskdale to Lingcove Bridge. Cross it ascending the path N to Scar Lathing veering W onto the Great Moss. Head N to an old wall and follow it alongside the River Esk past Esk Buttress to where the beck issuing from Little Narrowcove enters the river. Ford the Esk and climb the fellside on the southwest side of the beck to a shallow gully which is followed NW into Little Narrowcove proper. Contnue NW up through the cove to the col, then turn L and climb the rocky path SW to Scafell Pike.

Stockley Bridge, 0.75 miles (1.2km) south of Seathwaite, indicates the start of both the Grains Gill Path and the Sty Head bridleway

Descent: Head NE down to the col dropping SE into Little Narrowcove. Near the bottom the path becomes vague and is followed down a shallow gully on the southwest side of the cove. Drop down the fellside then ford the River Esk (difficult in spate) and turn S alongside the river and old wall to Scar Lathing. Follow the path E along the south side of Scar Lathing then head S to drop down to Lingcove Bridge. Cross it and follow the path SW along Upper Eskdale to Brotherilkeld.

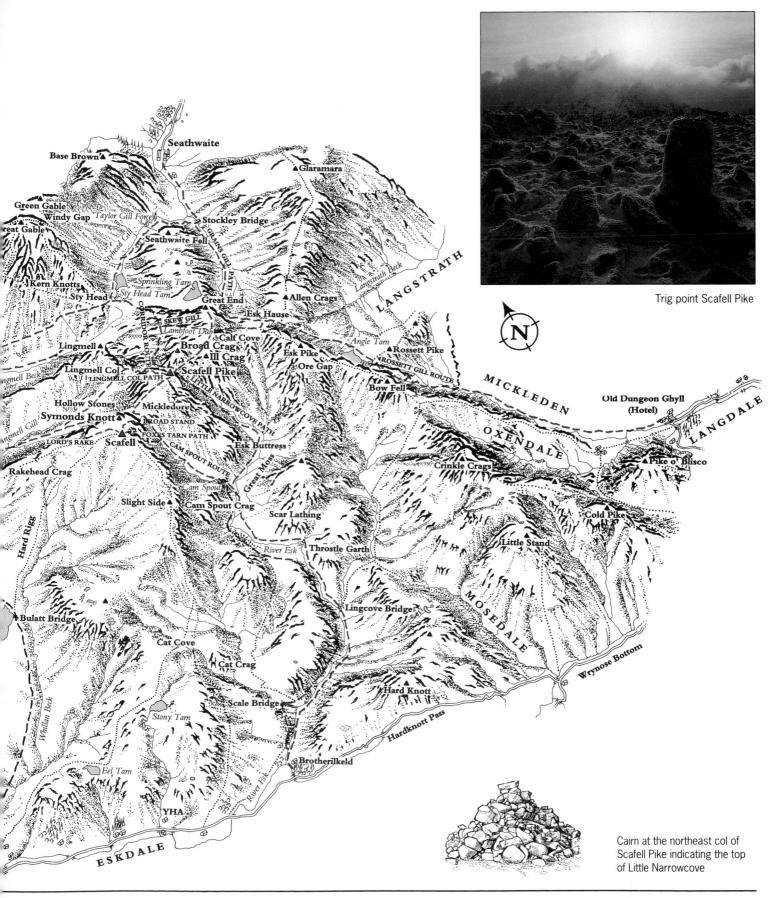

Trig point Scafell Pike

Seathwaite

Base Brown▲

▲Glaramara

Green Gable
Windy Gap   Taylor Gill Force
Great Gable   ▲Stockley Bridge
          Seathwaite Fell
Kern Knotts   Sprinkling Tarn
Sty Head   Sty Head Tarn   Great End   ▲Allen Crags
                    SKEW GILL
          Lambfoot Dub   Esk Hause
                 Calf Cove   Angle Tarn
Lingmell▲   Broad Crag▲   ▲Rossett Pike
          ▲Ill Crag   Esk Pike▲   ROSSETT GILL ROUTE
Lingmell Col ▲Scafell Pike   Ore Gap
     LINGMELL COL PATH   Bow Fell▲   MICKLEDEN
Hollow Stones   Mickledore   Old Dungeon Ghyll
Symonds Knott▲   (Hotel)
          BROAD STAND   OXENDALE
LORD'S RAKE   FOXES TARN PATH   ▲Pike o' Blisco
     ▲Scafell   Esk Buttress   Crinkle Crags
Rakehead Crag   CAM SPOUT ROUTE
                                                    Cold Pike
          Cam Spout   Great Moss
Slight Side▲ Cam Spout Crag   Little Stand
          Scar Lathing
                                              MOSEDALE
                         Throstle Garth
     River Esk

Bulatt Bridge
                    Lingcove Bridge

Cat Cove
     Cat Crag   Wrynose Bottom
                    Hard Knott
Scale Bridge
     Stony Tarn   Hardknott Pass

Eel Tarn   Brotherilkeld
     YHA   River Esk
ESKDALE

LANGSTRATH

Langstrath Beck

LANGDALE

N

Cairn at the northeast col of
Scafell Pike indicating the top
of Little Narrowcove

CAM SPOUT ROUTE

Grade: Strenuous
Time: 3 hours
Distance: 5 miles (8km)
Height Gain: 2900ft (884m)
Terrain: Long valley, boggy moss, rocky gill, scree and rocky summit
Variation: Alternative path to Cam Spout on the west side of the River Esk via Sampson's Stones.
Start: Brotherilkeld, GR212012

Summary: An easy scramble at the side of the spectacular Cam Spout Force is reached by an approach along Upper Eskdale and a traverse across the bogs of the Great Moss. Above Cam Spout Scafell Pike is reached via Mickledore.

Ascent: Follow the lane towards the farm taking the narrow path alongside the River Esk. Head NE along Upper Eskdale to Lingcove Bridge. Cross it and climb the path N to Scar Lathing turning W onto the Great Moss. Head N to an old wall and follow it to where How Beck enters the River Esk. Ford the river (difficult in spate) and head NW to Cam Spout. Climb the rocks on the east side of the waterfall continuing up the gill to Mickledore. At the stretcher box turn R and follow the rough path NE to Scafell Pike.

Descent: Take the rough path SW down to Mickledore turning SE and descend the gill to the top of Cam Spout. Scramble down the northeast side of the waterfall then follow How Beck until it joins the River Esk. Ford the river and then turn S alongside an old wall to Scar Lathing. Follow the path E along the south side of Scar Lathing then head S dropping down to Lingcove Bridge. Cross it and follow the path SW along Upper Eskdale to Brotherilkeld.

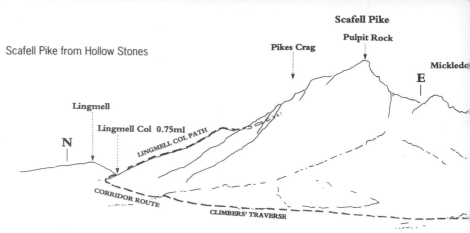

Scafell Pike from Hollow Stones

Esk Pike and Bow Fell from the waterfalls near Heron Crag in Upper Eskdale

Scafell Pike's trig point

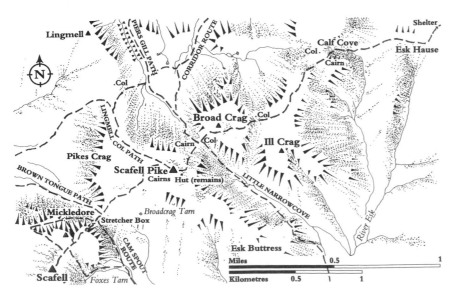

BROWN TONGUE PATH

Grade: Strenuous
Time: 2.5 hours
Distance: 2.5 miles (4km)
Height Gain: 2995ft (913m)
Terrain: Gill, steep moraine, boulders, scree and rocky summit
Variation: A traverse below Pikes Crag from Hollow Stones leads to Lingmell Col which gives direct access to Scafell Pike.
Start: National Trust Camp Site, Wasdale Head, GR181076

Summary: Follows the course of Lingmell Beck then climbs the steep unremitting moraine of Brown Tongue. Hard work, but a fine route with ever-expanding views of Pikes Crag and Scafell Crag.

Ascent: Take the permissive path past Brackenclose then cross Lingmell Gill by the footbridge. On the other side follow the path E alongside the beck to the ford at the foot of Brown Tongue. Cross the ford and climb the steep path up Brown Tongue to the boulders at Hollow Stones. Continue SE up the steep scree to Mickledore. Turn L at the stretcher box and follow the rough path NE to Scafell Pike.

Descent: Take the rough path SW down to Mickledore then turn NW and descend the scree to Hollow Stones. Make the steep descent down Brown Tongue to the ford, cross this and head W on the north side of Lingmell Gill to the footbridge. Cross this and take the permissive path past Brackenclose onto the camp site.

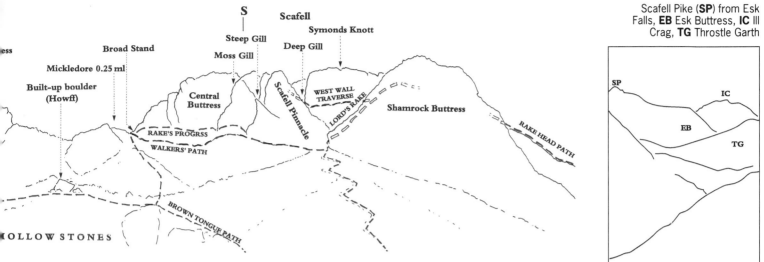

S
Scafell
Steep Gill
Symonds Knott
Moss Gill
Deep Gill
Broad Stand
Mickledore 0.25 ml
Built-up boulder
(Howff)
Central
Buttress
Scafell Pinnacle
WEST WALL
TRAVERSE
LORD'S RAKE
Shamrock Buttress
RAKE'S PROGRSS
WALKERS' PATH
RAKE HEAD PATH
BROWN TONGUE PATH
HOLLOW STONES

Scafell Pike (**SP**) from Esk
Falls, **EB** Esk Buttress, **IC** Ill
Crag, **TG** Throstle Garth

SP
IC
EB
TG

CORRIDOR ROUTE

Grade: Strenuous
Time: 3–3.5 hours
Distance: 4.5 miles (7.2km)
Height Gain: 2851ft (869m)
Terrain: Valley, rocky gill, rough craggy fellside, scree and rocky summit
Variation: Can be gained from Wasdale Head (GR186088) by following either the bridleway to Sty Head or the path alongside Lingmell Beck then on the east side of Piers Gill. The main ridge at a point between Great End and Ill Crag can easily be reached from the Corridor Route via either Greta Gill or Lambfoot Dub.
Start: Seathwaite, GR235121

Summary: Traverses the northwest side of the main Scafell Pike ridge from Sty Head to Lingmell Col then climbs direct to the summit. A particularly fine route taking in some of England's finest mountain scenery.

Ascent: Take the bridleway S to Stockley Bridge, cross it and climb the steep zig-zags W then head SW alongside Styhead Gill to Sty Head Tarn. Turn E at the stretcher box and follow the bridleway a short distance to a fork. Take the R branch and descend onto the Corridor Route which is followed as it climbs steadily SSW to Lingmell Col. Turn L and follow the rough path over scree and boulders SE to Scafell Pike.

Descent: Head NW down the boulders and scree to Lingmell Col and join the Corridor Route which is taken NNE to the Sty Head bridleway. Turn W and follow the bridleway to Sty Head. From Sty Head take the bridleway NE alongside the gill then E down to Stockley Bridge. Cross the bridge and head N to Seathwaite.

This cairn (left) at the head of
Calf Cove marks the start of
the descent to Esk Hause from
the main ridge, GR226080

The stretcher box at Sty Head – a major crossroads for access to the central fells

SKEW GILL AND GREAT END

Grade: Strenuous (Grade 1 and Grade 2 scrambles)
Time: 3 hours
Distance: 4.75 miles (7.6km)
Height Gain: 3021ft (921m)
Terrain: Valley, rocky gill, gullies, rough mountain ridge and rocky summit
Variation: Cust's Gully can be avoided by taking The Band, a broad ridge that climbs the north end of Great End Crag from the top of Skew Gill.
Start: Seathwaite, GR235121

Summary: An adventurous approach to the main Great End to Scafell Pike ridge. Skew Gill, which holds one steep section, gives access to the impressive depths of Cust's Gully capped with its famous chock stone.

Ascent: Take the bridleway S to Stockley Bridge, cross it and climb the steep zig-zags W then head SW alongside Styhead Gill to Sty Head Tarn. Turn E at the stretcher box and follow the bridleway a short distance to a fork. Take the R branch and descend onto the Corridor Route which is followed to Skew Gill. Climb SE up the bed of Skew Gill to the steeper section which is passed on the L and continue to the col. Cross it and descend across Great End Crag to the bottom of Cust's Gully which is climbed direct onto Great End. Descend SE to the head of Calf Cove then join the main ridge path past Ill Crag and Broad Crag to Scafell Pike.

Esk Hause shelter, alongside the Rossett Gill/Sty Head bridleway on the northeast side of Esk Hause, GR234083. A useful landmark for locating the path to Calf Cove

Scafell Pike from Sty Head

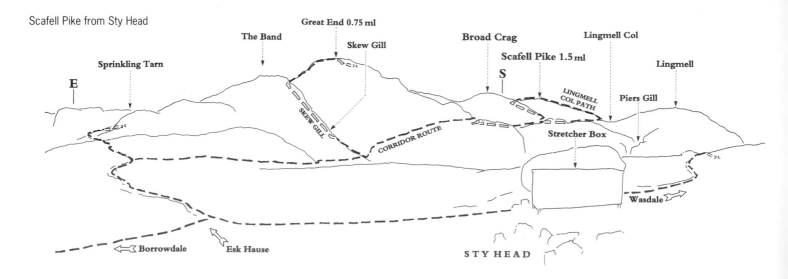

GRAINS GILL

Grade: Intermediate
Time: 2.5 hours
Distance: 4 miles (6.4km)
Height Gain: 2916ft (889m)
Terrain: Steep-sided valley, exposed col, stony cove, rough mountain ridge and rocky summit
Start: Seathwaite, GR235121

Summary: Direct route from Borrowdale to the north end of the Scafell massif via Esk Hause. Useful as a descent route or to avoid the crowds at Sty Head.

Ascent: Take the bridleway S past Stockley Bridge then L up Grains Gill to join the Esk Hause bridleway, turn L and follow it to the shelter near Esk Hause. Turn R and take the path W over Esk Hause and up through Calf Cove. At the top of the cove turn SW and follow the path past Ill Crag and Broad Crag to Scafell Pike.

Descent: Head NE along the main ridge past Broad Crag and Ill Crag to the top of Calf Cove. Drop down through the cove and follow the path to Esk Hause, then turn NE to join the bridleway by the shelter. Follow it NW to the head of Grains Gill which is then descended N past Stockley Bridge to Seathwaite.

FROM LANGDALE VIA ROSSETT GILL

Grade: Strenuous
Time: 3–3.5 hours
Distance: 5.5 miles (8.9km)
Height Gain: 3317ft (1011m)
Terrain: Long valley, steep fellside, rough mountain ridge and rocky summit
Start: Old Dungeon Ghyll Hotel, Langdale, GR285061

Summary: A long but logical route taking in some exceptional mountain scenery.

Ascent: Follow the bridleway at the back of the hotel W then NW the length of Mickleden to a fork after a footbridge. Take the L branch as it climbs the zig-zags alongside Rossett Gill W then NW to Angle Tarn. Pass the tarn and continue NW to the shelter near Esk Hause. Turn L and take the path W over Esk Hause up through Calf Cove. At the top of the cove head SW and follow the path past Ill Crag and Broad Crag to Scafell Pike.

Descent: Head NE along the main ridge past Broad Crag and Ill Crag to the top of Calf Cove. Drop down through the cove and follow the path to Esk Hause, then turn NE to join the bridleway by the shelter. Take the bridleway SE past Angle Tarn and follow it down the zig-zags to the R of Rossett Gill to the head of Mickleden. Follow the bridleway the length of Mickleden to the Old Dungeon Ghyll Hotel.

Scafell Pike from the summit of Great End

Great End Crag from Sprinkling Tarn

Scafell (**S**) and Scafell Pike (**SP**) from Upper Eskdale, **SS** Slight Side, **CSC** Cam Spout Crag, **SL** Scar Lathing, **IC** Ill Crag

Scafell's summit rocks are marked by a scrappy cairn. Many people mistakenly head for the more spectacularly situated but lower cairn on Symonds Knott

SCAFELL
3163FT (964M)

SYMONDS KNOTT
3146FT (959M)

ALTHOUGH NOT AS HIGH AS SCAFELL PIKE, Scafell is by far the more impressive of the two peaks. Its long southern ridge dominates Upper Eskdale and the wilderness of the Great Moss, while Scafell Crag's great north face is one of the most awe-inspiring cliffs in the Lake District. It draws the eye with its steep and complex geometry of dihedrals, blank walls and deep gullies. A mecca for climbers in both summer and winter it has produced routes of particularly high quality. From the very first days of rock climbing, routes have been put up on Scafell Crag which set the standard of the time.

Walkers too can find adventure among the acres of rock of Scafell's north face, for although the cliffs may seem impossibly steep, there are a number of breaks and weaknesses which can be followed without recourse to ropes and belays. Most popular of these is Lord's Rake which follows a diagonal line across the top of Shamrock Buttress. A variant to it is West Wall Traverse which takes an exposed line into the secretive depths of Deep Gill. Infamous rather than famous is Broad Stand, a fierce little scramble which climbs the low rocks at Mickledore – many people have come to grief on this short but problematic section of rock.

The western side of Scafell is unrecognisable as the same mountain, essentially one huge grassy slope, it descends uninterrupted to the bleak moorland plateau occupied by Burnmoor Tarn. The routes up this side are easy but a little monotonous. However, this does not detract from their quality, for although there is little of interest close at hand the views are superb. In the middle distance in the west is the restless prospect of Wast Water tucked behind the screes and crags of Illgill Head while to the south is the wooded softness of Eskdale. Filling the horizon is the Irish Sea – on clear days the mountains of Snowdonia, the Isle of Man and the Solway Firth are all visible.

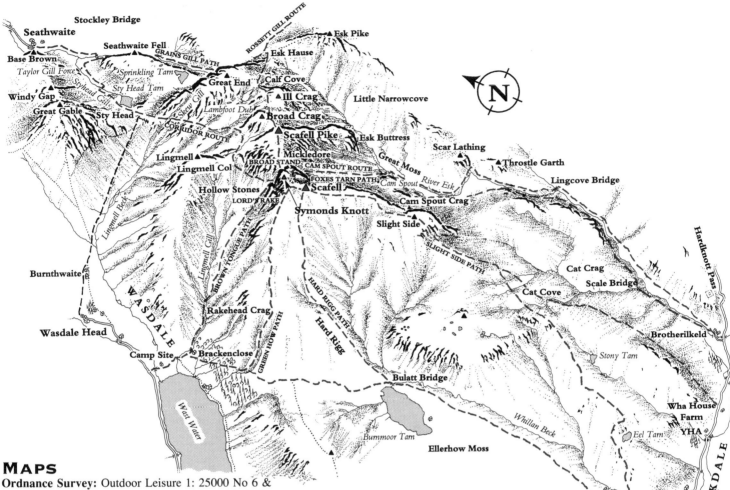

MAPS

Ordnance Survey: Outdoor Leisure 1: 25000 No 6 & No 4; Landranger 1: 50000 No 90 & No 89; Lake District Tourist Map 1: 63360.

Harvey Mountain Maps: Western Lakeland 1: 40000.

INFORMATION

Tourist Information Centres: Windermere: *Brockhole*; Ambleside; Keswick.

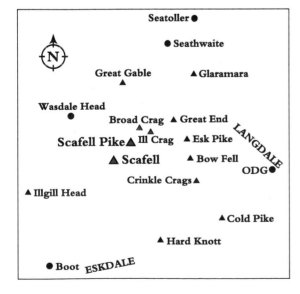

Scafell from the summit of Scafell Pike

ACCOMMODATION (SEE ALSO SCAFELL PIKE)

Youth Hostels: Eskdale: *Boot*; Wasdale; *Wasdale Hall*; Borrowdale: *Longthwaite*; Langdale: *Elterwater*.

Hotels and B&B: Eskdale: *Boot and Eskdale Green*; Wasdale: *Wasdale Head, Nether Wasdale and Santon Bridge*; Borrowdale: *Seathwaite, Seatoller, Stonethwaite, Rosthwaite and Grange*; Langdale: *Elterwater, Chapel Stile, New Dungeon Ghyll and Old Dungeon Ghyll*.

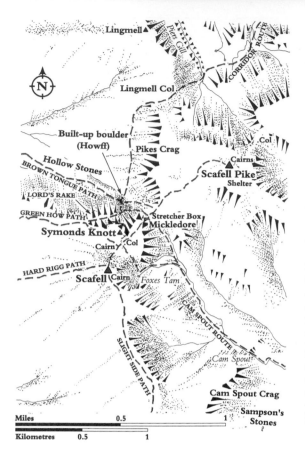

Miles 0.5 1

Kilometres 0.5 1

SLIGHT SIDE PATH

Grade: Intermediate
Time: 3 hours
Distance: 4 miles (6.4km)
Height Gain: 2890ft (881m)
Terrain: Craggy fellside, steep-sided ridge and rocky summit
Variation: Via Eel Tarn and Stony Tarn from Boot, GR176011.
Start: Near Wha House Farm in Eskdale, GR201009

Summary: Slight Side lies on the long southern ridge of Scafell which extends to the craggy broken fells of Eskdale. It provides a direct and straightforward route – useful as a descent route to Eskdale.

Ascent: From the road head NE along the top of the intake wall then N to Catcove Beck. Ford the beck and make the steady climb N across open fell; the gradient steepens as the path skirts the west side of Horn Crag. A short section of scree and rock steps leads NE onto Slight Side. The ridge line becomes more distinct and is followed NNW to Scafell.

Descent: Follow the path SSE from the summit rocks to the rocky knoll of Slight Side. A vague path descends SE through the rocks and is then followed S across fellside to Catcove Beck. Cross the beck and continue S along the path. Amongst the rocky fells the path becomes vague but swings SW to the top of the intake wall and is then followed down to the road.

Lingcove Bridge was originally a packhorse bridge built for the route to Esk Hause. Once across it the path steepens and climbs to Scar Lathing and then onto the Great Moss

Burnmoor Lodge. This old gamekeeper's and fishing lodge lies on the south side of Burnmoor Tarn

Kirk Fell, the Scafell Massif, Esk Pike, Bow Fell and Crinkle Crags from Birker Fell

HARD RIGG PATH

Grade: Intermediate
Time: 3 hours
Distance: 4.25 miles (6.8km)
Height Gain: 2992ft (912m)
Terrain: Open moorland, steep fellside and rocky summit
Variation: From Wasdale Head (National Trust Camp Site, GR182076) via the Burnmoor Tarn bridleway.
Start: Boot, GR176011

Summary: The steep western slopes of Scafell have few features, and of these few the most pronounced is Hard Rigg. This grassy ridge is separated from the fellside by Hardrigg Gill and gives easy access to the summit slopes.

Ascent: Take the Burnmoor Tarn bridleway N to a fork just over Bulatt Bridge. Take the vague R branch which climbs Hard Rigg NNE to a levelling near the top of Hardrigg Gill. The path then swings NE then E and is followed up the steep fellside to the summit rocks of Scafell.

Descent: Head W and descend the scree and grass to a levelling at the top of Hardrigg Gill. Descend the grassy ridge on the northwest side of the gill to Bulatt Bridge. Join the bridleway at Burnmoor Tarn and follow it S to Boot.

Seathwaite

Base Brown▲

Glaramara▲

Gable▲

Windy Gap

Taylor Gill Force

Stockley Bridge

Seathwaite Fell▲

Sprinkled Gill

Sty Head Tarn

Crains Gill

LANGSTRATH

Sprinkling Tarn

Allen Crags▲

Sty Head▲

Skew Gill

Great End▲

Langstrath Beck

Calf Cove

Esk Hause

Angle Tarn

Rossett Pike▲

Lingmell▲

Broad Crag▲

Ill Crag▲

Esk Pike▲

ROSSETT GILL ROUTE

CORRIDOR ROUTE

Scafell Pike▲

Ore Gap

MICKLEDEN

Lingmell Col

Bow Fell▲

Old Dungeon Ghyll
(Hotel)

Il Beck

Symonds Knott

Little Narrowcove

The Band

LANGDALE

Hollow Stones▲

Mickledore

BROAD STAND

Esk Buttress▲

OXENDALE

BROWN TONGUE PATH

LORD'S RAKE

FOXES TARN PATH

Great Moss

Crinkle Crags▲

Pike o' Blisco▲

CAM SPOUT ROUTE

Scafell▲

GREEN HOW PATH

Slight Side▲

Cam Spout

Cam Spout Crag▲

Cold Pike▲

d Rigg

Scar Lathing

Little Stand▲

HARD RIGG PATH

SLIGHT SIDE PATH

River Esk

Throstle Garth

MOSEDALE

Lingcove Bridge

Bulatt Bridge

Wrynose Bottom

Cat Cove

Cat Crag▲

Whillan Beck

Hard Knott▲

Scale Bridge

Stony Tarn

Hardknott Pass

Brotherilkeld

Eel Tarn

River Esk

YHA

Wha House
Farm

ESKDALE

Scafell from the summit of Scafell Pike

N

Scafell Pinnacle from the
head of Deep Gill with Great
Gable in the distance

Foxes Tarn Path cairn, 250yd (229m) NNE from Scafell's summit on a broad stony col, indicates the top of the excellent pitched path down to Foxes Tarn

GREEN HOW PATH

Grade: Intermediate
Time: 2–2.5 hours
Distance: 2.5 miles (4km)
Height Gain: 2949ft (899m)
Terrain: Woodland, steep grassy fellside, scree and rocky summit
Variation: From Boot, Eskdale (GR176011) via the Burnmoor Tarn bridleway.
Start: National Trust Camp Site, Wasdale Head, GR182076

Summary: Scafell's north face extends west from Scafell Crag through Shamrock Buttress and Black Crag then peters out amongst the broken rocks of Rakehead Crag. Running along the top of this long line of crags is the Green How Path which gives a steep direct approach from Wasdale Head – a good descent route.

Ascent: From the camp site take the Burnmoor Tarn bridleway SE then S up through Fence Wood. After the gate turn L on to the bridleway and follow the vague path(s) E up the steep fellside to Green How. Continue climbing E as the path becomes more distinct some way back from the edge of Scafell's north-facing crags. The last section ascends scree to arrive at a col between Scafell and Symonds Knott. Turn R and make the short pull S to Scafell.

Descent: Descend the short distance N to the col between Scafell and Symonds Knott, then turn L and head W down the scree. The path continues to descend W (well back from the edge of Scafell's north-facing crags) to the Burnmoor Tarn bridleway at Fence Wood. Join it and follow it N then NW to the camp site.

BROWN TONGUE PATH

Grade: Strenuous
Time: 2.5 hours
Distance: 2.5 miles (4km)
Height Gain: 2949ft (899m)
Terrain: Gill, steep moraine, boulders, scree, crags and rocky summit
Variation: Scafell Crags can also be climbed via Broad Stand (Grade 3 scramble) at Mickledore, which is approached from Hollow Stones either by the Walkers' Path or Rake's Progress along the base of the crags. On the east side of Mickledore climb through the cleft onto the first platform, then traverse L and climb the wall on smooth but sufficient holds onto the second platform. The wall at the back is climbed and easier ground leads across the top of Mickledore Chimney. A groove on the other side then leads to more easy scrambling to the top of the crag.
Start: National Trust Camp Site, Wasdale Head, GR182076

Summary: Follows the course of Lingmell Gill then climbs the steep unremitting moraine of Brown Tongue. Hard work but a fine route rewarded by the ever-expanding views of Scafell Crag and Pikes Crag.

Ascent: Take the permissive path past Brackenclose then cross Lingmell Gill over the footbridge. Once on the other side follow the path E alongside the beck to the ford at the foot of Brown Tongue. Cross the ford and climb the steep path up Brown Tongue to the boulders at Hollow Stones. Lord's Rake starts S at the top of the scree, follow it first up a loose gully then along a narrow path over two cols to the top of Scafell Crag. Head SE up the final steep and loose slope to a col between Scafell and Symonds Knott. Turn R and make the short pull S to Scafell.

Alternatively West Wall Traverse can be followed, it starts just below the first col of Lord's Rake and follows a very narrow path L into Deep Gill. Once in the bed of Deep Gill climb direct to the top of Scafell Crag then head SW across the col to Scafell.

Descent: Descend the short distance N to the col between Scafell and Symonds Knott, then turn L and head NW skirting the edge of the crags to the head of Lord's Rake. Drop E over the two cols then down the gully and scree to Hollow Stones. Turn W and make the steep descent down Brown Tongue to a ford, cross this and continue W on the north side of Lingmell Gill to the footbridge. Cross this and take the permissive path past Brackenclose onto the camp site.

Broad Stand (right) is the section of Scafell Crag at Mickledore which blocks a direct route between Scafell and Scafell Pike. The rocks are stepped and less than 50ft (15m) high but because of the exposed nature of the ground on either side any attempt to climb them requires utmost care. In wet or icy conditions a rope is highly recommended.
Broad Stand is a Grade 3 scramble; to start it climb through the narrow cleft onto the first platform, then traverse L and climb the wall on smooth but sufficient holds onto the second platform. The wall at the back is climbed and easier ground leads across the top of Mickledore Chimney. A groove on the other side then leads to easier scrambling to the top of the crag – Scafell is a short distance to the southwest.

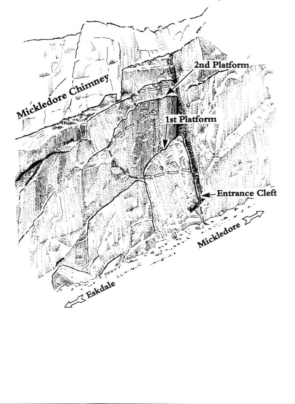

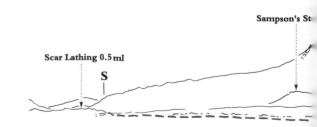

Scafell Pike from the Great Moss in Upper Eskdale

CORRIDOR ROUTE

Grade: Strenuous
Time: 3–3.5 hours
Distance: 5.25 miles (8.4km)
Height Gain: 3035ft (925m)
Terrain: Valley, rocky gill, rough craggy fellside, boulder field, scree, crags and rocky summit
Variation: Can be gained from Wasdale Head (GR186088) by following either the bridleway to Sty Head or the path alongside Lingmell Beck then on the east side of Piers Gill.
Start: Seathwaite, GR235121

Summary: Traverse the northwest side of the main Scafell Pike ridge from Sty Head to Lingmell Col, then skirt under Pikes Crag to Hollow Stones. Particularly fine route taking in some of England's finest mountain scenery.

Ascent: Take the bridleway S to Stockley Bridge, cross it and climb the steep zig-zags W, then head SE alongside Styhead Gill to Sty Head Tarn. Turn E at the stretcher box and follow the bridleway to a fork. Take the R branch and descend onto the Corridor Route which is followed as it climbs steadily SSW to Lingmell Col. Cross the col and traverse S below Pikes Crags to Hollow Stones. Lord's Rake starts at the top of the scree to the S. Follow it first up a loose gully then along a narrow path over two cols to the top of Scafell Crag. Head SE up the final slopes to a col between Scafell and Symonds Knott. Turn R and make the short pull S to Scafell.

Alternatively West Wall Traverse can be followed. It starts just below the first col of Lord's Rake and follows a very narrow path L into Deep Gill. Once in the bed of Deep Gill climb direct to the top of Scafell Crag then head SW across a col to Scafell.

Descent: Descend the short distance N to the col between Scafell and Symonds Knott then turn L and head NW skirting the edge of the crags to the head of Lord's Rake. Drop E over the two cols then down the gully and scree to Hollow Stones. Traverse N below Pikes Crags to Lingmell Col and join the Corridor Route which is taken NNE to the Sty Head bridleway. Turn W and follow the bridleway to Sty Head. From Sty Head take the bridleway NE alongside the gill then E down to Stockley Bridge. Cross the bridge and head N to Seathwaite.

Stretcher box – Mickledore

Scafell with the long ridge of Slight Side descending right to left

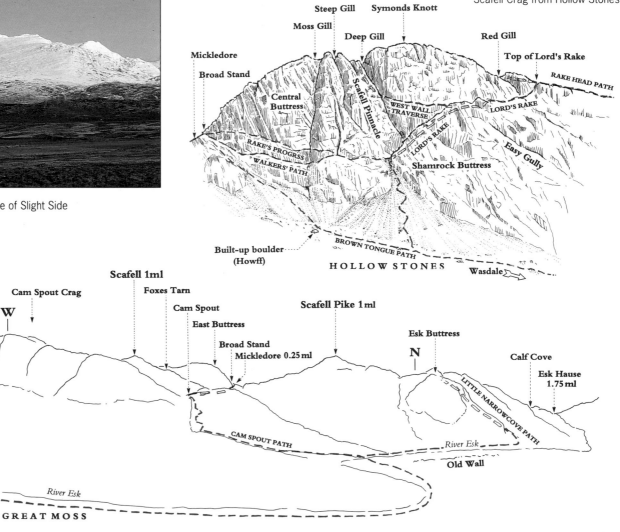

Scafell Crag from Hollow Stones

Scafell Crag from Pikes Crag, **SK** Symonds Knott, **Md** Mickledore, **DG** Deep Gill, **BS** Broad Stand, **SG** Steep Gill, **WWT** West Wall Traverse, **MG** Moss Gill, **RP** Rake's Progress, **LR** Lord's Rake, **SB** Shamrock Buttress, **WP** Walkers' Path, **PC** Pikes Crag, **HS** Hollow Stones

Broad Stand – climbing the difficult wall onto the second platform

FROM LANGDALE VIA ROSSETT GILL

Grade: Very strenuous
Time: 4–4.5 hours
Distance: 6.5 miles (10.5km)
Height Gain: 3727ft (1136m)
Terrain: Long valley, steep fellside, rough mountain ridge, crags and rocky summit
Variation: Can be joined from Seathwaite (GR235121) via Grains Gill.
Start: Old Dungeon Ghyll Hotel, Langdale, GR285061

Summary: A classic expedition. Takes a circuitous but logical route along the length of Mickleden then up Rossett Gill and over Scafell Pike via Esk Hause, Ill Crag and Broad Crag.

Ascent: Follow the bridleway at the back of the hotel W then NW the length of Mickleden to a fork after a footbridge. Take the R branch as it climbs the zig-zags alongside Rossett Gill W then NW to Angle Tarn. Pass the tarn and continue NW to the shelter near Esk Hause. Turn L and take the path W over Esk Hause turning R into Calf Cove. At the top of the cove head SW and follow the path past Ill Crag and Broad Crag to Scafell Pike. Descend SW from the summit cairn to Mickledore – from which there are three possible routes up Scafell Crag.

1. Foxes Tarn Path: Descend the east side of Mickledore skirting around the base of East Buttress to a gully line which leads SW to Foxes Tarn. Behind the tarn take the pitched path NW up the scree to the col between Scafell and Symonds Knott. Turn L and make the short pull to Scafell.

2. Broad Stand (Grade 3 scramble): On the east side of Mickledore climb through the cleft onto the first platform, then traverse L and climb the wall on smooth but sufficient holds onto the second platform. The wall at the back is climbed and easier ground leads across the top of Mickledore Chimney. A groove on the other side then leads to more easy scrambling to the top of the crag. Scafell is a short distance to the SW.

3. Lord's Rake: Traverse W along the base of Scafell Crag by either Rake's Progress or the lower Walkers' Path to the start of Lord's Rake. Follow it first up a loose gully then along a narrow path over two cols to the top of Scafell Crag. Head SE up the final slopes to a col between Scafell and Symonds Knott. Turn R and make the short pull S to Scafell.

Alternatively West Wall Traverse can be followed. It starts just below the first col of Lord's Rake and follows a very narrow path L into Deep Gill. Once in the bed of Deep Gill climb direct to the top of Scafell Crag then head SW across the col to Scafell.

Descent: Mickledore can be gained by two routes.

1. Lord's Rake: Descend the short distance N to the col between Scafell and Symonds Knott then turn L and head NW skirting the edge of the crags to the head of Lord's Rake. Drop E over the two cols then down the gully to join either Rake's Progress or the Walkers' Path, continuing E around the base of Scafell Crag to Mickledore.

2. Foxes Tarn Path: Descend the short distance N to the col between Scafell and Symonds Knott then turn R and drop SE down the pitched path to Foxes Tarn. At the tarn take the steep rocky path NE down the gully, then skirt the bottom of East Buttress and make the steep climb NW up to Mickledore. From Mickledore follow the path NE over Scafell Pike then past Broad Crag and Ill Crag to the top of Calf Cove. Drop down through the cove and follow the path to Esk Hause, then turn NE to join the bridleway by the shelter. Take the bridleway SE past Angle Tarn and follow it down the zig-zags at Rossett Gill to the head of Mickleden. Follow the bridleway the length of Mickleden to the Old Dungeon Ghyll Hotel.

CAM SPOUT ROUTE

Grade: Strenuous
Time: 3 hours
Distance: 5 miles (8km)
Height Gain: 2854ft (870m)
Terrain: Long valley, boggy moss, rocky gill, scree, crags and rocky summit
Variation: Alternative path to Cam Spout on the west side of the River Esk via Sampson's Stones.
Start: Brotherilkeld, GR212012

Footbridge – Lingmell Gill

Summary: An easy scramble at the side of the spectacular Cam Spout Force is reached by an approach along Upper Eskdale and a traverse across the bogs of the Great Moss. Above Cam Spout Scafell can be gained by either Foxes Tarn or Broad Stand.

Ascent: Follow the lane towards the farm then take the narrow path alongside the River Esk. Head NE along Upper Eskdale to Lingcove Bridge. Cross it and climb the path N passing underneath Scar Lathing then W onto the Great Moss. Head N to an old wall and follow it to where How Beck enters the River Esk. Ford the river (difficult in spate) and head NW to Cam Spout. Climb the rocks on the east side of the waterfall then follow the path up the gill. At the scree at the base of East Buttress is the Foxes Tarn Path. Follow it SW up the gully to the tarn, behind which take the pitched path NW up the scree to the col between Scafell and Symonds Knott. Turn L and make the short pull to Scafell

Alternatively continue up the gill to Mickledore to climb Broad Stand (Grade 3 scramble). Just on the east side of Mickledore climb through the cleft onto the first platform, then traverse L and climb the wall on smooth but sufficient holds onto the second platform. The wall at the back is climbed and easier ground leads across the top of Mickledore Chimney. A groove on the other side then leads to more easy scrambling to the top of the crag – Scafell is a short distance to the SW.

Descent: Descend the short distance N to the col between Scafell and Symonds Knott then turn R and drop SE down the pitched path to Foxes Tarn. At the tarn take the steep rocky path NE down the gully, then head SE down the gill to the top of Cam Spout. Scramble down the northeast side of the waterfall then follow How Beck until it joins the River Esk. Ford the river (difficult in spate) and then turn S alongside an old wall passing underneath to Scar Lathing. Follow the path E along the south side of Scar Lathing then head S and drop down to Lingcove Bridge. Cross it and follow the path SW along Upper Eskdale to Brotherilkeld.

The built-up boulder at Hollow Stones affords basic shelter. Two can just about be accommodated lying down, although headroom is limited

Climbers in Nethermost Gully
– on the left side of Striding
Edge where it abuts Helvellyn

HELVELLYN
3117FT (950M)

LOWER MAN
3035FT (925M)

HELVELLYN IS THE HIGHEST PEAK along the long ridge of mountains which runs north from the outskirts of Grasmere to Threlkeld Common just east of Keswick. Thirlmere marks the western boundary while to the east long arêtes and deep coves extend towards the shores of Ullswater.

The main section of the ridge centred around Helvellyn consists of Dollywaggon Pike, Nethermost Pike, Lower Man, Whiteside and Raise. These peaks are so closely linked in terms of both the character of terrain and proximity that any route to Helvellyn's summit inevitably crosses one or more of these satellite tops. The popularity of Helvellyn (perhaps the most climbed mountain in the Lake District) is due to the diversity of routes it offers, the convenience of access and the commanding views it affords.

The western and eastern sides of Helvellyn are as different as the proverbial chalk and cheese. To the west the slopes are generally uniform being wooded below 1700ft and very steep with few features save for fast-flowing becks which feed Thirlmere and the odd grassy hollow. Access is easy from either Wythburn, Thirlspot or Stanah along the main Lakes road the A591.

The eastern side is a different story: its shaded aspect has led to it being more heavily glaciated, creating long steep-sided dales with wild rocky corries at their heads separated by fine narrow ridges. The most famous of these features are Striding Edge and Swirral Edge, combined they make a justifiably popular round. The other routes on this side though should not be ignored; all are interesting throughout and will provide varying degrees of adventure in summer or winter. Patterdale and Glenridding are the start points for Helvellyn's eastern routes.

Although Helvellyn's crags are mostly too broken for rock climbing they do provide excellent winter climbing. The crags around Dollywaggon Cove, Nethermost Cove and those directly below Helvellyn's summit hold some of the most consistent snow-and-ice conditions in the Lake District.

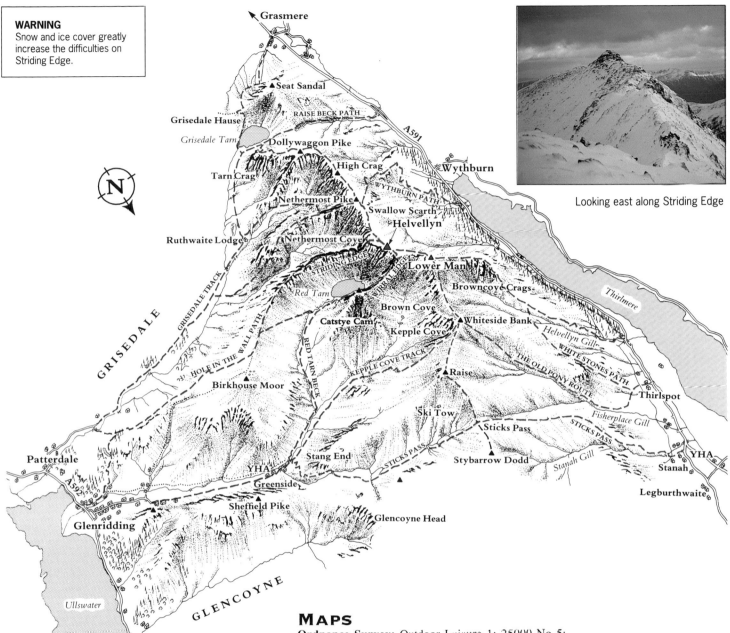

WARNING
Snow and ice cover greatly
increase the difficulties on
Striding Edge.

Grasmere

Seat Sandal

RAISE BECK PATH

Griesdale Hause

Grisedale Tarn

Dollywaggon Pike

High Crag

Tarn Crag

WYTHBURN PATH

Wythburn

Nethermost Pike

Swallow Scarth

Helvellyn

Ruthwaite Lodge

Nethermost Cove

STRIDING EDGE

Lower Man

SWIRRAL EDGE

Red Tarn

Browncove Crags

GRISEDALE TRACK

Brown Cove

GRISEDALE

Whiteside Bank

Helvellyn Gill

Catstye Cam

Kepple Cove

WHITE STONES PATH

HOLE IN THE WALL PATH

KEPPLE COVE TRACK

THE OLD PONY ROUTE

Thirlmere

RED TARN BECK

Raise

Birkhouse Moor

Thirlspot

Ski Tow

Fisherplace Gill

Sticks Pass

STICKS PASS

Stang End

STICKS PASS

Stybarrow Dodd

Stanah Gill

YHA

Stanah

Patterdale

YHA

Greenside

Legburthwaite

Sheffield Pike

Glencoyne Head

Glenridding

Ullswater

GLENCOYNE

Looking east along Striding Edge

Thirlmere from the Wythburn Path

MAPS

Ordnance Survey: Outdoor Leisure 1: 25000 No 5;
Landranger 1: 50000 No 90; Lake District Tourist Map
1: 63360.

Harvey Mountain Maps: Eastern Lakeland 1: 40000.

INFORMATION

Tourist Information Centres: Windermere:
Brockhole; Ambleside; Grasmere; Keswick;
Glenridding.

ACCOMMODATION

Youth Hostels: Grasmere: *Butharlyp How and
Thorney How*; Thirlmere: *Stanah*; Glenridding:
Greenside; Patterdale: *Goldrill House*.

Hotels and B&B: Grasmere; Thirlmere: *Thirlspot*;
Glenridding; Patterdale.

Camp sites: Thirlmere: *Legburthwaite*; Glenridding;
Patterdale.

Helvellyn (**H**) from High Spying How, **NC** Nethermost Cove, **NG** Nethermost Gully, **StE** Striding Edge, **SE** Swirral Edge, **RT** Red Tarn

GRISEDALE HAUSE TRACK

Grade: Intermediate
Time: 2.5–3 hours
Distance: 5 miles (8km)
Height Gain: 3001ft (915m)
Terrain: Broad open gill, bleak tarn, steep loose zig-zags and long summit ridge
Variation: Alternative path alongside Tongue Gill.
Start: Mill Bridge, Grasmere, GR336092

Summary: Attains the south end of the main Helvellyn ridge via Grisedale Hause and Grisedale Tarn. The ascent from Grisedale Tarn is steep and very loose but soon gives way to a pleasant ridge path.

Ascent: Take the narrow lane from the A591 at Mill Bridge NE to the water intake at the foot of Great Tongue. The main track climbs alongside Little Tongue on the northwest side of Great Tongue. Follow this NE then E to Grisedale Hause or alternatively take the path on the southwest side of Great Tongue. From Grisedale Hause drop down to Grisedale Tarn and cross the outlet at the northeast end. After the ford turn W and join the steep zig-zags which climb, on loose scree, NW to Dollywaggon Pike, then follow the good ridge path N to Helvellyn passing Nethermost Pike en route.

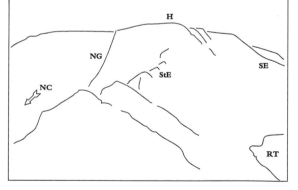

Descent: Follow the main ridge path S until it forks at Swallow Scarth; take the L branch and follow it S to Dollywaggon Pike. From Dollywaggon Pike the path turns SE; continue along it and descend the steep zig-zags to Grisedale Tarn. Cross the outlet at the northeast end of the tarn and climb SW to Grisedale Hause. From the top of the hause continue SW until the track forks. Either take the R branch alongside Little Tongue Gill or take the path on the L alongside Tongue Gill. Both descend to the water intake from where the lane back to Mill Bridge is joined.

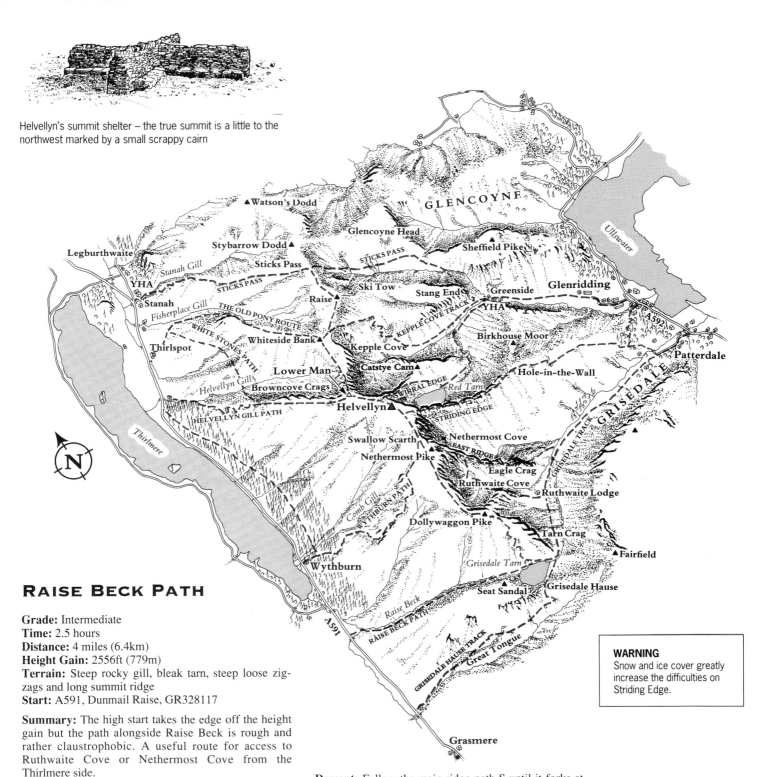

Helvellyn's summit shelter – the true summit is a little to the northwest marked by a small scrappy cairn

RAISE BECK PATH

Grade: Intermediate
Time: 2.5 hours
Distance: 4 miles (6.4km)
Height Gain: 2556ft (779m)
Terrain: Steep rocky gill, bleak tarn, steep loose zig-zags and long summit ridge
Start: A591, Dunmail Raise, GR328117

Summary: The high start takes the edge off the height gain but the path alongside Raise Beck is rough and rather claustrophobic. A useful route for access to Ruthwaite Cove or Nethermost Cove from the Thirlmere side.

Ascent: From the stile at the top of Dunmail Raise head NE a short distance across the fellside to join Raise Beck. Follow the beck on the south side to a low col overlooking Grisedale Tarn. Skirt the tarn on the north side and join the steep zig-zags which climb NW to Dollywaggon Pike, then follow the good ridge path N to Helvellyn.

Descent: Follow the main ridge path S until it forks at Swallow Scarth, take the L branch and follow it S to Dollywaggon Pike. From Dollywaggon Pike the path turns SE. Continue along it and descend the steep zig-zags to Grisedale Tarn. At the tarn turn W and follow the path across the low col to the head of Raise Beck. Join the path on the south side of Raise Beck and follow it down to Dunmail Raise.

WARNING
Snow and ice cover greatly increase the difficulties on Striding Edge.

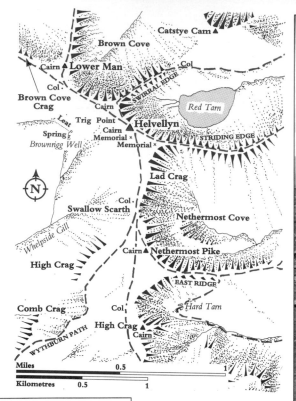

WARNING
Under snow cover considerable cornice build-up occurs at the edge of Helvellyn's east face. This should be taken into account when trying to find the start of Striding Edge and Swirral Edge or when visiting the summit.

Hard Tarn in Ruthwaite Cove

The Hinkler Memorial, 250yd (229m) south from Helvellyn's summit on the main ridge path. It commemorates the successful first landing and take-off by aeroplane on Helvellyn in 1926 by John Leeming and Bert Hinkler in an Avro 585 Gosport

WYTHBURN PATH

Grade: Intermediate
Time: 2 hours
Distance: 2.5 miles (4km)
Height Gain: 2523ft (769m)
Terrain: Rocky open fellside and summit ridge
Start: Car park behind the church at Wythburn, GR324136

Summary: Interesting open route with spectacular views over Thirlmere. Follows a devious line through Comb Crag then traverses the top of High Crag to join the main ridge path at Swallow Scarth.

Ascent: From the car park follow the bridleway steeply E through the plantation to the edge of the trees; then follow it NE into Comb Gill. Before the gill is reached the bridleway turns SE – continue along it as it zig-zags to the top of Comb Crag then traverses NE across the top of High Crag to Swallow Scarth. Join the main ridge path N to Helvellyn.

Descent: Follow the main ridge path S until it forks at Swallow Scarth, take the R fork and follow it SW across the top of High Crag and then NW as it zig-zags down into Comb Gill. Before the beck is reached turn W and follow the bridleway down to the trees and then back down to Wythburn Car Park.

THE OLD PONY ROUTE

Grade: Easy
Time: 2.5 hours
Distance: 3 miles (4.8km)
Height Gain: 2814ft (858m)
Terrain: Steep grass, open fellside and rocky ridge
Start: King's Head, Thirlspot, GR317177

Summary: The original tourist route, follows a pleasant meandering course via Whiteside Bank and the entertaining north ridge of Lower Man. The middle section above Brown Crag is a little indistinct and can be tricky to follow in mist.

Ascent: Take the bridleway behind the King's Head across the aqueduct and then NE to Fisherplace Gill. Ascend the the south side of Fisherplace Gill then follow Brund Gill SE past Brown Crag. The bridleway continues SE to Whiteside Bank across open fellside. The going is easy but its course on the ground is vague. From Whiteside Bank join the main ridge path and follow it S to make the short pull up the north ridge of Lower Man and then SE to Helvellyn.

Descent: Head NW then N along the summit ridge to Lower Man. Descend the rocky north ridge of Lower Man then follow the main path N to Whiteside Bank. From the summit cairn descend NW across open fellside to Brund Gill which is followed past Brown Crag to Fisherplace Gill. At Fisherplace Gill the bridleway becomes clearer and is followed down to the King's Head at Thirlspot.

HELVELLYN GILL PATH

Grade: Intermediate
Time: 2 hours
Distance: 2.25m (3.6km)
Height Gain: 2411ft (735m)
Terrain: Steep stony fellside and summit ridge
Variation: Can also be started from the King's Head at Thirlspot, GR317177, by following the white painted stones NE then SE to Helvellyn Gill.
Start: Highpark Wood Car Park, Thirlmere, GR316168

Summary: Continually steep, the path zig-zags alongside Helvellyn Gill then climbs the scree-covered shoulder of Browncove Crags. It provides the most direct route to Helvellyn's summit and can be followed in most conditions, although because of its exposed nature, it is less easily negotiated in high winds. Browncove Crags hold a number of winter climbs in the easier grades – well worth the short diversion en route.

Ascent: Cross the footbridge over Helvellyn Gill at the back of the car park then follow the path SE alongside the gill to another footbridge. Cross the footbridge, then climb the steep zig-zags to a wall. Through the gate continue climbing to the remains of another wall. From here the path ascends the steep scree-covered shoulder SE directly to Helvellyn's summit.

For access to Browncove Crags ignore the path and skirt E to the base of the climbs.

Descent: Head NW and skirt the south side of Lower Man to a fork, take the L branch and continue NW – this section passes close by top of Browncove Crags which can hold cornices under snow cover. Once past the crags descend the steep scree-covered shoulder and then follow the zig-zags down to the footbridge over Helvellyn Gill. A short section of path leads to another footbridge and Highpark Wood Car Park.

Helvellyn's trig point, just northwest of the true summit right at the edge of the crags

Thirlmere from the top of Comb Crags, Helvellyn

On Striding Edge

STICKS PASS
(FROM STANAH)

Grade: Intermediate
Time: 2.5–3 hours
Distance: 4 miles (6.4km)
Height Gain: 2956ft (901m)
Terrain: Grassy open fellside, broad undulating ridge and rocky ridge
Start: Stanah, GR318189

Summary: Originally a packhorse route, Sticks Pass gains an altitude of 2460ft (750m) giving easy access to the northern end of the main Helvellyn ridge.

Ascent: Take the bridleway E from Stanah and follow it across the aqueduct; then cross over the footbridge onto the south side of Stanah Beck. Continue along the bridleway as it climbs alongside Stanah Beck then swings SE across a broad spur. The route then bears back to the E and climbs directly to the top of the pass. Turn R onto the main ridge path and follow it S over the rocky top of Raise, over Whiteside Bank and up the rocky north ridge of Lower Man. From Lower Man turn SE and follow the bridleway to Helvellyn's summit.

Descent: Head NW then N along the summit ridge to Lower Man. Descend the rocky north ridge of Lower Man then follow the main path N over Whiteside Bank and Raise and then down to the top of Sticks Pass. Turn L and follow the bridleway W over a broad spur then down to Stanah Gill. Continue W on the south side of Stanah Gill down to the road at Stanah.

The buildings at Greenside were once part of a busy lead-mining complex. Most are now run as outdoor pursuits centres and climbing huts

STICKS PASS
(FROM GREENSIDE)

Grade: Intermediate
Time: 3 hours
Distance: 6 miles (9.7km)
Height Gain: 3012ft (918m)
Terrain: Old mine-workings amongst crags, hanging valley, broad undulating ridge and rocky ridge
Start: Glenridding Car Park, GR387169

Summary: Sticks Pass passes through the destruction and waste caused by the mines at Greenside and although dramatic these workings detract from what must have been a particularly beautiful valley. Once past the workings the route greatly improves and climbs pleasantly alongside Sticks Gill onto the main Helvellyn ridge.

Ascent: From Glenridding take the Greenside Road to the old mine-buildings. Pass the buildings to a fork, take the R branch and follow it as it zig-zags N around Stang End to a footbridge. Cross the footbridge and follow the narrow bridleway W alongside Sticks Gill to the top of the pass. Turn L onto the main ridge path and follow it S over the rocky top of Raise, over Whiteside Bank and up the rocky north ridge of Lower Man. From Lower Man turn SE to Helvellyn.

Descent: Head NW to Lower Man. Descend the rocky north ridge of Lower Man, then follow the main path N over Whiteside Bank and Raise and then down to the top of Sticks Pass. Turn R and follow the narrow bridleway E alongside Sticks Gill to a footbridge. Cross this and then descend the zig-zags S around Stang End to Greenside Mines. Pass the buildings and join the Greenside Road which is then followed down to Glenridding.

Red Tarn and Striding Edge

KEPPLE COVE TRACK

Grade: Intermediate
Time: 2.5–3 hours
Distance: 5 miles (8km)
Height Gain: 2874ft (868m)
Terrain: Old mine-workings amongst crags, corrie, grassy fellside and rocky ridge
Start: Glenridding Car Park, GR387169

Summary: Passes beneath the impressive north face of Catstye Cam and then winds its way above Kepple Cove, joining the main Helvellyn ridge at Whiteside Bank. Easy to follow, the route offers a quieter and more remote alternative to the Red Tarn routes.

Ascent: From Glenridding take the Greenside Road to the old mine-buildings, pass the buildings to a fork and take the L branch. Follow the track SW towards Kepple Cove then take the zig-zags NW to a terrace. The terrace skirts W above Kepple Cove; follow it to Whiteside Bank. Turn L onto the main ridge path and follow it S up the rocky north ridge of Lower Man. From Lower Man turn SE to Helvellyn.

Descent: Head NW around the edge to Lower Man. Descend the rocky north ridge of Lower Man, then follow the main path N to Whiteside Bank. Pick up the bridleway that heads NE to a terrace. Follow the terrace E as it skirts the top of Kepple Cove then drops SE down the zig-zags to join the Greenside track. Follow it E to the old mine-buildings, then join Greenside Road, continuing E to Glenridding.

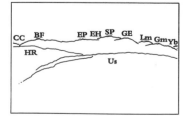

The sunset views from Helvellyn are equally impressive as the famed sunrises, **CC** Crinkle Crags, **HR** High Raise, **BF** Bow Fell, **EP** Esk Pike, **EH** Esk Hause, **SP** Scafell Pike, **Us** Ullscarf, **GE** Great End, **Lm** Lingmell, **Gm** Glaramara, **Yb** Yewbarrow

SWIRRAL EDGE

Grade: Intermediate
Time: 2.5 hours
Distance: 4 miles (6.4km)
Height Gain: 2625ft (800m)
Terrain: Steep valley, rocky corrie and narrow rocky ridge
Start: Glenridding Car Park, GR387169

Summary: Exposed ground on either side makes the steep rocky arête an exciting undertaking. It links Catstye Cam to Helvellyn and is easily gained by a narrow path from the side of Red Tarn. Although its difficulties are never excessive, enough people have come to grief to warrant a degree of caution particularly under snow cover or when visibility is poor.

Ascent: From Glenridding take the Greenside Road to the old mine-buildings. Pass the buildings to a fork and take the L branch. Continue a short distance to a footbridge on the left; cross it to the path on the other side. This is followed SW alongside Glenridding Beck to another footbridge; cross this and continue along the path first S then SW as it climbs to Red Tarn. The Swirral Edge Path traverses the steep fellside on the north side of Red Tarn. Take it to the col and then make the short steep scramble up Swirral Edge onto the summit plateau.

Descent: Locating the correct start of Swirral Edge is critical, the ground on either side of it is very steep and in parts loose. The top is marked by a small cairn at the lip of the crags 150yd (137m) NNW from the trig point. The initial section of Swirral Edge is quite steep but soon eases and leads down to a narrow col from which point the path descends to Red Tarn. Catstye Cam is a short distance E along the ridge. From the outlet of Red Tarn take the path NE then N as it descends to a footbridge. Cross this and follow the path to another footbridge. After crossing this, follow the track (then road) E to Glenridding.

Access to the Red Tarn Path is gained from Greenside via the footbridge over Glenridding Beck at the west end of the mining complex

Helvellyn from Birkhouse Moor

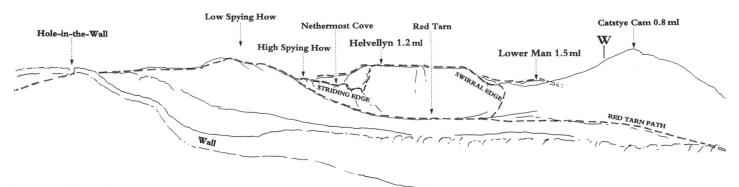

Hole-in-the-Wall · Low Spying How · High Spying How · Nethermost Cove · Helvellyn 1.2 ml · Red Tarn · Lower Man 1.5 ml · Catstye Cam 0.8 ml · STRIDING EDGE · SWIRRAL EDGE · RED TARN PATH · Wall

Sunset on Striding Edge

Swirral Edge cairn, 150yd (137m) northwest of Helvellyn's summit at the edge of the crags, indicates the top of Swirral Edge. It is particularly important to locate this cairn in snow or poor visibility as the ground either side of the correct route is steep and loose

STRIDING EDGE

Grade: Strenuous (Winter – Grade 1)
Time: 2.5 hours
Distance: 3.75 miles (6km)
Height Gain: 2690ft (820m)
Terrain: Woodland, steep fellside and narrow rocky ridge
Variation: From Patterdale, GR391162, via Grisedale.
Start: Glenridding Car Park, GR387169

Summary: Justifiably popular, Striding Edge is one of the Lake District's classic routes. A narrow arête set in a lofty position above Nethermost Cove and Red Tarn. The ridge can be followed either along its crest or more easily via the numerous and slightly lower paths on the Red Tarn side. The trickiest section is a rock chimney and step above the col where the edge abuts the summit crags. Under snow and ice Striding Edge becomes an exciting winter route.

Ascent: From the car park, cross the bridge and take the lane in front of the shops on the south side of Glenridding Beck W to the cottages at Westside. Then follow the path S to Lanty's Tarn. Past the tarn turn R and follow the path W as it traverses steeply up to the Hole-in-the-Wall. Pass through the hole and head SW along the crest of Bleaberry Crags and then W along Striding Edge. At the end of the edge make the steep loose climb up one of the numerous paths onto the summit plateau.

Descent: SE from the summit shelter the Gough Memorial marks the start of the descent to Striding Edge. The descent from the summit crags crosses much loose rock – avoid disturbing this as you drop E to a col. Continue E across Striding Edge then NE across Bleaberry Crags to the Hole-in-the-Wall. The path forks here, take the R branch which traverses E across the fellside down into Grisedale. At the bottom either turn R into Grisedale and then on to Patterdale or carry straight on and swing round to the N for Glenridding via Lanty's Tarn.

Striding Edge

(Left) Dollywaggon Pike, Nethermost Pike and Helvellyn from Fairfield

Striding Edge from Swallow Scarth

The Dixon Memorial. Halfway along Striding Edge on the Nethermost Cove side, a cast-iron memorial plaque commemorates Robert Dixon who fell to his death from Striding Edge whilst hunting in 1858

Ruthwaite Lodge (right) lies below Spout Crag at the entrance to Ruthwaite Cove, GR355135. Originally a shooting lodge, Ruthwaite Lodge is now run as a private climbing hut. The illustration was completed in the summer of 1992 whilst the lodge was being rebuilt after being damaged by fire

NETHERMOST PIKE – EAST RIDGE

Grade: Strenuous
Time: 3–3.5 hours
Distance: 5 miles (8km)
Height Gain: 2634ft (803m)
Terrain: Long valley, remote corrie and narrow rocky ridge
Variation: Via either Eagle Crag (Grade 2 scramble) or Nethermost Beck.
Start: A592, Patterdale, GR391162

Summary: Tucked away at the head of Grisedale between Ruthwaite Cove and Nethermost Cove is the East Ridge of Nethermost Pike. It lacks the pure quality of Striding Edge but this is more than made up for by its truly wild setting. There are three possible starts to the ridge via either Hard Tarn, Nethermostcove Beck or a scramble up Eagle Crag.

Ascent: From the A592 in Patterdale take the narrow lane SW (by the sports field) into Grisedale. Follow the track to join the bridleway. Continue SW past Crossing Plantation to the start of a vague path on the R. For access to the Nethermostcove Beck and Eagle Crag start, take this path W over Grisedale Beck. The Nethermostcove Beck route climbs the easy slopes behind Eagle Crag onto the flat lower section of the ridge. The Eagle Crag scramble climbs the R side of the gully/vein behind the mine-ruin over slabs, then up the steps and flakes, finally working L above the gully/vein to the flat lower section of the ridge. For the Hard Tarn

start ignore the path and continue along the bridleway to Ruthwaite Lodge. Behind the lodge take the vague zig-zags as they climb up into Ruthwaite Cove. Hard Tarn is high on the north side of the cove (hidden by a lip). Climb to it, then traverse NE below the crags onto the East Ridge proper. All three routes climb the top section of the ridge direct onto Nethermost Pike, from which the main Helvellyn ridge path can be joined and followed N to the summit.

GRISEDALE TRACK

Grade: Intermediate
Time: 3–3.5 hours
Distance: 6 miles (9.7km)
Height Gain: 2720ft (829m)
Terrain: Long valley, bleak tarn, steep loose zig-zags and long summit ridge
Start: A592, Patterdale, GR391162

Summary: Grisedale provides a convenient cross-country link between Patterdale and Grasmere via Grisedale Hause. It also gives access to the southern end of the main Helvellyn ridge. The track along it is in good order and allows short work to be made of the distance. A useful approach to Falcon Crag, Tarn Crag and Helvellyn's southern corries.

Ascent: From the A592 in Patterdale take the narrow lane SW (by the sports field) into Grisedale. Follow it and join the bridleway. Continue S passing Ruthwaite Lodge en route to the outlet at Grisedale Tarn. Climb the path past the outlet then turn NW and climb the steep zig-zags to Dollywaggon Pike. Follow the good ridge path N to Helvellyn.

Descent: Follow the main ridge path S until it forks at Swallow Scarth, take the L branch and follow it S to Dollywaggon Pike. From Dollywaggon Pike the path turns SE; continue along it and descend the steep zig-zags to Grisedale Tarn. Head NE past the outlet and follow the bridleway the length of Grisedale to join the road. Continue NE down the road to Patterdale.

Nethermost Pike from Grisedale

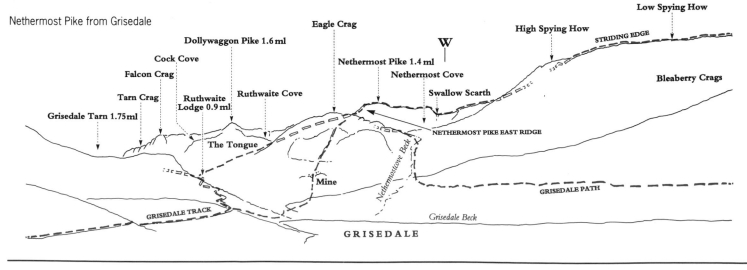

SKIDDAW
3054FT (931M)

SKIDDAW IS VISUALLY THE PERFECT MOUNTAIN. Its form is a simple combination of steep smooth flanks and deep shadowy gills; its slopes are covered with a patchwork of bracken, grass, heather and scree which from hour to hour are in a constant state of flux displaying an infinite variety of hues and tints.

The secret to Skiddaw's symmetry lies in its rocks; they are slates and shales from the Lower Ordovician period which tend to weather and decay in a homogeneous manner producing characteristically uniform terrain. This is of great frustration to climbers and some walkers as it leads to few crags and gives rather monotonous walking.

However, Skiddaw's qualities are more abstract than just the pure terrain. Being in an isolated position, set apart from its neighbours, the unrestricted views from its summit and south side are arguably the best in the Lake District. Across the Vale of Derwent the peaks of the eastern, central, southern and western fells are laid out in a magnificent panorama. For those who love solitude, the northern slopes which run down to the extensive upland valley of the River Caldew afford a wilderness comparable to corners of the Cairngorms or the Northern Pennines.

The most popular route to Skiddaw's exposed and wind-blasted summit is the Jenkin Hill Path. This route was established as a pony route for Victorian tourists and still attracts the greatest number of ascentionists, partly out of habit and partly because it can be started high, from the Latrigg Car Park. In one respect this is a pity as there are far better routes to choose, most notably the crossing of Longside Edge or ascent via Sale How's lonely fells. On the other hand it means that if you are enterprising enough to pick an alternative route you will quite probably have it to yourself.

MAPS

Ordnance Survey: Outdoor Leisure 1: 25000 No 4; Pathfinder 1: 25000 No 576; Landranger 1: 50000 No 90 & No 89; Lake District Tourist Map 1: 63360.

Harvey Mountain Maps: Northern Lakeland 1: 40000.

INFORMATION

Tourist Information Centres: Windermere: *Brockhole*; Keswick.

ACCOMMODATION

Youth Hostels: Keswick: *Station Road*; Skiddaw: *Skiddaw House*.

Hotels and B&B: Keswick; Underscar; Ormathwaite; Millbeck; Braithwaite; Ravenstone; High Side; Threlkeld.

Camp sites: Keswick; Braithwaite; Chapel; Bassenthwaite; Threlkeld.

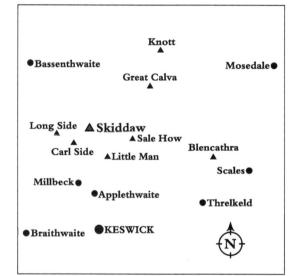

Skiddaw House (below left) lies east of Skiddaw on the flanks of Sale How (GR287291) and provides basic hostel-type accommodation. Formerly a row of shepherds' cottages, Skiddaw House is now run by the YHA. In a very lonely setting, although with good access from Latrigg Car Park or Melbecks

Skiddaw from Surprise View in Borrowdale

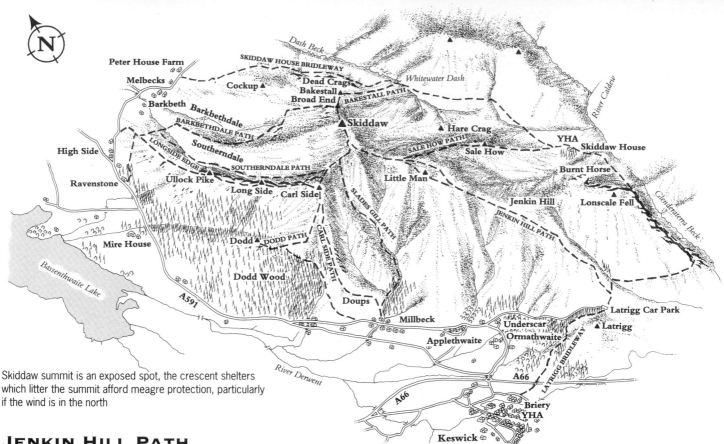

Skiddaw summit is an exposed spot, the crescent shelters which litter the summit afford meagre protection, particularly if the wind is in the north

JENKIN HILL PATH

Grade: Easy
Time: 2 hours
Distance: 3 miles (4.8km)
Height Gain: 2169ft (661m)
Terrain: Steep grassy fellside and stony summit ridge
Variation: Can also be started from Briar Rigg, Keswick GR267242 by taking the bridleway NE around Latrigg to Latrigg Car Park.
Start: Latrigg Car Park, GR281253

Summary: Steep start gives way to a pleasant amble past Little Man then up onto Skiddaw's summit ridge.

Ascent: From Latrigg Car Park follow the fenced bridleway NE then N to a fork. Take the L branch past the Hawell Monument and climb the steep fellside NW towards Jenkin Hill. As Jenkin Hill is approached the bridleway eases considerably; continue along it to a gate. At the gate either pass through it or turn W then NW and make the short diversion to Little Man. The bridleway skirts the northeast side of Little Man and is followed to another gate and up a final climb onto the summit ridge. Turn N and follow the crest to Skiddaw's summit.

Descent: Head S along the summit ridge then turn SE and descend to a fence and gate. Continue SE around the northeast flank of Little Man to another gate. Pass through this gate and follow the bridleway as it descends the steep fellside to the Hawell Monument and onto the intake wall. Join the fenced bridleway and follow this SW back to the car park.

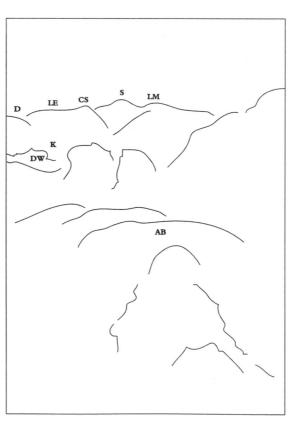

Skiddaw (**S**) from Ashness Bridge (**AB**), **D** Dodd, **DW** Derwent Water, **K** Keswick, **LE** Longside Edge, **CS** Carl Side, **LM** Little Man

Skiddaw from Millbeck

SLADES GILL PATH

Grade: Intermediate
Time: 2 hours
Distance: 2.25 miles (3.6km)
Height Gain: 2644ft (806m)
Terrain: Grassy fellside, steep rocky gill, scree and stony summit ridge
Start: Millbeck, GR256262

Summary: Follows Slades Beck in a deep gill between Carl Side and Skiddaw. The initial section through woodland is particularly pleasant but in misty conditions the gill is oppressive, best left for clear weather when the impressive southern slopes of Skiddaw can be viewed at close quarters.

Ascent: Starts along a narrow lane at Benny Crag. Follow the path N then NW around woodland to the side of Slades Beck. First on the west side of the beck then on the east side follow it N then NW to the flat col between Carl Side and Skiddaw. Turn NE and either climb direct up the scree onto the summit ridge (South Top) or follow the zig-zag. On the ridge follow it N to Skiddaw's summit.

Descent: Head S along the summit ridge; the zig-zag starts at the second saddle (cairn). The steep direct descent starts at the South Top (cairn and low shelter). Descend SW to a flat col between Carl Side and Skiddaw, then turn L at the small cairn and drop down the gill alongside Slades Beck. At the bottom follow the path on the northwest side of the beck past woodland and down to Millbeck.

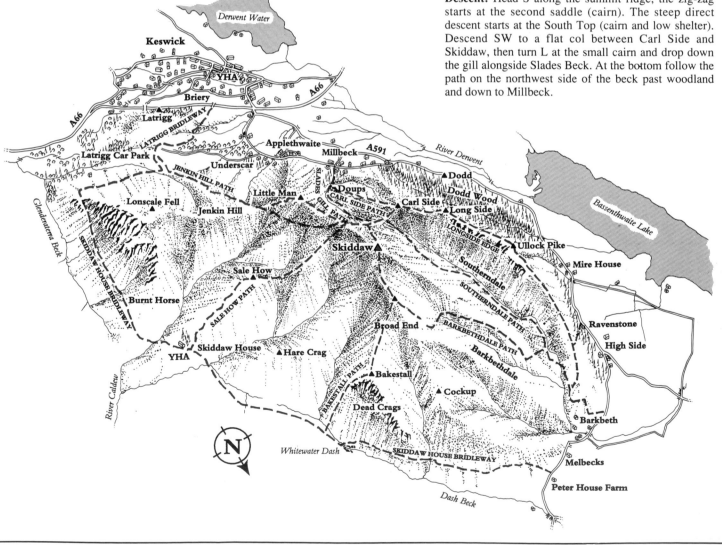

Skiddaw from the pencil factory in Keswick

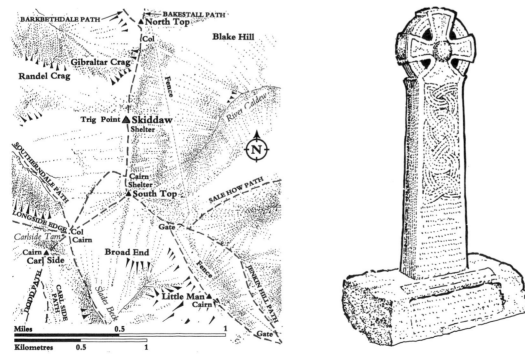

The Hawell Monument – a stone cross inscribed with an epitaph to three shepherds from the same family. Marks the start of the Jenkin Hill Path

CARL SIDE PATH

Grade: Intermediate
Time: 2 hours
Distance: 2.25 miles (3.6km)
Height Gain: 2726ft (831m)
Terrain: Steep fellside, grassy ridge, scree and stony summit ridge
Variation: Via Dodd – starts a short distance W along the road from Millbeck (GR254263). Take the path NW through Lyzzick Wood to the summit of Dodd then backtrack to the col east of Dodd. From the col climb NE up the steep fellside to the Carl Side Path.
Start: Millbeck, GR256262

Summary: Climbs over the subsidiary peak of Carl Side and then onto Skiddaw's South Top. Views from this route are particularly good from and towards Skiddaw.

Ascent: Starts along a narrow lane at Benny Crag. Follow the path N then NW straight up the steep fellside. The path works its way up a series of rock steps then continues up the steep rounded ridge towards the summit of Carl Side. Near the top the path splits; the traverse line on the east side is the easier of the two paths. From Carl Side drop NE down to a col and either climb directly up the scree onto the summit ridge (South Top) or follow the zig-zags. On the ridge follow it N to Skiddaw's summit.

Descent: Head S along the summit ridge; the zig-zag starts at the second saddle (cairn). The steep direct descent starts at the South Top (cairn and low shelter). Descend SW to the flat col, then continuing SW ascend the other side to Carl Side. Turn S and follow the steep broad ridge down to Benny Crag continuing onto the lane at Millbeck.

LONGSIDE EDGE

Grade: Intermediate
Time: 2.5–3 hours
Distance: 3.75 miles (6km)
Height Gain: 2818ft (859m)
Terrain: Long narrow ridge, scree and stony summit ridge
Variations: Instead of crossing Longside Edge, Southerndale can be followed to the col between Carl Side and Skiddaw. Can also be started from Ravenstone, GR235307.
Start: Near High Side, GR236310

Summary: A fine shapely ridge extends north from Carl Side separated from Skiddaw by Southerndale. From a distance the crest of Longside Edge looks deceptively narrow suggesting that there may be some scrambling involved. Closer inspection reveals otherwise; nevertheless still an excellent route.

Ascent: Join the bridleway which leaves the road and zig-zags SE to a fork at the lower end of Southerndale. Take the R branch and follow it S up Ullock Pike then SE across Longside Edge and finally E up Carl Side. From Carl Side drop NE down to the col and either climb direct up the scree onto the summit ridge (South Top) or follow the zig-zag. On the ridge follow it N to Skiddaw's summit.

Descent: Head S along the summit ridge; the zig zag starts at the second saddle (cairn). The steep direct descent starts at the South Top (cairn and low shelter). Descend SW to the flat col then climb the other side SW to Carl Side. Head NW and follow the crest of Longside Edge to Ullock Pike. Drop down the north ridge of Ullock Pike and follow the zig-zags NW to the road near High Side.

Carl Side summit cairn

Direction indicator, near Skiddaw's trig point

(Opposite) Whitewater Dash

Longside Edge from the summit of Skiddaw

BARKBETHDALE PATH

Grade: Easy
Time: 2.5 hours
Distance: 3.75 miles (6km)
Height Gain: 2562ft (781m)
Terrain: Steep grassy valleys, scree and stony summit
Start: Near High Side, GR236310

Summary: Contrived route which climbs by crossing the mouth of Southerndale then traverses around the head of Barkbethdale, finally reaching the North Top of Skiddaw via Broad End.

Ascent: Join the bridleway which leaves the road and zig-zags SE to a fork at the lower end of Southerndale. Take the L branch and follow it SE across Southerndale Beck then E as it winds up the fellside and over the ridge into Barkbethdale. The path then turns SE again, follow it right around the head of Barkbethdale until it climbs N onto Broad End. Amongst the scree the path becomes narrow and vague in places but generally climbs SE to the North Top of Skiddaw from which Skiddaw lies due S.

Descent: Head N to the North Top of Skiddaw then descend NW over scree to pick up the more distinct path on the west side of Broad End. Follow the path N then NW around the head of Barkbethdale then drop SW over the ridge and into Southerndale. Cross Southerndale Beck and head NW down the zig-zags to the road.

BAKESTALL PATH

Grade: Intermediate
Time: 2.5 hours
Distance: 3.5 miles (5.6km)
Height Gain: 2356ft (718m)
Terrain: Steep-sided valley, steep grassy ridge and stony summit
Variation: Via the long bridleway that starts at Latrigg Car Park (GR281254) and skirts around the back of Skiddaw.
Start: Near Peter House Farm, GR249323

Summary: Dead Crags form the impressive northeast face of Bakestall and although steep they are rough and very broken and hold no safe routes. The only alternative is the steep grassy ridge at the southern edge. This climbs directly from Whitewater Dash to the summit of Bakestall from which Skiddaw can be easily gained.

Ascent: Head SE along the Skiddaw House access track to the gate near the top of Whitewater Dash. Turn R and climb SW directly up the steep grassy ridge (Birkett Edge) alongside the fence to the summit of Bakestall. Head S then SE and climb the final slopes to the North Top of Skiddaw from which Skiddaw lies due S.

Descent: Head N to the North Top of Skiddaw then descend NE to Bakestall. Start descending from Bakestall by heading a short distance E to avoid the top of Dead Crags then descend NE alongside the fence to the Skiddaw House access track. Turn L onto the track and follow it NW to the road near Peter House Farm.

Salehow Beck footbridge – on the bridleway 0.25 miles (0.4km) southeast of Skiddaw House

Carrock Fell from the Salehow Beck footbridge

SALE HOW PATH

Grade: Easy
Time: 3 hours
Distance: 5.5 miles (8.9km)
Height Gain: 2188ft (667m)
Terrain: Steep-sided valley, open moorland and steep grassy fellside
Variation: Via the Skiddaw House access road from the road near Peter House Farm, GR249323.
Start: Latrigg Car Park, GR281253

Summary: Climbs to Skiddaw directly over the easy northeastern slopes of Sale How from Skiddaw House. Sale How itself is a little uninteresting but the surrounding hills, collectively known as the Back o' Skidda display a magnificent wild backdrop more reminiscent of the lonely parts of the Cairngorms than the Lake District.

Ascent: From Latrigg Car Park follow the fenced bridleway NE then N to a fork. Take the R branch and follow it N to Whit Beck; ford the beck and turn E along the bridleway. The bridleway then turns N and makes an airy traverse underneath Lonscale Crags to the broad ridge of Burnt Horse. Skirt NW around the ridge to Skiddaw House. From the back of the plantation climb the path WSW over Sale How to the fence on the east side of Skiddaw. At the fence join the main bridleway and follow it through the gate as it heads NW then N along the summit crest to Skiddaw.

Descent: Head S along the summit ridge then turn SE and descend to a fence and gate. Through the gate turn L and follow the broad ridge generally ENE over Sale How and then down the path to Skiddaw House. Join the bridleway and follow it SE to Burnt Horse then S across the steep slopes of Lonscale Fell. Once past the crags the bridleway turns W around the ridge and then S again at Whit Beck and is followed back to the car park at Latrigg.

Whitewater Dash from the bridleway below Dead Crags

Skiddaw's summit trig point

SCOTLAND'S 4000FT MOUNTAINS

SCOTLAND'S EIGHT 4000FT MOUNTAINS lie within two groupings. Ben Nevis, Aonach Beag, Aonach Mor and Carn Mor Dearg in the central highlands east of Fort William. Ben Macdui, Braeriach, Cairn Toul and Cairn Gorm in the Cairngorm Mountains between the River Spey and the River Dee.

Of a far greater altitude and lying at a more northerly latitude, Scotland's highest peaks experience more severe weather conditions than their English and Welsh counterparts. Through most years each of these giants will hold snow cover into the summer months and in some corries and gullies right through the year.

The routes which pass over these eight peaks are generally long and testing, requiring a high degree of experience in anything other than ideal conditions. For those confronting them the reward is some of Europe's finest mountain environment.

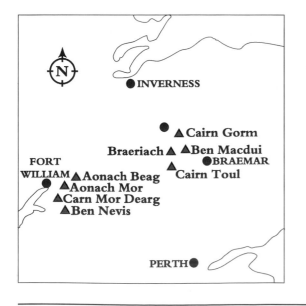

(Above) Aonach Beag viewed from Ben Nevis

(Right) Looking across Coire na Ciste, Ben Nevis

BEN NEVIS
4409FT (1344M)

CARN DEARG
NORTHWEST
4006FT (1221M)

The most striking feature of Ben Nevis, Britain's highest peak, is the steepness of its slopes. They climb directly from sea level to its lofty summit and are not reduced by the height of the surrounding land. The south and east flanks are craggy and cut into by deep gullies and steep-sided corries. The most dramatic side though is the northeast face. It extends for over 1.5 miles (2.4km) in a complex series of buttresses, gullies and ridges. At its highest point it towers more than 2000ft (610m) above the waters of the Allt a' Mhuilinn.

With its great height and exposure to the full fury of Atlantic weather systems Ben Nevis receives considerable and long-lasting snow cover. This provides climbers with reliable conditions for winter climbing making its northeast face Scotland's (and Britain's) premier crag and an internationally renowned forcing ground for snow and ice standards.

Surrounded by precipitous terrain there are few opportunities on Ben Nevis for walking or scrambling; however, those that exist are challenging and in winter potentially hazardous. Of the five main possible routes up Ben Nevis the Pony Track which climbs by the easier angled northwest flank gets the majority of the traffic. It was constructed to service the summit meteorological observatory which operated between 1883 and 1904 – the remains of which are still visible at the summit when not buried by snow – and provides a long but well-graded route. In its time it has seen a wide variety of objects ridden, driven, carried and walked up it – mostly in aid of charity. By contrast the other routes see very little traffic and you can expect to have them to yourself on most occasions.

The Brenva Face of Ben Nevis from the top of the Abseil Posts

MAPS

Ordnance Survey: Outdoor Leisure 1: 25000 No 32 (Mountainmaster of Ben Nevis); Landranger 1: 50000 No 41; Tourist Map 1: 63360 Ben Nevis and Glen Coe.

INFORMATION

Tourist Information Centre: Fort William.

ACCOMMODATION

Youth Hostels: Glen Nevis.

Hotels and B&B: Fort William and Glen Nevis.

Camp sites: Glen Nevis and Camaghael.

Bothies and Howffs: There are shelters on the summit of Ben Nevis (GR167713), on Carn Dearg Northwest (GR158719) and in Coire Leis (GR173714), but they are for emergencies and should not be used for planned overnight stays. The CIC Hut (GR168722) alongside the Allt a' Mhuilinn and the Steall Hut (GR178684) in Glen Nevis are locked private huts and need to be booked through either the Scottish Mountaineering Club or the British Mountaineering Council.

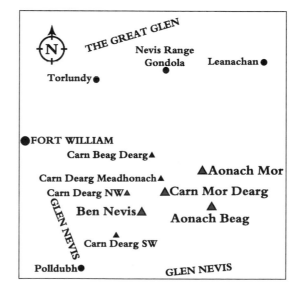

Water intake – part of the Lochaber Water Power Scheme

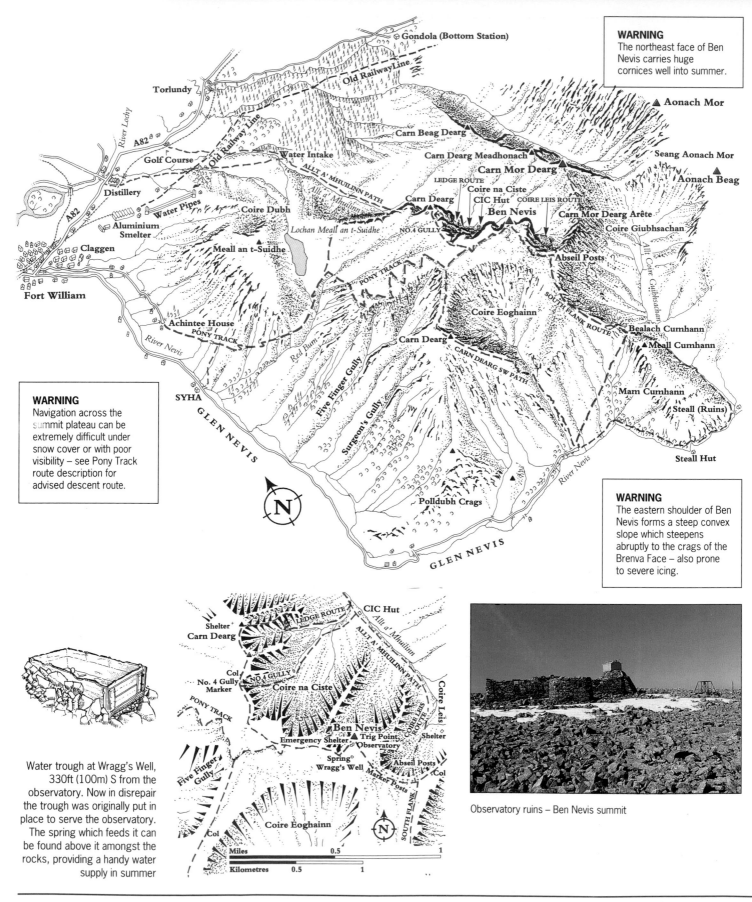

Gondola (Bottom Station)

Torlundy

Old Railway Line

▲ Aonach Mor

River Lochy

A82

Carn Beag Dearg ▲

Old Railway Line

Seang Aonach Mor

Golf Course

Water Intake

Carn Dearg Meadhonach ▲

ALLT A' MHUILINN PATH

Carn Mor Dearg

Aonach Beag ▲

Distillery

Allt a' Mhuilinn

LEDGE ROUTE

Coire na Ciste

Carn Dearg ▲

CIC Hut

COIRE LEIS ROUTE

Water Pipes

Coire Dubh

Ben Nevis ▲

Carn Mor Dearg Arête

Aluminium Smelter

Lochan Meall an t-Suidhe

NO.4 GULLY

Coire Giubhsachan

Claggen

Meall an t-Suidhe ▲

Abseil Posts

Allt Coire Giubhsachan

Fort William

PONY TRACK

SOUTH FLANK ROUTE

Coire Eoghainn

Bealach Cumhann

Achintee House

Meall Cumhann ▲

PONY TRACK

River Nevis

Carn Dearg ▲

CARN DEARG SW PATH

Mam Cumhann

SYHA

Five Finger Gully

Steall (Ruins)

GLEN NEVIS

Red Burn

Surgeon's Gully

Steall Hut

River Nevis

N

Polldubh Crags

GLEN NEVIS

Water trough at Wragg's Well, 330ft (100m) S from the observatory. Now in disrepair the trough was originally put in place to serve the observatory. The spring which feeds it can be found above it amongst the rocks, providing a handy water supply in summer

CIC Hut

Shelter

Carn Dearg

LEDGE ROUTE

ALLT A' MHUILINN PATH

Coire Leis

Col
No. 4 Gully Marker

NO. 4 GULLY

Coire na Ciste

COIRE LEIS ROUTE

PONY TRACK

Ben Nevis ▲

Shelter

Emergency Shelter

Trig Point

Observatory

Five Finger Gully

Spring

Abseil Posts

Wragg's Well

Col

Marker Posts

Coire Eoghainn

SOUTH FLANK

Col

N

| Miles | 0.5 | 1 |
| Kilometres | 0.5 | 1 |

Observatory ruins – Ben Nevis summit

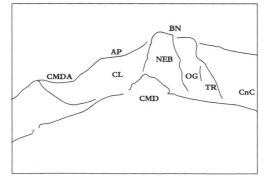

Ben Nevis (**BN**) from Carn Mor Dearg (**CMD**), **CMDA** Carn Mor Dearg Arête, **AP** Abseil Posts, **CL** Coire Leis, **NEB** Northeast Buttress, **OG** Observatory Gully, **TR** Tower Ridge, **CnC** Coire na Ciste

Former direction indicator, Ben Nevis summit

SOUTH FLANK ROUTE

Grade: Very strenuous
Time: 2.5–3 hours
Distance: 2.25 miles (3.6km)
Height Gain: 3950ft (1204m)
Terrain: Steep grassy slope, rock outcrops, steep boulders and scree
Variation: Bealach Cumhann can also be gained from Steall via the lower reaches of Coire Giubhsachan.
Start: Glen Nevis Car Park, GR167692

Summary: The South Flank of Ben Nevis is very steep and a little monotonous but it does provide the shortest approach.

Ascent: From the car park traverse NE up to the Bealach Cumhann. From the Bealach climb the ridge NW then NNE past the top of Sloc nan Uan to the sign at the top of the Abseil Posts (the start of the Carn Mor Dearg Arête). Turn L and climb the steep path by the marker posts which swings NW onto the summit plateau.

Descent: Descend SE then E by the marker post path to the Abseil Posts at the head of Coire Leis. From the sign at the top of the posts descend steeply SSW to the head of Sloc nan Uan then SE down the steep ridge to Bealach Cumhann. In poor visibility and under snow cover this route cannot be recommended as a descent route.

(Opposite) Northeast Buttress, Minus Face, Orion Face, Observatory Gully and the Douglas Boulder from the CIC Hut

Ben Nevis from Carn Dearg (Northwest)

Peace Cairn – Ben Nevis summit

Summit cairn, Carn Dearg
Southwest (Ben Nevis)

CARN DEARG
(SOUTHWEST) PATH

Grade: Very strenuous
Time: 3 hours
Distance: 2.75 miles (4.4km)
Height Gain: 4064ft (1239m)
Terrain: Steep grassy slope, rocky corrie, narrow ridges, scree and exposed summit plateau
Start: Glen Nevis Car Park, GR167692

Summary: Coire Eoghainn on the south side of Ben Nevis is bounded by the minor peak Carn Dearg (Southwest). Its east ridge and the ridge linking it with Ben Nevis set high above Glen Nevis with expansive views makes it a superb route.

Ascent: From the car park climb the steep path on the east side of the Allt Coire Eoghainn into Coire Eoghainn. Head W to climb the steep slopes onto the east ridge of Carn Dearg. From the cairn on Carn Dearg head NNW along the ridge to the col. Cross the col then turn NE and climb the broad ridge to join the Pony Track. Turn E and follow the Pony Track to the summit of Ben Nevis (taking care to avoid the heads of Tower Gully and Gardyloo Gully).

Descent: Descend the Pony Track W (taking care to avoid the heads of Gardyloo Gully and Tower Gully) to the big bend at the head of Five Finger Gully. Descend the broad ridge first S then SW to the col on the north side of Carn Dearg. Cross the col and climb easily SSE to Carn Dearg. From the summit cairn descend the narrow ridge E then the steep slopes NE into Coire Eoghainn. From the corrie descend the path on the east side of the Allt Coire Eoghainn to the car park.

Tower Ridge and Northeast Buttress from the large perched boulder on Ledge Route

The summit of Ben Nevis from the top of the Trident Buttresses

PONY TRACK

Grade: Intermediate
Time: 3 hours
Distance: 4.75 miles (7.6km)
Height Gain: 4347ft (1325m)
Terrain: Rocky slopes, moorland, steep expansive slopes, boulder fields and exposed summit plateau
Start: Youth Hostel, Glen Nevis, GR128718, or Achintee House, Glen Nevis, GR126729

Summary: Constructed to service the summit meteorological observatory which opened in 1883 the Pony Track remains almost wholly intact. It traverses the southwest side of Meall an t-Suidhe, then zig-zags the broad west slopes of Ben Nevis to the summit plateau. In summer its course is easy to follow but once the winter snows arrive much of it is obliterated. The hazards in winter on the Pony Track are not as obvious as on Ben Nevis's other routes; for this reason walkers and climbers regularly get into difficulty on it. The problems encountered en route include the cornices at the head of Gardyloo Gully and Tower Gully, mistaken descent into Five Finger Gully and crossing the top of the Red Burn. Despite all these problems, the Pony Track is still the safest route to take in winter.

Ascent: Cross the River Nevis by the footbridge opposite the youth hostel then climb the steep path NE to join the Pony Track. Turn R onto it and follow it along the terrace first SE then NE to the moorland at the south end of Lochan Meall an t-Suidhe. At the cairn head S and cross the top of Red Burn (in winter this can involve a short section of steep snow). Once past the Red Burn the Pony Track zig-zags ESE between Coire na h-Urchaire and the top of Five Finger Gully onto the summit plateau. Turn E across the plateau to the summit taking care to avoid the edge of the northeast face and the heads of Tower and Gardyloo Gullies.

Descent: Head W from the summit avoiding the heads of Gardyloo and Tower Gullies then descend the zig-zags down the broad slopes between Five Finger Gully and Coire na h-Urchaire. Cross the Red Burn and head N to the cairn overlooking Lochan Meall an t-Suidhe. Turn L and head SW then NW down the terrace to the top of the youth hostel path. Descend it SW and cross the River Nevis by the footbridge to the Glen Nevis road.

Clearing the summit plateau in winter or in poor visibility is particularly hazardous. The recommended route is:

1. From the summit trig point follow a bearing of 231° (grid) for 164yd (150m).

2. Then turn to a bearing of 281° (grid). This will take you to the Pony Track 109yd (100m) N of the top of Five Finger Gully. (*Note:* magnetic N decreases by 1° every six years.)

Emergency shelter, Carn Dearg Northwest – on the west side of Carn Dearg's summit, GR158719 (an identical shelter is located in Coire Leis, GR174713). Holds eight (seated). Of dubious value, there has been debate about the removal of such shelters

LEDGE ROUTE

Grade: Strenuous (Grade 1 scramble; Grade 2 winter climb)
Time: 3.5–4 hours
Distance: 5.5miles (8.8km)
Height Gain: 4383ft (1336m)
Terrain: Woodland, moorland, craggy glen, rock slabs, scree, rock buttress, narrow rocky ridge and exposed summit plateau
Variation: No. 4 Gully provides a slightly easier (but loose) alternative out of Coire na Ciste although it is not often snow free – under full snow cover it is a Grade 1 winter climb and usually carries a cornice. The Allt a' Mhuilinn can also be gained from Glen Nevis, first along the Pony Track then via the path along the east side of Lochan Meall an t-Suidhe.
Start: A82, Distillery, GR126757, or A82, Golf Course, GR136762

Summary: The northeast face of Ben Nevis extends for 1.5 miles (2.4km) in a complex series of corries and ridges high above the Allt a' Mhuilinn. The first most striking feature is the Great Buttress of Carn Dearg. The Ledge Route climbs a devious meandering line up its south side (No. 5 Gully Buttress) to the top of the Great Buttress, then follows the crest of the superb connecting ridge to Carn Dearg (Northwest). Snow regularly lies through summer in No. 5 Gully (the approach route), in which circumstances an ice axe is recommended.

Negotiating the snow in No. 5 Gully at the start of Ledge Route – considerable quantities remain well into the summer

Ascent: From the A82 gain the water intake on the Allt a' Mhuilinn via the path from either the Distillery or the Golf Course. Head up the Allt a' Mhuilinn on the northeast side to the CIC Hut. Cross the Allt a' Mhuilinn and climb WSW up the slabs and scree to the foot of the Great Buttress of Carn Dearg. Continue WSW up the south side of the buttress into No. 5 Gully. Climb the gully to the ramp (third from the entrance of the gully) on the R. Ascend it across a slab then around the ledge to a gully/groove system. Climb this as it trends L to gain another ledge. Turn R along this ledge and follow it to a platform (large perched boulder). From here gain the crest of the ridge and follow it as it winds its way W to Carn Dearg. From Carn Dearg skirt S around the edge of the crags to join the Pony Track which is then followed E to the summit of Ben Nevis.

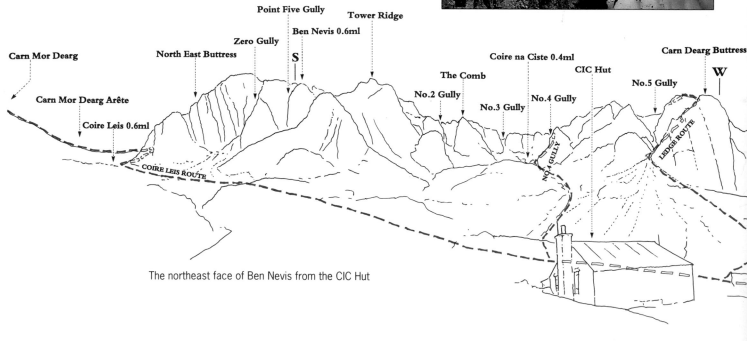

The northeast face of Ben Nevis from the CIC Hut

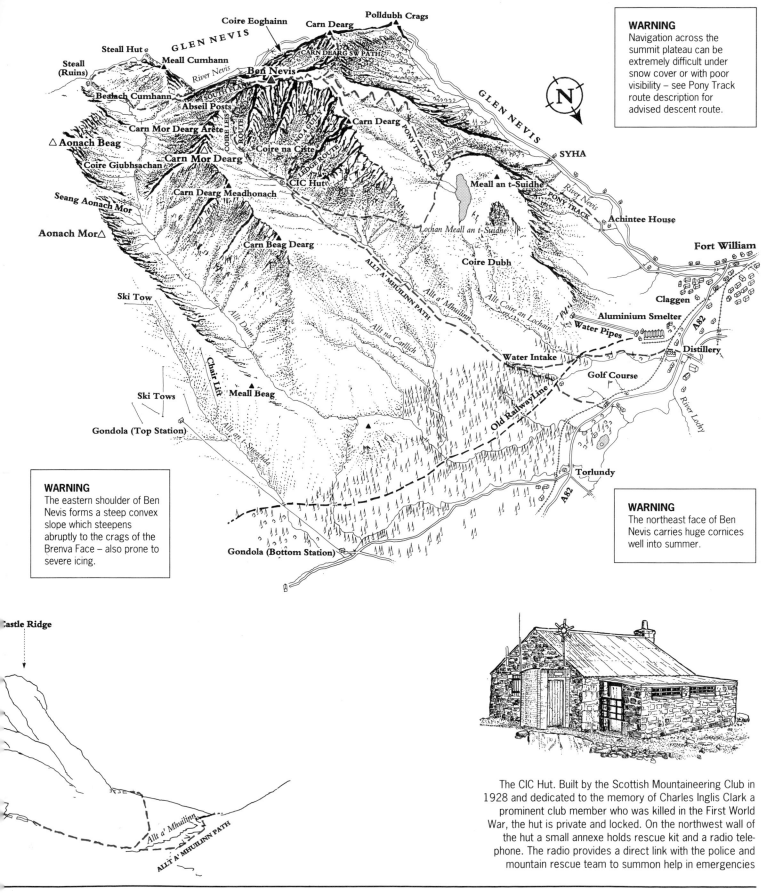

Polldubh Crags
Coire Eoghainn
Carn Dearg
GLEN NEVIS
Steall Hut
Steall (Ruins)
Meall Cumhann
CARN DEARG SW PATH
Ben Nevis
River Nevis
Bealach Cumhann
Abseil Posts
SOUTH
Carn Mor Dearg Arête
△ Aonach Beag
Coire Giubhsachan
Coire na Ciste
Carn Mor Dearg
CIC Hut
Carn Dearg Meadhonach
Seang Aonach Mor
Aonach Mor △
Carn Beag Dearg
Ski Tow
Coire Dubh
Chair Lift
Meall Beag
Ski Tows
Gondola (Top Station)
Gondola (Bottom Station)

Carn Dearg
GLEN NEVIS
SYHA
Meall an t-Suidhe
PONY TRACK
Achintee House
Fort William
Claggen
Lochan Meall an t-Suidhe
Aluminium Smelter
Water Pipes
Water Intake
Distillery
Golf Course
Old Railway Line
River Lochy
Torlundy
A82

CARN DEARG PONY TRACK
COIRE LEIS
LEDGE ROUTE
NO4 GULLY
Red Burn
ALLT A' MHUILINN PATH
Allt a' Mhuilinn
Allt Coire an Lochain
Allt na Carlich
Allt Daim
Allt an t-Sneachda

Castle Ridge
Allt a' Mhuilinn
ALLT A' MHUILINN PATH

The CIC Hut. Built by the Scottish Mountaineering Club in 1928 and dedicated to the memory of Charles Inglis Clark a prominent club member who was killed in the First World War, the hut is private and locked. On the northwest wall of the hut a small annexe holds rescue kit and a radio telephone. The radio provides a direct link with the police and mountain rescue team to summon help in emergencies

COIRE LEIS ROUTE

Grade: Strenuous (Grade 1 winter climb)
Time: 4 hours
Distance: 5.25 miles (8.4km)
Height Gain: 4383ft (1336m)
Terrain: Woodland, moorland, craggy glen, rough scree-filled corrie, steep head wall, boulder-strewn ridge and exposed summit plateau
Variation: The Allt a' Mhuilinn can also be gained from Glen Nevis, first along the Pony Track then via the path along the east side of Lochan Meall an t-Suidhe.
Start: A82, Distillery, GR126757, or A82, Golf Course, GR136762

Summary: Follows the course of the Allt a' Mhuilinn then climbs the head wall of Coire Leis (close by the Abseil Posts) onto the southeast shoulder of Ben Nevis. An ideal route to view the entire northeast face at close quarters. The head wall of Coire Leis holds a considerable quantity of snow into the summer months – in winter it is prone to avalanche and very severe icing.

Ascent: From the A82 gain the water intake on the Allt a' Mhuilinn via the path from either the Distillery or the Golf Course. Head up the Allt a' Mhuilinn on the northeast side to the CIC Hut then cross it and follow it up into Coire Leis. Head SW through the corrie then turn S and ascend the head wall. The best line is slightly W of the Abseil Posts to the col at the start of the Carn Mor Dearg Arête. Turn R and climb the steep path by the marker posts which swings NW onto the summit plateau.

Descent: Descend SE then E by the marker post path to the Abseil Posts at the head of Coire Leis. From the sign at the top of the posts descend steeply N into Coire Leis (best line lies slightly W of the posts), then follow the southwest side of the Allt a' Mhuilinn NW down to the CIC Hut. Once past the hut join the path on the northeast side and descend to the intake. Cross the Allt a' Mhuilinn again and take either the Distillery path or the Golf Course path down to the A82. In poor visibility or under snow cover this route cannot be recommended as a descent route.

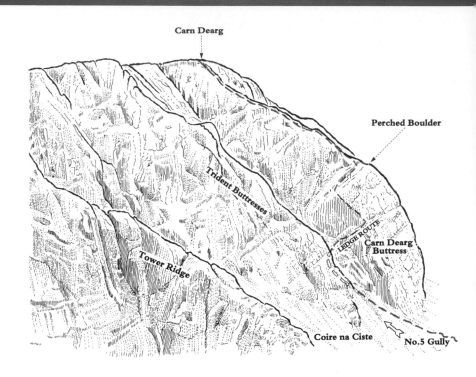

The remains of the meteorological observatory with new emergency shelter in position on top of the tower (during construction, summer 1992). The shelter contains rescue kit and is strictly for emergency use only – no overnight stays in it should be planned. In winter, snow usually covers the remains of the observatory to the top of the tower

The Carn Mor Dearg Arête and the Brenva Face

CARN MOR DEARG ARÊTE

Grade: Strenuous (Grade 1 winter climb)
Time: 1–1.5 hours
Distance: 1.5 miles (2.4km)
Height Gain: 531ft (162m)
Terrain: Steep boulder-strewn ridge and rocky arête
Start: Ben Nevis, GR167713

Summary: One of the finest ridges in Britain though more for the setting than the actual route.

Route: Descend SE then E by the marker post path to the Abseil Posts at the head of Coire Leis. This is the start of the Carn Mor Dearg Arête. Follow its crest NE then climb it N direct to the summit of Carn Mor Dearg. In poor visibility or with snow cover locating the correct line of descent down the southeast shoulder of Ben Nevis is very difficult.

Ben Nevis summit trig point

On the Carn Mor Dearg Arête

BEN MACDUI
4295FT (1309M)

NORTH TOP
4249FT (1295M)

STOB COIRE SPUTAN
DEARG
4098FT (1249M)

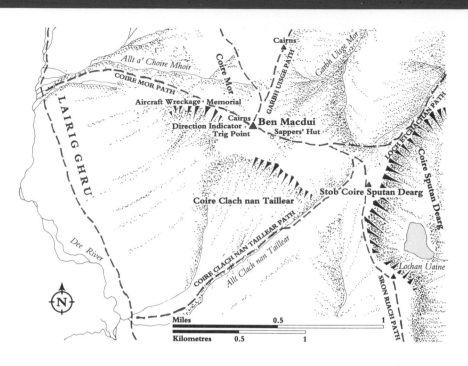

UNTIL THE ORDNANCE SURVEY FINALLY SETTLED the matter in 1847 many people believed that Ben Macdui was the highest peak in Scotland (and Britain). It may now be relegated to second place, but it is, nevertheless, a big mountain in all respects. Its bulk dominates the east side of the Lairig Ghru with its outlying ridges extending north to Creag an Leth-choin and south to Carn a' Mhaim. To the east its influence is cast over the Loch Avon Basin, the broad corrie occupied by Loch Etchachan and the shapely upper reaches of Glen Luibeg.

Ben Macdui has an ill-defined shape. It looks impressive from most view points, but its attractiveness lies in its detail rather than in the mountain as a whole. Lost amongst the clutter of subsidiary tops, ridges and corries it is a mountain better explored than viewed.

Lying at the centre of a subarctic plateau Ben Macdui experiences atrociously bad weather. All routes to its summit involve either traversing precipitous ground or passing close by it, and although they may not be very demanding technically they are notoriously difficult to retreat from.

Sapper's Bothy lies 100yd ESE or so of the summit trig point. Built in 1847 for surveyors of the Ordnance Survey it is now in ruins and affords only limited shelter from the wind

(Right) Luibeg Bridge

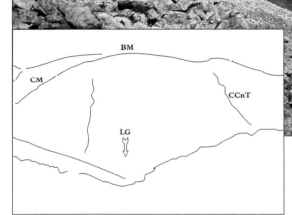

Ben Macdui (**BM**) from Cairn Toul, **CM** Coire Mor, **LG** Lairig Ghru, **CCnT** Coire Clach nan Taillear

MAPS

Ordnance Survey: Outdoor Leisure 1: 25000 No 3; Landranger 1: 50000 No 36 & No 43.

INFORMATION

Tourist Information Centres: Aviemore, Glenmore, Tomintoul and Braemar.

ACCOMMODATION

Youth Hostels: Aviemore, Glenmore, Tomintoul, Braemar and Inverey (near the Linn of Dee).

Hotels and B&B: Aviemore, Coylumbridge, Glenmore, Tomintoul and Braemar

Camp sites: Aviemore, Coylumbridge and Glenmore.

Bothies and Howffs: Bob Scott's Bothy, GR042931; Corrour Bothy, GR982958; The Shelter Stone, GR002016; The Hutchison Memorial Hut, GR023998; Fords of Avon Refuge, GR042032; Bynack Stable, GR105031; Ryvoan Bothy, GR006115. The Sinclair Memorial Hut was removed in 1991.

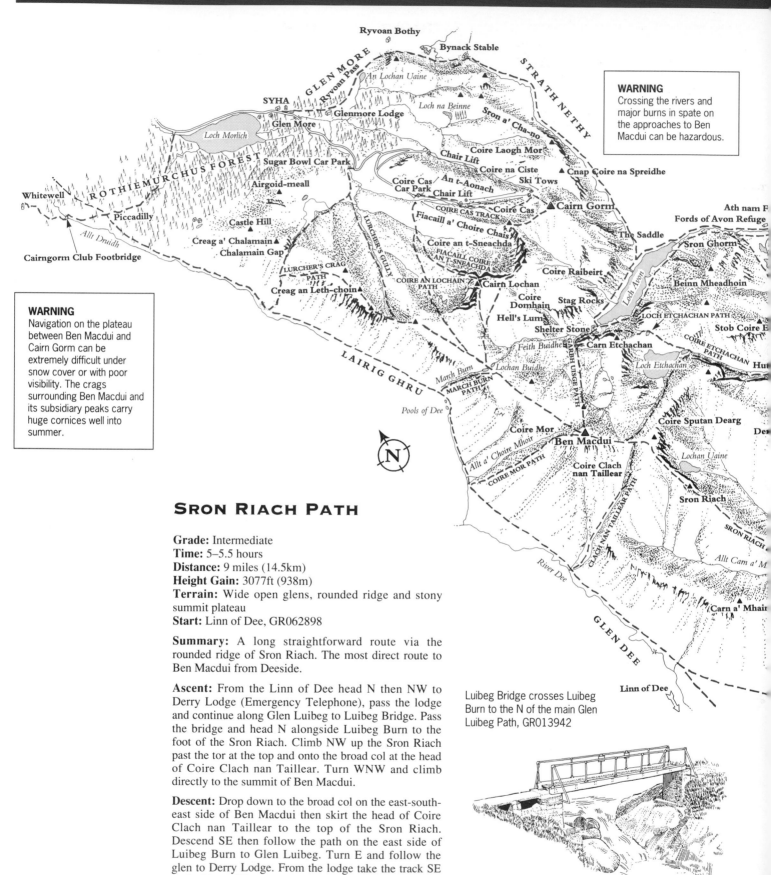

SRON RIACH PATH

Grade: Intermediate
Time: 5–5.5 hours
Distance: 9 miles (14.5km)
Height Gain: 3077ft (938m)
Terrain: Wide open glens, rounded ridge and stony summit plateau
Start: Linn of Dee, GR062898

Summary: A long straightforward route via the rounded ridge of Sron Riach. The most direct route to Ben Macdui from Deeside.

Ascent: From the Linn of Dee head N then NW to Derry Lodge (Emergency Telephone), pass the lodge and continue along Glen Luibeg to Luibeg Bridge. Pass the bridge and head N alongside Luibeg Burn to the foot of the Sron Riach. Climb NW up the Sron Riach past the tor at the top and onto the broad col at the head of Coire Clach nan Taillear. Turn WNW and climb directly to the summit of Ben Macdui.

Descent: Drop down to the broad col on the east-south-east side of Ben Macdui then skirt the head of Coire Clach nan Taillear to the top of the Sron Riach. Descend SE then follow the path on the east side of Luibeg Burn to Glen Luibeg. Turn E and follow the glen to Derry Lodge. From the lodge take the track SE to the Linn of Dee.

Luibeg Bridge crosses Luibeg Burn to the N of the main Glen Luibeg Path, GR013942

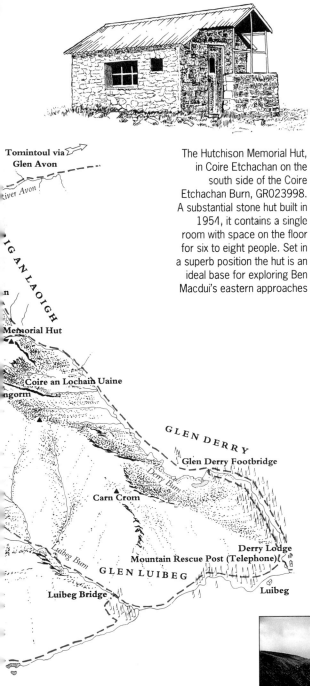

The Hutchison Memorial Hut, in Coire Etchachan on the south side of the Coire Etchachan Burn, GR023998. A substantial stone hut built in 1954, it contains a single room with space on the floor for six to eight people. Set in a superb position the hut is an ideal base for exploring Ben Macdui's eastern approaches

COIRE CLACH NAN TAILLEAR PATH

Grade: Strenuous
Time: 5.5–6 hours
Distance: 10.5 miles (16.9km)
Height Gain: 3209ft (978m)
Terrain: Wide open glens, steep rocky corrie and stony summit plateau.
Variation: From the Linn of Dee an alternative route is to take the Glen Dee track past White Bridge then on to the Lairig Ghru Path. Can also be started from Speyside from either Whitewell, GR916086, or Loch Morlich, GR957097.
Start: Linn of Dee, GR062898

Summary: On the south side of Ben Macdui directly below the summit dome Coire Clach nan Taillear falls away steeply into Glen Dee. It derives its name from the ribbed boulders (Clach nan Taillear) further S down the glen where tradition has it that three tailors died in a snow storm on New Year's Eve as they traversed the Lairig Ghru between Speyside and Deeside. It is particularly useful as an approach from Corrour Bothy. The corrie is steep and loose in parts – under snow cover it is prone to avalanche.

Ascent: From the Linn of Dee head N then NW to Derry Lodge (Emergency Telephone), pass the lodge and continue along Glen Luibeg to Luibeg Bridge. Cross the bridge then swing W over the col into Glen Dee.

Join the Lairig Ghru Path and follow it N up Glen Dee to the Allt Clach nan Taillear. Turn NE and follow the burn steeply up Coire Clach nan Taillear. Continue NE to the crest of the col then turn W to the summit of Ben Macdui.

Descent: Head E down onto the broad col at the head of Coire Clach nan Taillear. From the col descend steeply SW down the corrie; first on the left bank then on the right; until the Lairig Ghru Path is reached. Take it S down Glen Dee until the start of the Glen Luibeg Path. Follow it SE then E over the col and over Luibeg Bridge to Derry Lodge. From the lodge take the track SE to the Linn of Dee.

Creagan Coire Etchachan from Coire Etchachan – Hutchison Memorial Hut in the middle distance

COIRE MOR PATH

The memorial at the head of the Coire Mor Path

Grade: Strenuous
Time: 6 hours
Distance: 11 miles (17.7km)
Height Gain: 3209ft (978m)
Terrain: Wide open glens, steep rocky corrie and stony summit plateau
Variation: From the Linn of Dee an alternative is to take the Glen Dee track past White Bridge then on to the Lairig Ghru Path. Can also be started from Speyside from either Whitewell, GR916086, or Loch Morlich, GR957097.
Start: Linn of Dee, GR062898

Summary: Boulder strewn and fairly steep, the Coire Mor Path is not the most obvious route on Ben Macdui. It does though provide a direct link with An Garbh Choire, across the Lairig Ghru, and for that purpose is useful as a through route.

Ascent: From the Linn of Dee head N then NW to Derry Lodge (Emergency Telephone), pass the lodge and continue along Glen Luibeg to Luibeg Bridge. Cross the bridge then swing W over the col into Glen Dee. Join the Lairig Ghru Path and follow it N up Glen Dee to the Allt a' Choire Mhoir. Turn E and climb the steep broad ridge on the south side of Coire Mor. As the angle eases (near the aircraft wreckage and memorial) turn SE to the summit of Ben Macdui.

Ben Macdui from upper Glen Dee

Descent: Head NW across the summit dome as the slope steepens (near the aircraft wreckage and memorial) turn W and follow the broad ridge steeply down the south side of Coire Mor. At the bottom join the Lairig Ghru Path and follow it S down Glen Dee until the start of the Glen Luibeg Path. Take it and follow it SE then E over the col and over Luibeg Bridge to Derry Lodge. From the lodge take the track SE to the Linn of Dee.

MARCH BURN PATH

Grade: Very strenuous
Time: 4.5–5 hours
Distance: 8.5 miles (13.7km)
Height Gain: 3343ft (1019m)
Terrain: Forest, steep-sided glen, very steep rocky slope and stony summit plateau
Variation: Can also be started from Whitewell, GR916086, Sugar Bowl Car Park, GR985074, or from the Linn of Dee on Deeside, GR062898.
Start: Loch Morlich, GR957097

Summary: An unremittingly steep slog from the top of the Lairig Ghru to Lochan Buidhe on the north shoulder of Ben Macdui – for masochists only!

Ascent: Cross the Allt Mor at the Sugar Bowl and follow the path SW to the Chalamain Gap. Pass through the gap and follow the path S down to the Allt Druidh. Head SE through the Lairig Ghru and cross over the top of the pass to the March Burn. Follow its course and climb very steeply E until the gradient relents at Lochan Buidhe. Turn S at the lochan and follow the main path to Ben Macdui.

Direction indicator, near Ben Macdui's trig point (right)

Loch Avon from the top of Shelter Stone Crag

LURCHER'S CRAG PATH

Grade: Intermediate
Time: 5 hours
Distance: 9 miles (14.5km)
Height Gain: 3343ft (1019m)
Terrain: Forest, steep-sided glen, high ridge and stony summit plateau
Variation: Can also be started from Loch Morlich, GR957097, or the Sugar Bowl Car Park, GR985074. If starting at the Sugar Bowl, Lurcher's Gully provides an easier alternative line.
Start: Whitewell, GR916086

Summary: Forming the impressive east wall of the Lairig Ghru the long ridge of Creag an Leth-choin can be easily gained from Rothiemurchus via the easy slopes of the Chalamain Gap. it gives a fine high-level approach to Ben Macdui via the western shoulder of Cairn Lochan.

Ascent: Take the Gleann Einich track S to Lochan Deo then turn E and follow the path over the Cairngorm Club Footbridge to the junction at Piccadilly. Take the Lairig Ghru Path SE to the junction with the Chalamain Gap Path. Join it and follow it N, then turn SE and climb the steep slopes to Creag an Leth-choin. Continue SE past the head of Lurcher's Gully to the col on the west side of Cairn Lochan. From the col head SSE past Lochan Buidhe to Ben Macdui.

Descent: Take the main plateau path NNW past Lochan Buidhe then cross the southwest shoulder of Cairn Lochan to the broad col on its west side. Cross the col and head NW over Creag an Leth-choin then descend to the Chalamain Gap. Drop S to join the Lairig Ghru track which is then followed NW to Piccadilly. Take the path SW then NW to the Cairngorm Club Footbridge. Cross it and head W along the path to join the Gleann Einich track which is then followed N to Whitewell.

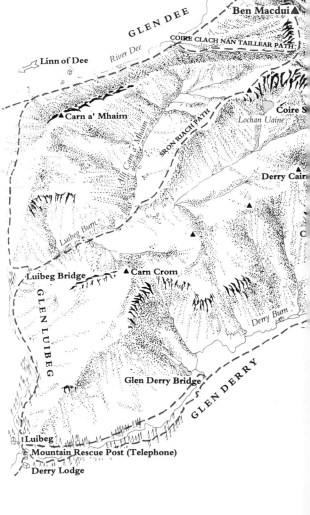

Ben Macdui from upper Glen Dee

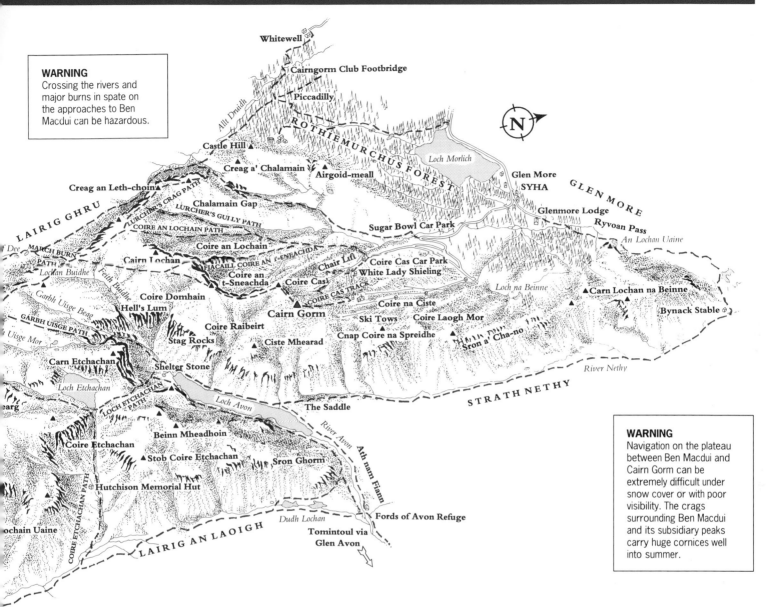

WARNING
Crossing the rivers and major burns in spate on the approaches to Ben Macdui can be hazardous.

WARNING
Navigation on the plateau between Ben Macdui and Cairn Gorm can be extremely difficult under snow cover or with poor visibility. The crags surrounding Ben Macdui and its subsidiary peaks carry huge cornices well into summer.

FIACAILL COIRE AN T-SNEACHDA

Grade: Strenuous (Grade 1 scramble; Grade 1 winter climb)
Time: 3 hours
Distance: 5 miles (8km)
Height Gain: 2460ft (750m)
Terrain: Broad corrie floor, narrow rocky ridge and high mountain plateau
Start: Coire Cas Car Park, GR990060

Summary: The Fiacaill Coire an t-Sneachda extends N between the steep crags of Coire Lochain and Coire an t-Sneachda. An easy scramble it gives an adventurous approach to Ben Macdui via the slopes of Cairn Lochan.

Ascent: From the car park cross the Allt a' Choire Chais and follow the constructed path SW across the mouth of Coire an t-Sneachda. After crossing the Allt Coire an t-Sneachda turn S and climb the broad ridge to the Fiacaill Coire an t-Sneachda. Continue S up the Fiacaill on to the slopes east of Cairn Lochan. Descend S to join the main plateau path. Take it and head SSE past Lochan Buidhe to Ben Macdui.

Descent: Take the main plateau path NNW past Lochan Buidhe to the col at the top of Coire Domhain. Climb W to the top of the Fiacaill Coire an t-Sneachda (there is a cairn, but in winter it is usually obliterated by snow – under such conditions the Fiacaill cannot be recommended as a descent). Descend N down it and continue down the broad ridge to join the main corries path. Follow it NE to Coire Cas Car Park.

COIRE CAS TRACK

Clach nan Taillear

Grade: Intermediate
Time: 3.5–4 hours
Distance: 7 miles – 4.5 miles from the top of the chair lift (11.3km or 7.2km)
Height Gain: 2881ft – 1476ft from the top of the chair lift (878m or 450m)
Terrain: Broad open corrie, stony summit slopes and high mountain plateau
Start: Coire Cas Car Park, GR990060, or chair lift top station, GR005049

Summary: A broad constructed track that winds its way through the ski grounds to the summit of Cairn Gorm. From Cairn Gorm a well-trodden path meanders S across the plateau to Ben Macdui. In good conditions an easy walk; in a blizzard near-impossible.

Ascent: From the car park follow the track SE up through Coire Cas then traverse NE to the Ptarmigan Restaurant. Turn S and follow the waymarked track to Cairn Gorm. Descend W from the radio relay station and follow the main plateau path as it skirts the top of Coire Raibeirt and Coire and t-Sneachda to the head of Coire Domhain. Turn S then SW and traverse the southeast side of Cairn Lochan to Lochan Buidhe. The path then swings to the SSE; follow it as it winds its way up the summit slopes of Ben Macdui.

Descent: Take the main plateau path NNW past Lochan Buidhe to the col at the top of Coire Domhain then skirt the heads of Coire an t-Sneachda and Coire Raibeirt NE to Cairn Gorm. Descend N from the radio relay station and follow the waymarked path to the Ptarmigan Restaurant. Turn W and follow the track as it traverses around to the S and into Coire Cas. Continue along the track and follow it NW through Coire Cas to the car park.

GARBH UISGE PATH

Grade: Very strenuous
Time: 6 hours
Distance: 11.75 miles (18.9km)
Height Gain: 3399ft (1036m)
Terrain: Forest, long narrow glen, exposed pass, high mountain loch, rocky corrie head wall and high mountain plateau
Variation: Loch Avon can be gained via Glen Avon by an extremely long approach from Delnabo, near Tomintoul, GR161171.
Start: Glenmore, GR977098

Summary: Garbh Uisge tumbles into the Loch Avon Basin in a series of dashes and cascades. The easy scramble up its east side makes a magnificent route to Ben Macdui. The surrounding rock architecture is superb and the views over Loch Avon are simply stunning. Under snow cover, which can extend well into summer, this is considerably more difficult.

Ascent: Take the Glenmore Lodge road and follow it E past the lodge, then NE and take the Ryvoan Pass Track. After An Lochan Uaine the track splits. Take the right-hand branch and follow it E then SE to Bynack Stable. Cross the River Nethy and follow the narrow path S down Strath Nethy to The Saddle. Cross over the broad col and follow the path SW above Loch Avon to the head of the loch. Follow the Feith Buidhe to its junction with the Garbh Uisge. Then scramble S up the east side of Garbh Uisge. At the top head SW across the huge open corrie and make the final ascent up the broad ridge to Ben Macdui's summit.

Descent: Head NE down the broad ridge then across the huge open corrie to the confluence of the Garbh Uisge Beag and the Garbh Uisge Mor. Follow the east side of the Garbh Uisge and scramble down alongside it into the Loch Avon Basin. At the bottom join the path on the north side of the loch to The Saddle. Cross the broad col and head N the length of Strath Nethy to the bridge near Bynack Stable. Cross it and take the path NW then W to join the Ryvoan Pass Track. Turn L onto it and follow it to Glenmore.

The crags and corries of Loch Avon

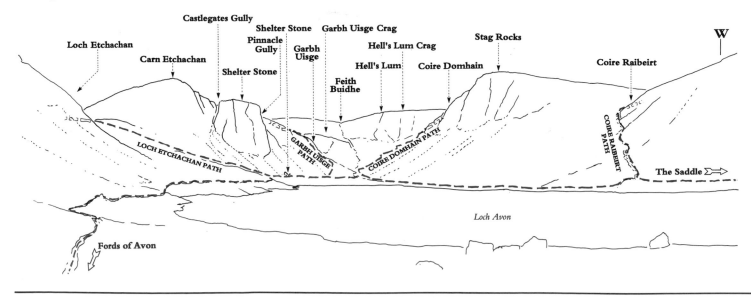

LOCH ETCHACHAN PATH

Grade: Strenuous
Time: 6 hours
Distance: 12.5 miles (20.1km)
Height Gain: 3394ft (1034m)
Terrain: Forest, long narrow glen, exposed pass, high mountain loch, rocky corrie head wall and high mountain plateau
Variation: Loch Avon can be gained via Glen Avon by an extremely long approach from Delnabo, near Tomintoul, GR161171.

Start: Glenmore, GR977098

Summary: A popular path that climbs the south side of the Loch Avon Basin to Loch Etchachan from the Shelter Stone.

Ascent: Take the Glenmore Lodge road and follow it E past the lodge then NE and take the Ryvoan Pass Track. After An Lochan Uaine the track splits. Take the right-hand branch and follow it E then SE to Bynack Stable. Cross the River Nethy and follow the narrow path S down Strath Nethy to The Saddle. Cross over the broad col and follow the path SW above Loch Avon to the Shelter Stone at the head of the loch. Climb the path that traverses ESE to the col on the east side of Cairn Etchachan then cross the open ground SSE to the outlet of Loch Etchachan. Cross the burn and join the path on the other side which is taken SW then W to Ben Macdui.

Descent: Take the path E down to the broad col then follow the path as it swings NE and steadily descends to Loch Etchachan. Cross the outlet burn and head NNW across open ground to the col on the east side of Cairn Etchachan. Turn WNW and traverse down to the Shelter Stone. Join the path on the north side of the loch and follow it to The Saddle. Cross the broad col and head N the length of Strath Nethy to the bridge near Bynack Stable. Cross it and take the path NW then W to join the Ryvoan Pass Track. Turn L onto it and follow it to Glenmore.

Shelter Stone Crag and Carn Etchachan from the head of Coire Domhain

COIRE ETCHACHAN PATH

Grade: Strenuous
Time: 4.5–5 hours
Distance: 10.75 miles (17.3km)
Height Gain: 3077ft (938m)
Terrain: Long open glen, steep craggy corrie, high mountain loch and high summit plateau
Variation: Coire Etchachan can be gained via Lairig an Laoigh and Glen Avon by an extremely long approach from Delnabo, near Tomintoul, GR161171.
Start: Linn of Dee, GR062898

Summary: The route up Glen Derry and then through Coire Etchachan is a pleasant undertaking. Although the approach is long the gradients are never particularly steep and the scenery is particularly beautiful – less harsh than the normal Cairngorm terrain.

Ascent: From the Linn of Dee head N then NW to Derry Lodge (Emergency Telephone), pass the lodge and head N into Glen Derry. Continue N the length of Glen Derry then fork L and take the Coire Etchachan Path over the footbridge and W up through the corrie. At the Loch Etchachan outlet turn L and follow the path SW then W to Ben Macdui.

Descent: Take the path E down to the broad col then follow it as it swings NE and steadily descends to Loch Etchachan. From the outlet descend SE into Coire Etchachan. Follow the path across the corrie floor E then SE to the footbridge. Cross it and continue SE and join the Glen Derry Path. Head S down Glen Derry to Derry Lodge. From the lodge take the track SE to the Linn of Dee.

Clach Dhion (Shelter Stone) is found amongst the scree and boulders at the foot of the Shelter Stone Crag at the west end of Loch Avon, GR012016. A roomy cave underneath a massive boulder with floor space for around six, more in an emergency (illustrated in red). It enjoys a magnificent situation amongst wild scenery and is a popular base for approaches to Ben Macdui and Cairn Gorm. If the Shelter Stone is occupied there are numerous other boulders nearby which provide adequate shelter

BRAERIACH
4252FT (1296M)

SOUTH PLATEAU
4150FT (1265M)

EINICH CAIRN
4058FT (1237M)

NORTH PLATEAU
4052FT (1235M)

RINGED BY A COMPLEX SYSTEM OF CORRIES the high plateau on the west side of the Lairig Ghru is the most extensive area of land above 4000ft in Britain. The highest point on this Arctic-like plateau is the rounded dome of Braeriach. Set amongst gravel beds and boulder fields this rather bland-looking summit has a wonderful variety of routes to it.

In the broad hollow between Braeriach and the subsidiary top Einich Cairn the source of the River Dee percolates from a series of springs and tumbles over the plateau edge into Garbh Choire Dhaidh which, along with Coire Bhrochain, Garbh Choire Mor and Coire an Lochain, makes up the inner recesses of the huge An Garbh Choire. This remote complex of corries holds the longest-lying snow beds in Britain – they amount to the nearest thing Britain has to a glacier. Most years they survive from winter to winter and display bergschrunds and even small crevasses. The snow that feeds these snow fields is blown off the plateau and from the barren expanse of Moine Mhor By mid-winter the whole corrie system is ringed by an almost continuous cornice,

and until they decay routes to Braeriach from the corrie floors are the domain of climbers. Mid-summer usually sees most routes clear of snow at which time the remote depths of An Garbh Choire provide a magnificent place to explore.

With the exception of the Creag an Loch Ridge and the Coire an Lochain Ridge the corries and their separating ridges on the north and west sides of the Braeriach plateau tend to be less dramatic than their eastern counterparts. Gleann Einich with its access track gives a long but easy approach to the west while to the north the traverse over the top of the Sron na Lairig gives a fine walk high above the Lairig Ghru.

MAPS
Ordnance Survey: Outdoor Leisure 1: 25000 No 3; Landranger 1: 50000 No 36 & No 43.

INFORMATION
Tourist Information Centres: Aviemore, Glenmore and Braemar.

ACCOMMODATION
Youth Hostels: Aviemore, Glenmore, Braemar and Inverey (near the Linn of Dee).

Hotels and B&B: Aviemore, Coylumbridge, Glenmore and Braemar.

Camp sites: Aviemore, Coylumbridge and Glenmore.

Bothies and Howffs: Bob Scott's Bothy, GR042931; Corrour Bothy, GR982958; Garbh Choire Bothy, GR959986 (on the south side of the Allt a' Garbh-choire below the Lochan Uaine Waterfall); and the Dey-Smith Bivouac, GR946985 (a built-up cave which can just about hold two – too uncomfortable to use for a planned stay). The Sinclair Memorial Hut was removed in 1991.

GCD Garbh Choire Dhaidh,
FoD Falls of Dee, **Br** Braeriach

SOUTHWEST RIDGE

Grade: Intermediate
Time: 6 hours
Distance: 14 miles (22.5km)
Height Gain: 3527ft (1075m)
Terrain: Woodland, wide glens, featureless mountainside, high mountain plateau and stony summit
Variation: From the Linn of Dee an alternative is to take the Glen Dee track past White Bridge to join the route near Corrour Bridge.
Start: Linn of Dee, GR062898

Summary: Approached via the lovely Glen Geusachan, this route climbs the rounded and featureless southwest ridge of Sgor an Lochain Uaine then skirts the crags of Garbh Choire Mor and Garbh Choire Dhaidh.

Ascent: From the Linn of Dee head N then NW to Derry Lodge (Emergency Telephone), pass the lodge and continue along Glen Luibeg to Luibeg Bridge. Cross the bridge then swing W over the col into Glen Dee. Cross the River Dee (if in spate use Corrour Bridge) and head W then NW up Glen Geusachan. From Loch nan Stuirteag climb the broad ridge NE towards Sgor an Lochain Uaine. Traverse NW before the top to the col on the west side of Sgor an Lochain Uaine. Skirt W, NW then NE around the edge of Garbh Choire Mor and Garbh Choire Dhaidh to the head of the Falls of Dee. From the infant Dee climb steadily NE to Braeriach.

Descent: Descend steadily SW to the head of the Falls of Dee. Cross the infant Dee and skirt SW, SE then E around the edge of Garbh Choire Dhaidh and Garbh Choire Mor to the col on the west side of Sgor an Lochain Uaine. Traverse S across the slopes then descend SW down the broad ridge to Loch nan Stuirteag. From the loch descend SE into Glen Geusachan then head E along it to the River Dee. Cross the river (if in spate use Corrour Bridge) and make the short climb on the east side to the Glen Luibeg Path. Join the path and follow it E over Luibeg Bridge to Derry Lodge. From the lodge take the track SE to the Linn of Dee.

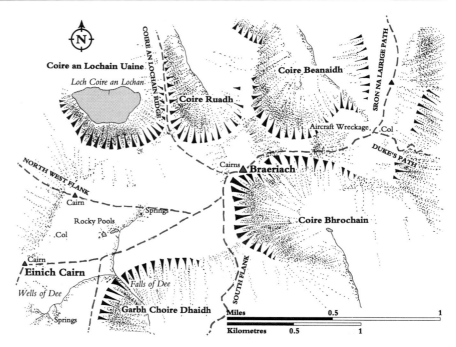

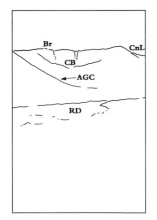

Braeriach from Glen Dee, **Br** Braeriach, **CB** Coire Bhrochain, **AGC** An Garbh Choire, **CnL** Coire na Lairige, **RD** River Dee

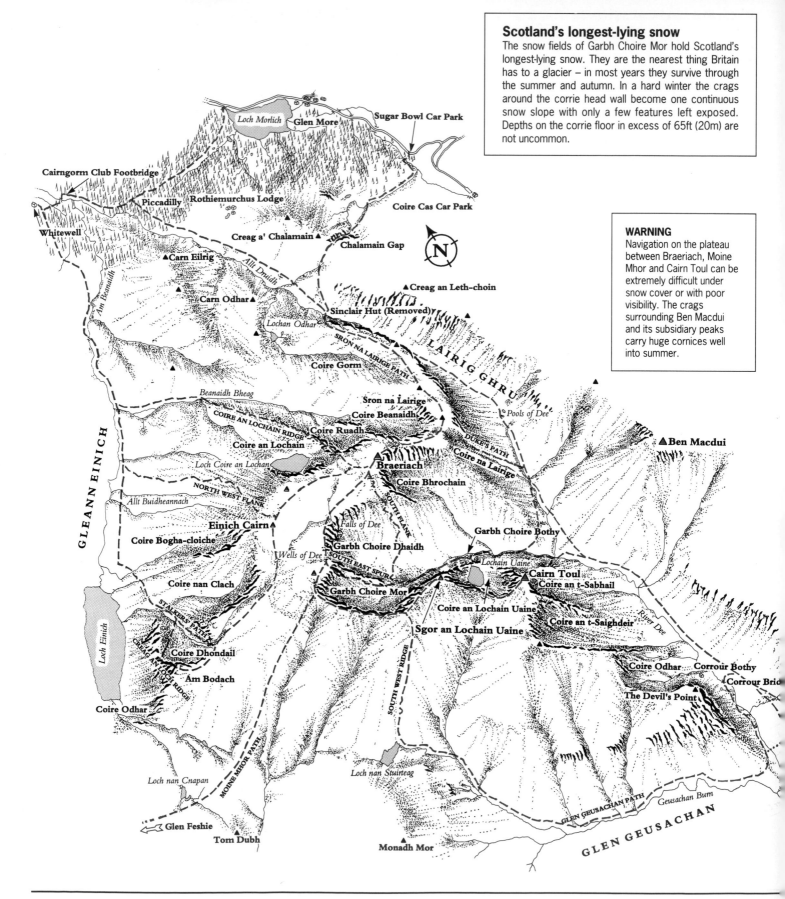

Scotland's longest-lying snow
The snow fields of Garbh Choire Mor hold Scotland's longest-lying snow. They are the nearest thing Britain has to a glacier – in most years they survive through the summer and autumn. In a hard winter the crags around the corrie head wall become one continuous snow slope with only a few features left exposed. Depths on the corrie floor in excess of 65ft (20m) are not uncommon.

WARNING
Navigation on the plateau between Braeriach, Moine Mhor and Cairn Toul can be extremely difficult under snow cover or with poor visibility. The crags surrounding Ben Macdui and its subsidiary peaks carry huge cornices well into summer.

Loch Morlich
Glen More
Sugar Bowl Car Park
Cairngorm Club Footbridge
Piccadilly
Rothiemurchus Lodge
Coire Cas Car Park
Whitewell
Creag a' Chalamain
Chalamain Gap
Carn Eilrig
Am Beanaidh
Allt Druidh
Creag an Leth-choin
Carn Odhar
Sinclair Hut (Removed)
Lochan Odhar
SRON NA LAIRIGE PATH
LAIRIG GHRU
Coire Gorm
N
Beanaidh Bheag
Sron na Lairige
Coire Beanaidh
Pools of Dee
COIRE AN LOCHAIN RIDGE
Coire Ruadh
Ben Macdui
Coire an Lochain
DUKE'S PATH
Loch Coire an Lochain
Coire na Lairige
NORTH WEST FLANK
Braeriach
Allt Buidheannach
Coire Bhrochain
SOUTH FLANK
GLEANN EINICH
Einich Cairn
Falls of Dee
Coire Bogha-cloiche
Garbh Choire Bothy
Garbh Choire Dhaidh
Wells of Dee
SOUTH EAST SPUR
Coire nan Clach
Lochain Uaine
Cairn Toul
Coire an t-Sabhail
Garbh Choire Mor
Coire an Lochain Uaine
River Dee
STALKER'S PATH
Sgor an Lochain Uaine
Coire an t-Saighdeir
CREAG AN RIDGE
Loch Einich
Coire Dhondail
Coire Odhar
Corrour Bothy
Am Bodach
Corrour Brid
The Devil's Point
Coire Odhar
SOUTH WEST RIDGE
MOINE MHOR PATH
Loch nan Cnapan
Loch nan Stuirteag
Glen Feshie
GLEN GEUSACHAN PATH
Geusachan Burn
Tom Dubh
Monadh Mor
GLEN GEUSACHAN

MOINE MHOR PATH

Grade: Intermediate
Time: 4.5–5 hours
Distance: 8 miles (12.9km)
Height Gain: 3960ft (1207m)
Terrain: Steep open corrie, high exposed moorland, featureless slope, high mountain plateau and stony summit
Start: Achlean, Glen Feshie, GR853975

Summary: A novel route which starts in Glen Feshie and takes advantage of the high-level link provided by Moine Mhor. The crossing of this high and exposed moorland is a unique experience – with a covering of soft snow or with poor visibility it can be a nightmare!

Ascent: From Achlean take the path that works its way unremittingly E up the north side of the Allt Fhearnagan to Carn Ban Mor. From Carn Ban Mor descend SE to join the access track then head E to Loch nan Cnapan. From the loch swing NE and climb onto the plateau S of Cairn Einich. Skirt the edge of Garbh Choire Dhaidh to the head of the Falls of Dee. From the infant Dee climb steadily NE to Braeriach.

Descent: Descend steadily SW to the head of the Falls of Dee. Cross the infant Dee and skirt S around the head of Garbh Choire Dhaidh then descend SW to Loch nan Cnapan. From the loch continue W to the Allt Sgairnich and join the access track. Follow it to the Carn Ban Mor Path which is then taken NW. From Carn Ban Mor descend W on the north side of Allt Fhearnagan to the road at Achlean.

CREAG AN LOCH RIDGE

Grade: Strenuous (Grade 1 scramble; Grade 1 winter climb)
Time: 4.5–5 hours
Distance: 10 miles (16km)
Height Gain: 3317ft (1011m)
Terrain: Long remote glen, heather-covered hillside, high rocky corrie, exposed rocky ridge, high mountain plateau and stony summit
Start: Whitewell, GR916086
Summary: Perched at the head of Gleann Einich the fine ridge of Creag an Loch is a superb route onto the south end of the Braeriach plateau. It climbs high above the dark waters of Loch Einich and although only short gives an exciting scramble.

Ascent: Follow the access track S the full length of Gleann Einich. Just before Loch Einich take the Stalkers' Path that climbs SE then S into Coire Dhondail. Cross the corrie floor SW to the foot of Creag Loch Ridge and climb the crest of the ridge SE to Am Bodach. Skirt the head of Coire Dhondail and climb NE onto the plateau. Continue NE across the plateau to the head of the Falls of Dee. From the infant Dee climb steadily NE to Braeriach.

The Wells of Dee

▲ Carn a' Mhaim

Mountain Rescue Post (Telephone)
GLEN LUIBEG
Luibeg Bridge
Luibeg Burn
Luibeg
Derry Lodge

GLEN DEE

er Dee

WARNING
Crossing the rivers and major burns in spate on the approaches to Braeriach can be hazardous.

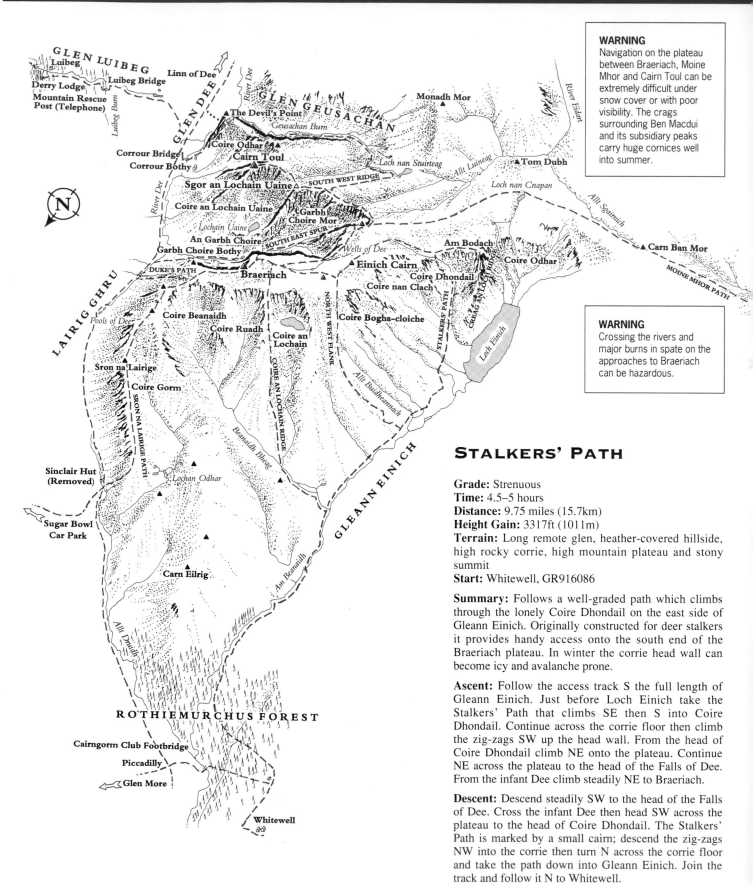

WARNING
Navigation on the plateau between Braeriach, Moine Mhor and Cairn Toul can be extremely difficult under snow cover or with poor visibility. The crags surrounding Ben Macdui and its subsidiary peaks carry huge cornices well into summer.

WARNING
Crossing the rivers and major burns in spate on the approaches to Braeriach can be hazardous.

STALKERS' PATH

Grade: Strenuous
Time: 4.5–5 hours
Distance: 9.75 miles (15.7km)
Height Gain: 3317ft (1011m)
Terrain: Long remote glen, heather-covered hillside, high rocky corrie, high mountain plateau and stony summit
Start: Whitewell, GR916086

Summary: Follows a well-graded path which climbs through the lonely Coire Dhondail on the east side of Gleann Einich. Originally constructed for deer stalkers it provides handy access onto the south end of the Braeriach plateau. In winter the corrie head wall can become icy and avalanche prone.

Ascent: Follow the access track S the full length of Gleann Einich. Just before Loch Einich take the Stalkers' Path that climbs SE then S into Coire Dhondail. Continue across the corrie floor then climb the zig-zags SW up the head wall. From the head of Coire Dhondail climb NE onto the plateau. Continue NE across the plateau to the head of the Falls of Dee. From the infant Dee climb steadily NE to Braeriach.

Descent: Descend steadily SW to the head of the Falls of Dee. Cross the infant Dee then head SW across the plateau to the head of Coire Dhondail. The Stalkers' Path is marked by a small cairn; descend the zig-zags NW into the corrie then turn N across the corrie floor and take the path down into Gleann Einich. Join the track and follow it N to Whitewell.

NORTHWEST FLANK

Grade: Intermediate
Time: 3.5–4 hours
Distance: 7.25 miles (11.7km)
Height Gain: 3268ft (996m)
Terrain: Long remote glen, exposed heather moorland, pathless mountainside, high mountain plateau and stony summit
Start: Whitewell, GR916086

Summary: The featureless Northwest Flank of Braeriach provides an undramatic but relatively safe route between Gleann Einich and the Braeriach plateau.

Ascent: Follow the access track S up Gleann Einich then strike SE alongside Allt Buidheannach and climb the vague zig-zags onto the Braeriach plateau. Once on the plateau head E across the flats and then make the steady climb to Braeriach's summit.

Descent: Head W from the summit cairn and make the short descent onto the plateau. Continue W across the plateau to the head of the broad slope between Coire an Lochain and Coire Bogha-cloiche. Descent NW down the slope (there is a vague zig-zag path but it is difficult to locate from above) and follow the Allt Buidheannach down to Gleann Einich. Join the track and follow it N to Whitewell.

Falls of Dee

Loch Einich and Sgor Gaoith from the top of Creag an Loch Ridge

COIRE AN LOCHAIN RIDGE

Grade: Strenuous
Time: 3.5–4 hours
Distance: 7 miles (11.3km)
Height Gain: 3268ft (996m)
Terrain: Long remote glen, exposed heather moorland, narrow rocky ridge, scree and stony summit
Start: Whitewell, GR916085

Summary: Loch Coire an Lochain occupies the cold craggy corrie on the north side of Braeriach. Rising above its icy waters on the east side is a steep rocky ridge. Not technically difficult, it nevertheless provides an airy and exciting route with superb views back over the Spey Valley.

Ascent: Follow the access track S up Gleann Einich then take the vague path SE along the north side of Beanaidh Bheag. At the junction with the Allt Coire an Lochain cross the Beanaidh Bheag and climb SE to the foot of Coire an Lochain Ridge. Climb the ridge S onto the plateau. Then turn SE and climb direct to the summit of Braeriach.

Descent: The top of Coire an Lochain Ridge is best located by descending W from the summit cairn then turning N at the change in angle between the summit slopes and the plateau. Descend the ridge N then turn NW at its foot and continue NW until the Beanaidh Bheag is reached. Cross it and follow it down to Gleann Einich. Join the track and follow it N to Whitewell.

Braeriach's summit cairn

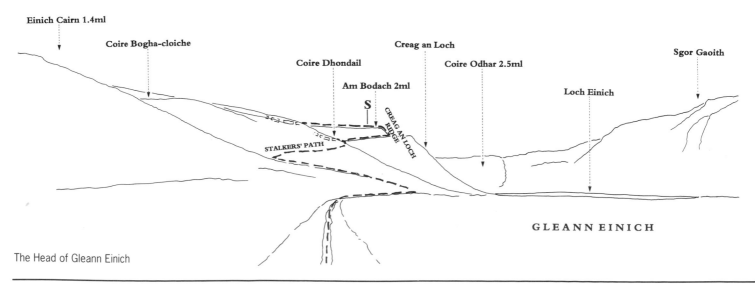

The Head of Gleann Einich

Einich Cairn 1.4ml

Coire Bogha-cloiche

Coire Dhondail

Am Bodach 2ml

S

CREAG AN LOCH RIDGE

STALKERS' PATH

Creag an Loch

Coire Odhar 2.5ml

Loch Einich

Sgor Gaoith

GLEANN EINICH

SRON NA LAIRIGE PATH

Grade: Intermediate
Time: 4 hours
Distance: 7 miles (11.3km)
Height Gain: 3279ft (1005m)
Terrain: Exposed moorland, boulder-choked valley, craggy glen, broad stony ridge and stony summit
Variation: From Whitewell, GR916085, or Loch Morlich, GR957097.
Start: Sugar Bowl Car Park, GR985074

Summary: An excellent introductory route. It has the least arduous approach and takes in some classic Cairngorm scenery – particularly the final section to the summit with views into the wild corries of An Garbh Choire.

Ascent: Cross the Allt Mor at the Sugar Bowl and follow the path SW to the Chalamain Gap. Pass through the gap and follow the path S down to the Allt Druidh then up to the old site of the Sinclair Hut (removed 1991). Climb the hillside behind it SW then SE up the Sron na Lairige. From the Sron na Lairige head S descending slightly to a broad col. From the col swing W and make the final climb to Braeriach.

Descent: Head E around the plateau edge then drop NE down to the col at the head of Coire Ruadh. Cross the col climbing N onto the Sron na Lairige. From the summit continue N then swing NW to avoid the crags on the east side of the ridge. As the slope eases turn NE and descend to the old site of the Sinclair Hut (removed 1991). Cross the Allt Druidh and climb N then NE to the Chalamain Gap. Once through the gap head NE to the Sugar Bowl Car Park.

DUKE'S PATH

Grade: Strenuous
Time: 4.5 hours
Distance: 7.25 miles (11.7km)
Height Gain: 3379ft (1030m)
Terrain: Exposed moorland, boulder-choked valley, craggy glen, boulder field, steep rocky corrie and stony summit
Variation: Can also be started from Whitewell, GR916086, or Loch Morlich, GR957097, or the Linn of Dee, GR062898.
Start: Sugar Bowl Car Park, GR985074

Summary: Crosses the top of Lairig Ghru then climbs directly onto the plateau via Coire Ruadh. The corrie is very steep, with zig-zags up the head wall – avalanche prone when snow covered.

Ascent: Cross the Allt Mor at the Sugar Bowl and follow the path SW to the Chalamain Gap. Pass through the gap and follow the path S down to the Allt Druidh. Head S through the Lairig Ghru over the top to the Pools of Dee. From the pools skirt the slope on the west side of the Lairig Ghru to a burn issuing from Coire Ruadh. Climb NW alongside the burn and up through the corrie, then follow the zig-zags onto the col. Turn W and climb the summit slopes to Braeriach.

Descent: Head E around the plateau edge then drop NE down to the col at the head of Coire Ruadh. From the cairn on the east side of the col descend the zig-zags SE into Coire Ruadh; as the angle eases continue SE alongside the burn. Before the bottom is reached traverse N towards the Pools of Dee. Continue N through the Lairig Ghru until the path forks below the old site of the Sinclair Hut. Take the right-hand branch N as it climbs to the Chalamain Gap. Once through the gap head NE to the Sugar Bowl Car Park.

An Garbh Choire ringed by Cairn Toul, Sgor an Lochain Uaine, Einich Cairn and Braeriach – from Ben Macdui

SOUTH FLANK

Grade: Very strenuous
Time: 5 hours
Distance: 9.5 miles (15.3km)
Height Gain: 3497ft (1066m)
Terrain: Exposed moorland, boulder-choked valley, craggy glen, boulder field, remote corries, steep scree-covered slopes and stony summit
Variation: Can also be started from Speyside at Whitewell, GR916086, or Loch Morlich, GR957097, or from Deeside at the Linn of Dee, GR062898.
Start: Sugar Bowl Car Park, GR985074

Summary: Steep and boulder strewn, the South Flank of Braeriach provides access to Garbh Choire Dhaidh. In itself it is not a very exciting route, its qualities lie in views into the vast An Garbh Choire, particularly towards the Falls of Dee.

Ascent: Cross Allt Mor at the Sugar Bowl and follow the path SW to the Chalamain Gap. Pass through the gap and follow the path down to the Allt Druidh. Head S through the Lairig Ghru over the top to the Pools of Dee. From the pools skirt the slope on the west side of the Lairig Ghru and continue traversing into An Garbh Choire. Follow the Allt a' Gharbh-choire past Garbh Choire Bothy then turn NW climbing into the Garbh Choire Dhaidh. Head N across the corrie floor then climb steeply up the South Flank of Braeriach onto the plateau. Continues N up the easy summit slopes then E to the summit cairn.

Descent: Head W then S around the crags of Coire Bhrochain to the edge of the plateau. Descend the steep scree and boulders of the South Flank into Garbh Choire Dhaidh. Continue S across the corrie floor and drop into An Garbh Choire. Turn L and head NE then E to Garbh Choire Bothy. Past the bothy traverse NE into the Lairig Ghru. Head N past the Pools of Dee and descend to the start of the Chalamain Gap Path (below the old site of the Sinclair Hut). Turn R and follow it N to the gap. Once through head NE to the Sugar Bowl Car Park.

SOUTHEAST SPUR

Grade: Very strenuous (Grade 1 scramble; Grade 1 winter climb)
Time: 6 hours
Distance: 13.25 miles (21.3km)
Height Gain: 3209ft (978m)
Terrain: Woodland, wide open glens, high remote corries, steep scree, short steep ridge, high mountain plateau and stony summit
Variation: Can also be started from Speyside at Whitewell, GR916086, or Loch Morlich, GR957097, or the Sugar Bowl Car Park, GR985074.
Start: Linn of Dee, GR062898

Summary: From below, the dramatically situated Southeast Spur at the head of An Garbh Choire seems an unlikely route. It looks very steep, and is located between two major crags. Its difficulties though are short and considerably fewer than may first appear (snow cover on this route can exist throughout summer).

Ascent: Cross Allt Mor at the Sugar Bowl and follow the path SW to the Chalamain Gap. Pass through the gap and follow the path down to the Allt Druidh. Head S through the Lairig Ghru over the top to the Pools of Dee. From the pools skirt the slope on the west side of the Lairig Ghru and continue traversing into An Garbh Choire. Follow the Allt a' Gharbh-choire past Garbh Choire Bothy to the mouth of Garbh Choire Mor. Turn R and climb the steep slope NW to the foot of the Southeast Spur – the easiest way is up the left-hand side. Once on the plateau walk N to the head of the Falls of Dee. From the infant Dee climb steadily NE to Braeriach.

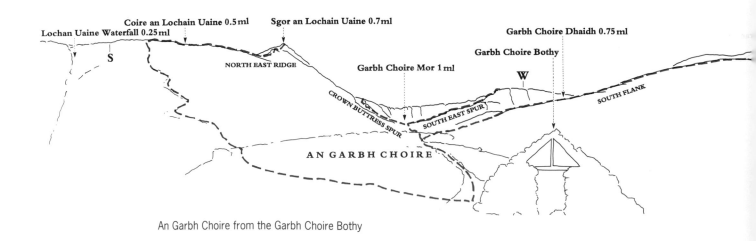

An Garbh Choire from the Garbh Choire Bothy

Garbh Choire Mor from the top of the Southeast Spur

CAIRN TOUL LINK

Grade: Intermediate
Time: 1.5 hours
Distance: 3.5 miles (5.6km)
Height Gain: 1083ft (330m)
Terrain: High mountain plateau and scree-covered ridges
Start: Braeriach, GR953999

Summary: A high-level walk around one of Scotland's most impressive corrie systems.

Route: Descend SW to the head of the Falls of Dee. Cross the infant Dee then skirt SW, SE then E around the edge of Garbh Choire Dhaidh and Garbh Choire Mor to the col on the west side of Sgor an Lochain Uaine. Continue E and climb Sgor an Lochain Uaine. Descend SE to the col and make the short pull E to Cairn Toul.

(Above) Derry Lodge at the confluence of Derry Burn and Luibeg Burn, GR041934. Formerly a shooting lodge, this fine building is now redundant and boarded up. Just behind it is a mountain rescue post which has an emergency telephone

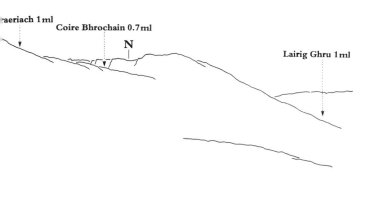

Garbh Choire Bothy 1 mile (1.6km) west of the Lairig Ghru in An Garbh Choire on the south bank of the Allt a' Garbh Choire below the Lochain Uaine Waterfall, GR959986. A waterproofed cage within a built-up cairn, it holds six at a push. An ideal bothy, imaginatively designed, it blends beautifully into its wild surroundings – an excellent base for Braeriach and Cairn Toul or for exploring the corries of An Garbh Choire.

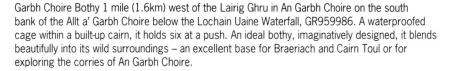

Braeriach 1 ml   Coire Bhrochain 0.7 ml   N   Lairig Ghru 1 ml

Near 'White-out' conditions on the plateau between Einich Cairn and Braeriach – common enough in winter, making navigation extremely difficult

CAIRN TOUL
4236FT (1291M)
SGOR AN LOCHAIN UAINE
4127FT (1258M)

CAIRN TOUL IS ALMOST ENTIRELY SURROUNDED by the headwaters of the Dee. To the north the rushing waters of the Allt a' Garbh-choire issue from the long-lying snow beds of Garbh Choire Mor and Garbh Choire Dhaidh draining east through An Garbh Choire to join the Dee in the Lairig Ghru. The River Dee in turn drains south to form the eastern boundary through the deep trench of the Lairig Ghru. Bounding the southern edge the Geusachan Burn meanders the length of the lovely Glen Geusachan to meet the Dee at the flats below the crags of The Devil's Point. Cairn Toul's only high-level link with its neighbours is to the west where it abuts Sgor an Lochain Uaine and the extensive Braeriach plateau – the most extensive area of land above 4000ft in Britain.

Arguably the most elegant of all the Cairngorm mountains, Cairn Toul's well-defined shape is instantly recognisable. Presiding over the Lairig

Cairn Toul from the side of Glen Dee – on the Glen Luibeg Path

Ghru its steep boulder-strewn slopes are cut into by high hanging corries which are separated by long ridges. On the Lairig Ghru side they form steep narrow arêtes which provide easy but entertaining scrambles, while to the west they are broad and open.

Cairn Toul is most commonly approached via the Lairig Ghru either from Deeside via Glen Luibeg or Glen Dee, or from Speyside via the Rothiemurchus Forest or the Chalamain Gap. There are, however, two less obvious alternatives, one from Glen Feshie over the high exposed moorland of Moine Mhor, the other via Gleann Einich and the remote Coire Dhondail.

MAPS
Ordnance Survey: Outdoor Leisure 1: 25000 No 3; Landranger 1: 50000 No 36 & No 43.

INFORMATION
Tourist Information Centres: Aviemore, Glenmore and Braemar.

ACCOMMODATION
Youth Hostels: Aviemore, Glenmore, Braemar and Inverey (near the Linn of Dee).

Hotels and B&B: Aviemore, Coylumbridge, Glenmore and Braemar.

Camp sites: Aviemore, Coylumbridge and Glenmore.

Bothies and Howffs: Bob Scott's Bothy, GR042931; Corrour Bothy, GR982958; Garbh Coire Bothy, GR959986 (on the south side of the Allt a' Garbh-choire below the Lochan Uaine Waterfall); and the Dey-Smith Bivouac, GR946985 (a built-up cave which can just about hold two – too uncomfortable to use for a planned stay). The Sinclair Memorial Hut was removed in 1991.

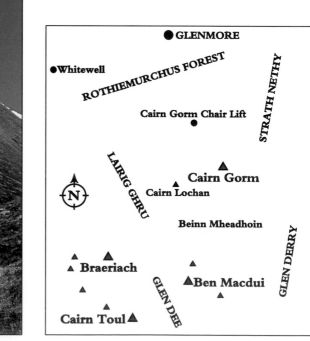

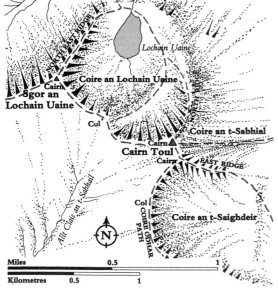

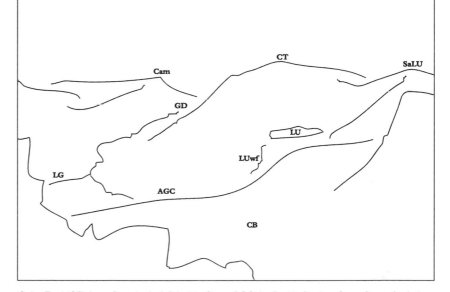

Cairn Toul (**CT**) from Braeriach, **LG** Lairig Ghru, **AGC** An Garbh Choire, **Cam** Carn a' mhaim, **GD** Glen Dee, **LUwf** Lochan Uaine Waterfall, **CB** Coire Bhrochain, **CT** Cairn Toul, **LU** Lochan Uaine, **SaLU** Sgor an Lochain Uaine

Glen Dee with Devil's Peak
and Cairn Toul in the distance

SOUTHWEST RIDGE

Grade: Intermediate
Time: 5–5.5 hours
Distance: 12.5 miles (20.1km)
Height Gain: 3635ft (1108m)
Terrain: Woodland, wide glens, featureless mountain-side, high ridge and narrow stony summit
Variation: Allt Clais an t-Sabhail provides an alternative route between the head of Glen Geusachan and the col on the west side of Cairn Toul. From the Linn of Dee another alternative is to take the Glen Dee track past White Bridge to join the route near Corrour Bridge.
Start: Linn of Dee, GR062898

White Bridge (above) gives access to Glen Feshie and Glen Tilt

Summary: Approached via the lovely Glen Geusachan this route climbs the rounded and featureless southwest ridge of Sgor an Lochain Uaine. Although not the most direct line it provides a relatively easy route to follow in poor conditions.

Ascent: From the Linn of Dee head N then NW to Derry Lodge (Emergency Telephone), pass the lodge and continue along Glen Luibeg to Luibeg Bridge. Cross the bridge then swing W over the col into Glen Dee. Cross the River Dee (if in spate use Corrour Bridge) and head W then NW up Glen Geusachan. From Loch nan Stuirteag climb the broad ridge NE towards Sgor an Lochain Uaine. Traverse E before the top to the col on the west side of Cairn Toul. From the col continue E and climb to Cairn Toul's summit.

Descent: Head W and drop down to the col. From the col traverse W across the slopes of Sgor an Lochain Uaine then descend SW down the broad ridge to Loch nan Stuirteag. From the loch descend SE into Glen Geusachan then head E along it to the River Dee. Cross the river (if in spate use Corrour Bridge) and make the short climb on the east side to the Glen Luibeg path. Join the path and follow it E over Luibeg Bridge to Derry Lodge. From the lodge take the track SE to the Linn of Dee.

Corrour Bridge crosses the
River Dee at the flats below
The Devil's Point, GR983956.
The River Dee can be very
difficult to ford – Corrour
Bridge provides the only safe
crossing in upper Glen Dee

⟵ Linn of I

MOINE MHOR PATH

Grade: Intermediate
Time: 5 hours
Distance: 8 miles (12.9km)
Height Gain: 4238ft (1292m)
Terrain: Steep open corrie, high exposed moorland, featureless slope, high ridge and narrow stony summit
Variation: Sgor an Lochain Uaine can be avoided by crossing Moine Mhor via Loch nan Stuirteag.
Start: Achlean, Glen Feshie, GR853975

Summary: A novel route which starts in Glen Feshie and takes advantage of the high-level link provided by Moine Mhor. The crossing of this high and exposed moorland is a unique experience – with a covering of soft snow or with poor visibility it can be a nightmare!

Ascent: From Achlean take the path that works its way unremittingly E up the north side of the Allt Fhearnagan to Carn Ban Mor. From Carn Ban Mor descend SE to join the access track then head E to Loch nan Cnapan. From the loch swing NE then ENE and traverse the slopes to the col on the west side of Sgor an Lochain Uaine. Climb E to Sgor an Lochain Uaine then descend SE to the col. Finally from the col make the short pull E to Cairn Toul.

Descent: From Cairn Toul head W then NW to Sgor an Lochain Uaine. Descend W to the col then make a descending traverse WSW then SW to Loch nan Cnapan. From the loch continue W to the Allt Sgairnich and join the access track. Follow it to the Carn Ban Mor Path which is then taken NW. From Carn Ban Mor descend W on the north side of Allt Fhearnagan to the road at Achlean.

Cairn Toul from the snow fields at the top of the Falls of Dee

CREAG AN LOCH RIDGE

Grade: Strenuous (Grade 1 scramble; Grade 1 winter climb)
Time: 4.5–5 hours
Distance: 10.5 miles (16.9km)
Height Gain: 3766ft (1148m)
Terrain: Long remote glen, heather-covered hillside, high rocky corrie, exposed rocky ridge, high mountain ridge and narrow stony summit
Start: Whitewell, GR916086

Summary: Perched at the head of Gleann Einich the fine ridge of Creag an Loch is a superb route onto the Braeriach/Cairn Toul massif. It climbs high above the dark waters of Loch Einich and although only short gives an exciting scramble.

Ascent: Follow the access track S the full length of Gleann Einich. Just before Loch Einich take the Stalkers' Path which climbs SE then S into Coire Dhondail. Cross the corrie floor SW to the foot of Creag an Loch Ridge and climb the crest of the ridge SE to Am Bodach. Skirt the head of Coire Dhondail and climb E onto the plateau. Head SE then E and skirt around the crags of Garbh Choire Mor to Sgor an Lochain Uaine. Descend SE to the col and make the short pull E to Cairn Toul.

Cairn Toul from upper Glen Dee

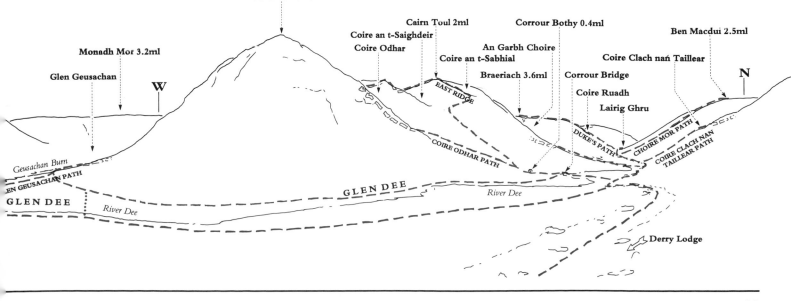

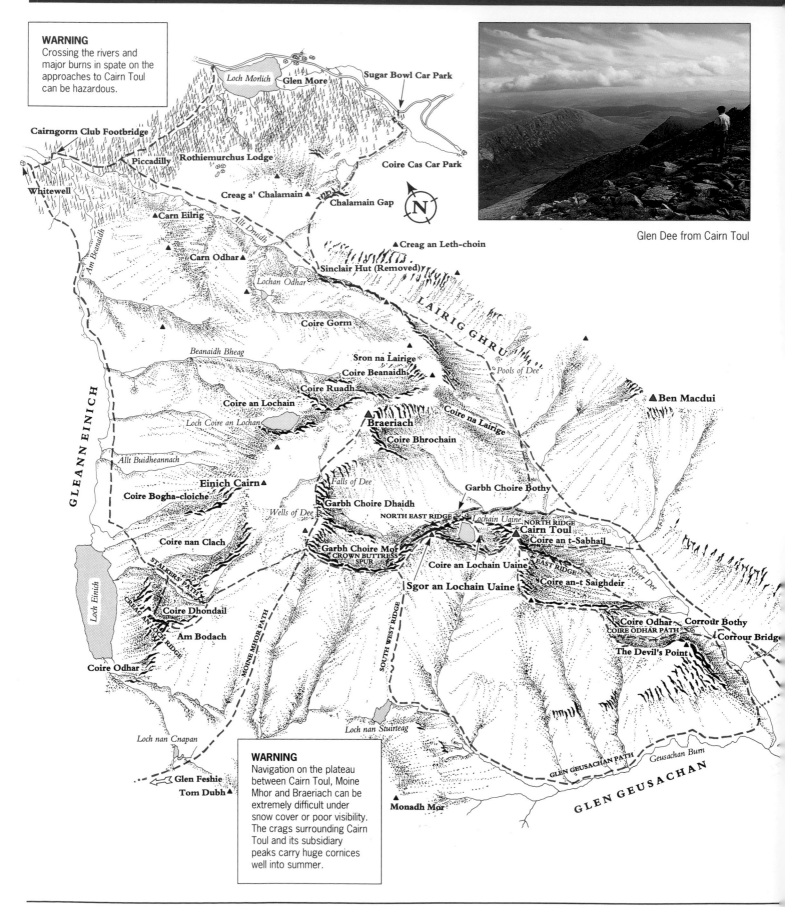

Loch Morlich
Glen More
Sugar Bowl Car Park
Coire Cas Car Park

Glen Dee from Cairn Toul

Cairngorm Club Footbridge
Piccadilly
Rothiemurchus Lodge
Whitewell
Creag a' Chalamain
Chalamain Gap
N

Carn Eilrig
Carn Odhar
Creag an Leth-choin
Sinclair Hut (Removed)
Lochan Odhar

Am Beanaidh
Allt Druidh

Coire Gorm
LAIRIG GHRU

Beanaidh Bheag
Sron na Lairige
Coire Beanaidh
Pools of Dee
Coire Ruadh
Coire an Lochain
Coire na Lairige
Ben Macdui
Loch Coire an Lochan
Braeriach
Coire Bhrochain

GLEANN EINICH
Allt Buidheannach
Einich Cairn
Falls of Dee
Garbh Choire Bothy
Coire Bogha-cloiche
Garbh Choire Dhaidh
Wells of Dee
NORTH EAST RIDGE
Lochain Uaine
NORTH RIDGE
Cairn Toul
Coire an t-Sabhail
Coire nan Clach
Garbh Choire Mor
CROWN BUTTRESS SPUR
Coire an Lochain Uaine
EAST RIDGE
River Dee
Sgor an Lochain Uaine
Coire an-t Saighdeir

STALKERS PATH
Loch Einich
CREAG NAN LOCH RIDGE
Coire Dhondail
Am Bodach
MOINE MHOR PATH
Coire Odhar
COIRE ODHAR PATH
Corrour Bothy
Corrour Bridge

Coire Odhar
SOUTH WEST RIDGE
The Devil's Point

Loch nan Cnapan
Loch nan Stuirteag

Glen Feshie
Tom Dubh
Monadh Mor
GLEN GEUSACHAN PATH
Geusachan Burn
GLEN GEUSACHAN

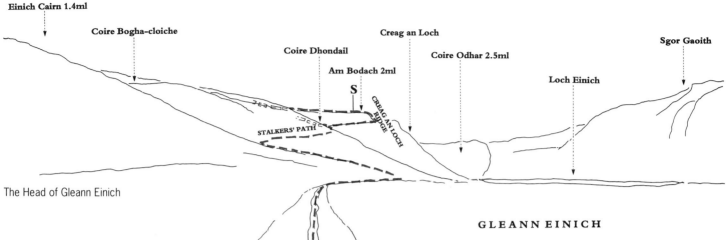

Einich Cairn 1.4ml

Coire Bogha-cloiche

Coire Dhondail

Creag an Loch

Sgor Gaoith

Coire Odhar 2.5ml

Am Bodach 2ml

S

Loch Einich

STALKERS' PATH

CREAG AN LOCH RIDGE

The Head of Gleann Einich

GLEANN EINICH

Cairn Toul and Sgor an Lochain Uaine from the flats between Braeriach and Einich Cairn

▲ Carn a' Mhaim

Mountain Rescue Post (Telephone)

GLEN LUIBEG

Luibeg Bridge

Luibeg Burn

Luibeg
Derry Lodge

GLEN DEE

r Dee

STALKERS' PATH

Grade: Intermediate
Time: 4.5–5 hours
Distance: 10.25 miles (16.5km)
Height Gain: 3766ft (1148m)
Terrain: Long remote glen, heather-covered hillside, high rocky corrie, high ridge and narrow stony summit
Start: Whitewell, GR916086

Summary: A well-graded path which climbs through the lonely Coire Dhondail on the east side of Gleann Einich. Originally constructed for deer stalkers, it provides handy access onto the Braeriach/Cairn Toul massif. In winter the corrie head wall can become icy and avalanche prone.

Ascent: Follow the access track S the full length of Gleann Einich. Just before Loch Einich take the Stalkers' Path that climbs SE then S into Coire Dhondail. Continue across the corrie floor then climb the zig-zags SW up the head wall. From the head of Coire Dhondail climb E onto the plateau. Head SE then E and skirt around the crags of Garbh Choire Mor to Sgor an Lochain Uaine. Descend SE to the col and make the short pull E to Cairn Toul.

Descent: Head W then NW over Sgor an Lochain Uaine then drop W down to the col. From the col skirt W then NW around the crags of Garbh Choire Mor and then descend W to the head of Coire Dhondail. The Stalkers' Path is marked by a small cairn; descend the zig-zags NW into the corrie then turn N across the corrie floor and take the path down into Gleann Einich. Join the track and follow it N to Whitewell.

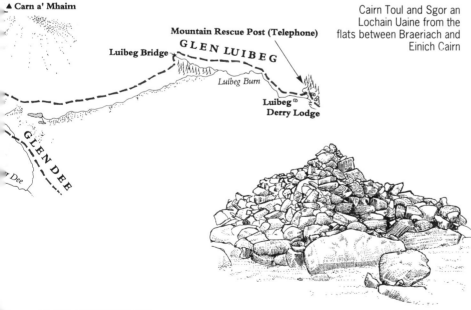

Cairn Toul's summit cairn

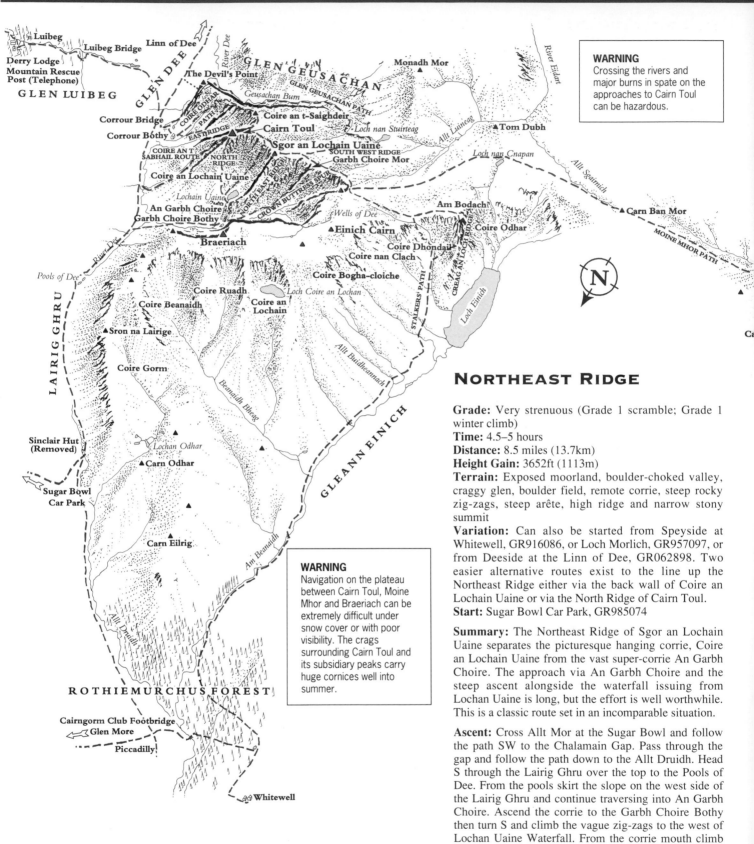

WARNING
Crossing the rivers and major burns in spate on the approaches to Cairn Toul can be hazardous.

WARNING
Navigation on the plateau between Cairn Toul, Moine Mhor and Braeriach can be extremely difficult under snow cover or with poor visibility. The crags surrounding Cairn Toul and its subsidiary peaks carry huge cornices well into summer.

NORTHEAST RIDGE

Grade: Very strenuous (Grade 1 scramble; Grade 1 winter climb)
Time: 4.5–5 hours
Distance: 8.5 miles (13.7km)
Height Gain: 3652ft (1113m)
Terrain: Exposed moorland, boulder-choked valley, craggy glen, boulder field, remote corrie, steep rocky zig-zags, steep arête, high ridge and narrow stony summit
Variation: Can also be started from Speyside at Whitewell, GR916086, or Loch Morlich, GR957097, or from Deeside at the Linn of Dee, GR062898. Two easier alternative routes exist to the line up the Northeast Ridge either via the back wall of Coire an Lochain Uaine or via the North Ridge of Cairn Toul.
Start: Sugar Bowl Car Park, GR985074

Summary: The Northeast Ridge of Sgor an Lochain Uaine separates the picturesque hanging corrie, Coire an Lochain Uaine from the vast super-corrie An Garbh Choire. The approach via An Garbh Choire and the steep ascent alongside the waterfall issuing from Lochan Uaine is long, but the effort is well worthwhile. This is a classic route set in an incomparable situation.

Ascent: Cross Allt Mor at the Sugar Bowl and follow the path SW to the Chalamain Gap. Pass through the gap and follow the path down to the Allt Druidh. Head S through the Lairig Ghru over the top to the Pools of Dee. From the pools skirt the slope on the west side of the Lairig Ghru and continue traversing into An Garbh Choire. Ascend the corrie to the Garbh Choire Bothy then turn S and climb the vague zig-zags to the west of Lochan Uaine Waterfall. From the corrie mouth climb the Northeast Ridge direct to the summit of Sgor an Lochain Uaine. Descend SE to the col and make the short pull E to Cairn Toul.

BRAERIACH LINK

Grade: Intermediate
Time: 1.5 hours
Distance: 3.5 miles (5.6km)
Height Gain: 1049ft (320m)
Terrain: Scree-covered ridges and high mountain plateau
Start: Cairn Toul, GR964973

Summary: A high-level walk around one of Scotland's most impressive corrie systems.

Route: Head W then NW over Sgor an Lochain Uaine, then drop W down to the col. Skirt W, NW then NE around the edge of Garbh Choire Mor and Garbh Choire Dhaidh to the head of the Falls of Dee. From the infant Dee climb steadily NE to Braeriach.

Sgor an Lochain Uaine from Allt a' Gharbh-choire (near Garbh Choire Bothy)

CROWN BUTTRESS SPUR

Grade: Strenuous
Time: 4.5–5 hours
Distance: 9 miles (14.5km)
Height Gain: 3652ft (1113m)
Terrain: Exposed moorland, boulder-choked valley, craggy glen, boulder field, remote corrie, scree-covered spur, high ridge and narrow stony summit
Variation: Can also be started from Speyside at Whitewell, GR916086, or Loch Morlich, GR957097, or from Deeside at the Linn of Dee, GR062898.
Start: Sugar Bowl Car Park, GR985074

Summary: The ring of crags at the head of Garbh Choire Mor have precious few lines that can be attempted by walkers. The easiest line is the spur/shelf above Crown Buttress on the south side of the corrie (this part of Garbh Choire Mor is known as Corrie of the Chockstone Gully). In winter the top of this route is one of the few places between Cairn Toul and Braeriach that generally does not carry a cornice.

Ascent: Cross Allt Mor at the Sugar Bowl and follow the path SW to the Chalamain Gap. Pass through the gap and follow the path down to the Allt Druidh. Head S through the Lairig Ghru over the top to the Pools of Dee. From the pools skirt the slope on the west side of the Lairig Ghru and continue traversing into An Garbh Choire. Ascend the corrie past the bothy then climb SW below the Corrie of the Chockstone Gully. At the west end of the bay ascend the shelf, then spur, onto the plateau. Turn E and climb Sgor an Lochain Uaine. Descend SE to the col and make the short pull E to Cairn Toul.

Descent: Head W then NW over Sgor an Lochain Uaine then drop W towards the col. Just before the col the Crown Buttress Spur abuts the plateau edge (GR947976); descend NE down it into An Garbh Choire. Continue NW then W past Garbh Choire Bothy then traverse NW into the Lairig Ghru. Head N past the Pools of Dee and descend to the start of the Chalamain Gap Path (below the old site of the Sinclair Hut). Turn R and follow it N to the gap. Once through head NE to the Sugar Bowl.

Corrour Bothy, below Coire Odhar on the west side of the River Dee at the north end of Glen Dee, GR981958. A stone hut that formerly accommodated stalkers in the season, it is now a popular open bothy with room for ten

EAST RIDGE

Grade: Strenuous (Grade 1 scramble; Grade 1 winter climb)
Time: 4.5–5 hours
Distance: 9.75 miles (15.7km)
Height Gain: 3209ft (978m)
Terrain: Woodland, wide open glens, steep scree-strewn slope, high remote corrie, rocky arête and narrow stony summit
Variation: An easier alternative is via Coire an t-Sabhail. Can also be started from Linn of Dee by taking the Glen Dee track past White Bridge to join the route near Corrour Bridge.
Start: Linn of Dee, GR062898

Summary: Climbs the fine arête between Coire an t-Saighdeir and Coire and t-Sabhail on the east side of Cairn Toul. Affords superb views of the Lairig Ghru. The most direct route to Cairn Toul from Deeside.

Ascent: From the Linn of Dee head N then NW to Derry Lodge (Emergency Telephone), pass the lodge and continue along Glen Luibeg to Luibeg Bridge. Cross the bridge then swing W over the col into Glen Dee. Cross the river at Corrour Bridge and head NW past Corrour Bothy up the steep slope behind to Coire an t-Saighdeir. Head N across the mouth of the corrie to the foot of the East Ridge. Climb the ridge direct to Cairn Toul's summit.

COIRE ODHAR PATH

Grade: Intermediate
Time: 5 hours
Distance: 10 miles (16km)
Height Gain: 3372ft (1028m)
Terrain: Woodland, wide open glens, remote corrie, high ridge and narrow stony summit
Variation: An alternative to the zig-zag path is the rocky ridge at the north side of Coire Odhar – a safer route under icy or avalanche conditions. Can also be started from Linn of Dee by taking the Glen Dee track past White Bridge to join the route near Corrour Bridge.
Start: Linn of Dee, GR062898

Summary: A popular and straightforward route that climbs the steep head wall of Coire Odhar via a series of zig-zags to emerge onto the verdant flats between The Devil's Point and Cairn Toul.

Ascent: From the Linn of Dee head N then NW to Derry Lodge (Emergency Telephone), pass the lodge and continue along Glen Luibeg to Luibeg Bridge. Cross the bridge then swing W over the col into Glen Dee. Cross the river at Corrour Bridge, pass Corrour Bothy and head NW then W up into Coire Odhar. Climb the head wall via the zig-zags onto the flats at the top. Turn R and climb steadily NW then N, skirting the crags, to Cairn Toul.

Descent: Head S then SE, skirting the crags, to the flats on the northwest side of The Devil's Point. Descend E via the zig-zags into Coire Odhar. Pass Corrour Bothy and turn SE to cross the River Dee at Corrour Bridge. Make the short climb on the east side to the Glen Luibeg path. Join the path and follow it E over Luibeg Bridge to Derry Lodge. From the lodge take the track SE to the Linn of Dee.

The top section of the East Ridge

CAIRN GORM
4081FT (1244M)

CAIRN GORM HAS DEVELOPED A REPUTATION as the easiest of 4000ft peaks to climb. Since the arrival in 1961 of the chair lift and all the ski-grounds paraphernalia this sentiment may well be true, but it can only be applied to the Coire Cas Track. Elsewhere on the mountain there is a wide selection of routes, some long, some short, all of which offer superb outings through some classic high-mountain terrain.

Cairn Gorm shares the high plateau on the east side of the Lairig Ghru with Ben Macdui. To the south its slopes descend steeply to the cold waters of Loch Avon while to the north long ridges intersected by deep corries extend towards Glen More. Two deep and long glens bound Cairn Gorm's east and west fringes. Lairig Ghru to the west is a popular and well documented route but Strath Nethy is less well known; its high point is at The Saddle below Cairn Gorm's summit from which it runs due north to the open moorland by the Ryvoan Pass – over which it is linked to Glen More.

The popular northern corries of Cairn Gorm attract walkers and climbers as well as skiers in considerable numbers; easy access and attractive climbing have ensured this. To the south is altogether a different story. Cairn Gorm's main ridge line marks the start of some of Britain's wildest country. Numerous parties have set off south from Cairn Gorm only to be overtaken by vicious storms which can arrive with frightening speed. This very difficult terrain requires a high degree of competence to navigate through and survive in.

MAPS
Ordnance Survey: Outdoor Leisure 1: 25000 No 3; Landranger 1: 50000 No 36 & No 43.

INFORMATION
Tourist Information Centres: Aviemore, Glenmore, Tomintoul and Braemar.

ACCOMMODATION
Youth Hostels: Aviemore, Glenmore, Tomintoul, Braemar and Inverey (near the Linn of Dee).

Hotels and B&B: Aviemore, Coylumbridge, Glenmore, Tomintoul and Braemar.

Camp sites: Aviemore, Coylumbridge and Glenmore.

Bothies and Howffs: Bob Scott's Bothy, GR042931; Corrour Bothy, GR982958; The Shelter Stone, GR002016; The Hutchison Memorial Hut, GR023998; Fords of Avon Refuge, GR042032; Bynack Stable, GR105031; Ryvoan Bothy, GR006115. The Sinclair Memorial Hut was removed in 1991.

Cairn Gorm (**CG**) from the head of Coire an t-Sneachda, **CaS** Coire an t-Sneachda, **CR** Coire Raibeirt

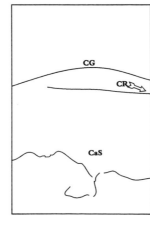

Bynack Stable at the north end of Strath Nethy on the west bank of the River Nethy, GR021105. An unappealing corrugated steel shed with two rooms, it can hold about six people

SOUTHEAST FLANK

Grade: Strenuous
Time: 4.5–5 hours
Distance: 12.25 miles (19.7km)
Height Gain: 3041ft (927m)
Terrain: Woodland, wide open glens, exposed moorland, boulder-strewn col, steep rocky slopes and stony summit
Variation: The Saddle can be reached from Speyside via Strath Nethy starting at Glenmore, GR977098. An extremely long approach can also be made via Glen Avon from Delnabo, near Tomintoul, GR161171.
Start: Linn of Dee, GR062898

Summary: The Southeast Flank of Cairn Gorm is steep and a little monotonous but provides a useful route as it can be climbed from the high start point of The Saddle. The Saddle is a broad col which separates the head of Strath Nethy from Loch Avon.

Ascent: From the Linn of Dee head N then NW to Derry Lodge (Emergency Telephone), pass the lodge and head N into Glen Derry. Continue N the length of Glen Derry then cross over the Lairig an Laoigh and finally descend to the Fords of Avon. Cross the ford to the Fords of Avon Refuge and follow the River Avon W to Loch Avon. Once alongside the loch continue W making a rising traverse to The Saddle. From The Saddle climb the steep slope W. As the angle eases turn NW and climb steadily to Cairn Gorm's summit.

Descent: Descend SE from the radio relay station, then E as the ground steepens to The Saddle. From The Saddle make a descending traverse E to the path at the side of Loch Avon, then follow it to the Fords of Avon Refuge. Cross the Fords of Avon and head S over the Lairig an Laoigh. Continue S down Glen Derry to Derry Lodge. From the lodge take the track SE to the Linn of Dee.

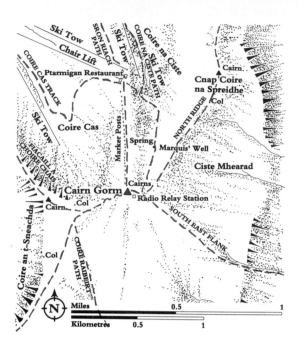

COIRE RAIBEIRT PATH

Grade: Strenuous
Time: 4.5–5 hours
Distance: 10.5 miles (16.9km)
Height Gain: 3189ft (972m)
Terrain: Forest, long narrow glen, exposed col, high mountain loch, steep rocky corrie, scree and stony summit
Variation: Access from Deeside can be had from Linn of Dee, GR062898, via Glen Derry, Lairig an Laoigh and the Fords of Avon.
Start: Glenmore, GR977098

Summary: Coire Raibeirt Path provides the most direct access to the crags at the head of Loch Avon and is popular with climbers approaching from Speyside (in descent).

Ascent: Take the Glenmore Lodge road and follow it E past the lodge, then NE to take the Ryvoan Pass Track. After An Lochan Uaine the track splits. Take the right-hand branch and follow it E then SE to Bynack Stable. Cross the River Nethy and follow the narrow path S down Strath Nethy to The Saddle. Cross over the broad col and follow the path SW above Loch Avon. Continue along it until the Allt Coire Raibeirt then turn NW and climb the steep path into the Coire Raibeirt. At the head of the corrie turn R and follow the path E to the summit of Cairn Gorm.

Descent: Head W to the head of Coire Raibeirt and take the path SSE down through the corrie to the side of Loch Avon. Turn L and follow the path NE to The Saddle. Cross the broad col and head N the length of Strath Nethy to the bridge near Bynack Stable. Cross it and take the path NW then W to join the Ryvoan Pass Track. Turn L onto it and follow it to Glenmore.

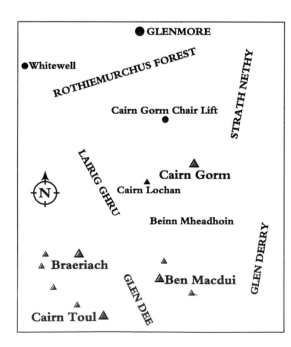

COIRE DOMHAIN PATH

Grade: Strenuous
Time: 5 hours
Distance: 11.5 miles (18.5km)
Height Gain: 3189ft (972m)
Terrain: Forest, long narrow glen, exposed col, high mountain loch, steep rocky corrie, high ridge, scree and stony summit
Variation: Access from Deeside can be had from Linn of Dee, GR062898, via Glen Derry, Lairig an Laoigh and the Fords of Avon.
Start: Glenmore, GR977098

Summary: The Loch Avon Basin has an impressive ring of crags; particularly striking is the towering prow of the Shelter Stone Crag. The best through route to pass by them is through Coire Domhain.

Ascent: Take the Glenmore Lodge road and follow it E past the lodge then NE to take the Ryvoan Pass Track. After An Lochan Uaine the track splits. Take the right-hand branch and follow it E then SE to Bynack Stable. Cross the River Nethy and follow the narrow path S down Strath Nethy to The Saddle. Cross over the broad col and follow the path SW above Loch Avon to the head of the loch. Follow the Feith Buidhe to its junction with the Allt Coire Domhain. Turn NW and climb steeply between Hell's Lum Crag and Stag Rocks into Coire Domhain. At head of the corrie turn R and follow the path NE around the top of Coire Raibeirt then E to the summit of Cairn Gorm.

Radio relay station, Cairn Gorm summit

Descent: Descend W from the radio relay station and follow the main plateau path as it skirts the top of Coire Raibeirt and Coire an t-Sneachda to the head of Coire Domhain. Drop into the corrie and follow the Allt Coire Domhain SE into the Loch Avon Basin. Turn E at the bottom and follow the path on the north side of the loch to The Saddle. Cross the broad col and head N the length of Strath Nethy to the bridge near Bynack Stable. Cross it and take the path NW then W to join the Ryvoan Pass Track. Turn L on to it and follow it to Glenmore.

Fords of Avon

LURCHER'S CRAG PATH

Grade: Intermediate
Time: 5 hours
Distance: 9 miles (14.5km)
Height Gain: 3848ft (1173m)
Terrain: Forest, steep-sided glen, high ridges, scree and stony summit
Variation: Can also be started from Loch Morlich, GR977098, or the Sugar Bowl Car Park, GR985074. If starting at the Sugar Bowl, Lurcher's Gully provides an easier alternative line.
Start: Whitewell, GR916085

Summary: Forming the impressive east wall of the Lairig Ghru the long ridge of Creag an Leth-choin can be easily gained from Rothiemurchus via the easy slopes of the Chalamain Gap. It gives a long steady approach to Cairn Gorm and passes through the complete range of terrain for which the Cairngorms are famous.

Ascent: Take the Gleann Einich track S to Lochan Deo then turn E and follow the path over the Cairngorm Club Footbridge to the junction at Piccadilly. Take the Lairig Ghru Path SE to the junction with the Chalamain Gap Path. Join it and follow it N, then turn SE and climb the steep slopes to Creag an Leth-choin. Continue SE past the head of Lurcher's Gully to the col on the west side of Cairn Lochan. Climb E to Cairn Lochan and then descend ENE to join the main plateau path at the head of Coire Domhain. Take the path NE as it skirts over the top of Coire an t-Sneachda and Coire Raibeirt to Cairn Gorm.

Descent: Descend W from the radio relay station and follow the main plateau path as it skirts the top of Coire Raibeirt and Coire an t-Sneachda to the head of Coire Domhain. Turn WSW and climb over Cairn Lochan to the col on the west side. Cross the col and head NE over Creag an Leth-choin then descend to the Chalamain Gap. Drop S to join the Lairig Ghru Path which is then followed NW to Piccadilly. Take the path SW then NW to the Cairngorm Club Footbridge. Cross it and head W along the path to join the Gleann Einich track which is then followed N to Whitewell.

BEN MACDUI LINK

Grade: Intermediate
Time: 1.5 hours
Distance: 4 miles (6.4km)
Height Gain: 721ft (220m)
Terrain: High mountain plateau
Start: Cairn Gorm, GR006040

Summary: A well-trodden path across the Cairn Gorm plateau to Britain's second-highest peak. In good conditions an easy walk, in a blizzard, near-impossible.

Route: Descend W from the radio relay station and follow the main plateau path as it skirts the top of Coire Raibeirt and Coire an t-Sneachda to the head of Coire Domhain. Turn S then SW and traverse the east side of Cairn Lochan to Lochan Buidhe. The path then swings SSE; follow it as its winds its way up to the summit slopes of Ben Macdui.

> **WARNING**
> Crossing the rivers and major burns in spate on the approaches to Cairn Gorm can be hazardous.

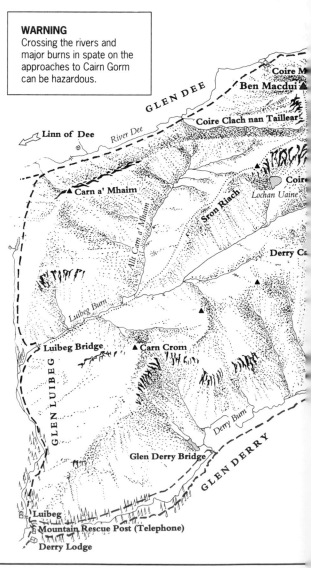

Descending into Coire Raibeirt

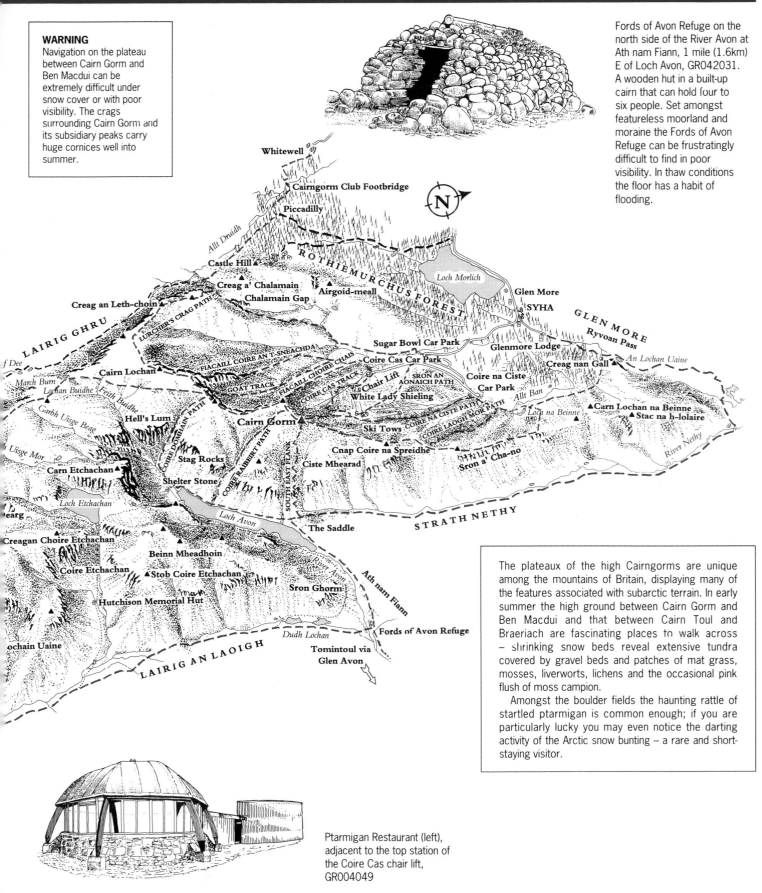

WARNING
Navigation on the plateau between Cairn Gorm and Ben Macdui can be extremely difficult under snow cover or with poor visibility. The crags surrounding Cairn Gorm and its subsidiary peaks carry huge cornices well into summer.

Fords of Avon Refuge on the north side of the River Avon at Ath nam Fiann, 1 mile (1.6km) E of Loch Avon, GR042031. A wooden hut in a built-up cairn that can hold four to six people. Set amongst featureless moorland and moraine the Fords of Avon Refuge can be frustratingly difficult to find in poor visibility. In thaw conditions the floor has a habit of flooding.

The plateaux of the high Cairngorms are unique among the mountains of Britain, displaying many of the features associated with subarctic terrain. In early summer the high ground between Cairn Gorm and Ben Macdui and that between Cairn Toul and Braeriach are fascinating places to walk across – shrinking snow beds reveal extensive tundra covered by gravel beds and patches of mat grass, mosses, liverworts, lichens and the occasional pink flush of moss campion.

Amongst the boulder fields the haunting rattle of startled ptarmigan is common enough; if you are particularly lucky you may even notice the darting activity of the Arctic snow bunting – a rare and short-staying visitor.

Ptarmigan Restaurant (left), adjacent to the top station of the Coire Cas chair lift, GR004049

FIACAILL COIRE AN T-SNEACHDA

Grade: Strenuous (Easy scramble; Grade 1 winter climb)
Time: 2.5 hours
Distance: 4 miles (6.4km)
Height Gain: 2493ft (760m)
Terrain: Broad corrie floor, narrow rocky ridge, high ridge, scree and stony summit
Variation: The col on the east side of Cairn Lochan can be gained from Coire an t-Sneachda by the Goat Track. This steep series of zig-zags is, however, rather unattractive, being loose in summer and avalanche prone in winter.
Start: Coire Cas Car Park, GR990060

Summary: Easy access has ensured that the northern corries of Cairn Gorm – Coire Lochain and Coire an t-Sneachda - are popular climbing venues. Between the crags of these two steep-walled corries a narrow ridge projects N at an easier angle. The Fiacaill Coire an t-Sneachda gives an adventurous scramble to the west side of Cairn Gorm.

Ascent: From the car park cross the Allt a' Choire Chais and follow the constructed path SW across the mouth of Coire an t-Sneachda. After crossing the Allt Coire an t-Sneachda, turn S and climb the broad ridge to the Fiacaill Coire an t-Sneachda. Continue S up the Fiacaill onto the slopes east of Cairn Lochan. Descend E to the col at the head of Coire Domhain then skirt the heads of Coire an t-Sneachda and Coire Raibeirt NE to Cairn Gorm.

Descent: Descend W from the radio relay station and follow the main plateau path as it skirts the top of Coire Raibeirt and Coire an t-Sneachda to the head of Coire Domhain. Climb W to the top of the Fiacaill Coire an t-Sneachda (there is a cairn, but in winter it is usually obliterated by snow – under such conditions the Fiacaill cannot be recommended as a descent). Descend N onto the ridge dropping down to meet up with the main corries path. Follow it NE to Coire Cas Car Park.

FIACAILL A' COIRE CHAIS

Grade: Easy
Time: 1.5–2 hours
Distance: 2 miles (3.2km)
Height Gain: 1984ft (605m)
Terrain: Narrow ridge, scree and stony summit
Start: Coire Cas Car Park, GR990060

Summary: The west edge of Coire Cas is bounded by a slender ridge which climbs direct to the west shoulder of Cairn Gorm. It provides a pleasant route with fine views into Coire an t-Sneachda.

Ascent: From the car park cross the Allt a' Choire Chais to the start of the constructed path. Turn immediately SE and climb the Fiacaill a' Choire Chais to the shoulder on the west side of Cairn Gorm's summit slopes. Turn E and climb direct to the summit.

Descent: Descend W from the radio relay station and follow the main plateau path to the cairn at the top of Fiacaill a' Choire Chais. Drop NW down the Fiacaill then cross the Allt a' Choire Chais to the Coire Cas Car Park.

COIRE CAS TRACK

Grade: Easy
Time: 1.5–2 hours
Distance: 2.25 miles (3.6km)
Height Gain: 1984ft (605m)
Terrain: Broad open corrie and stony summit
Variation: The worst of the destruction caused by the ski grounds can be avoided by the Sron an Aonaich path (starts at GR987069) up the east side of Coire Cas.
Start: Coire Cas Car Park, GR990060

Summary: A broad constructed track that winds its way through the ski ground paraphernalia to the igloo-shaped Ptarmigan Restaurant then climbs a stone staircase to Cairn Gorm's summit.

Ascent: From the car park follow the track SE up through Coire Cas then traverse NE to the Ptarmigan Restaurant. Turn S and follow the waymarked (stone staircase) track to Cairn Gorm.

Descent: Descend N from the radio relay station and follow the waymarked path to the Ptarmigan Restaurant. Turn W and follow the track as it traverses to the S into Coire Cas. Continue along the track and follow it NW through Coire Cas to the car park.

Fiacaill Coire an t-Sneachda from Coire an Lochain

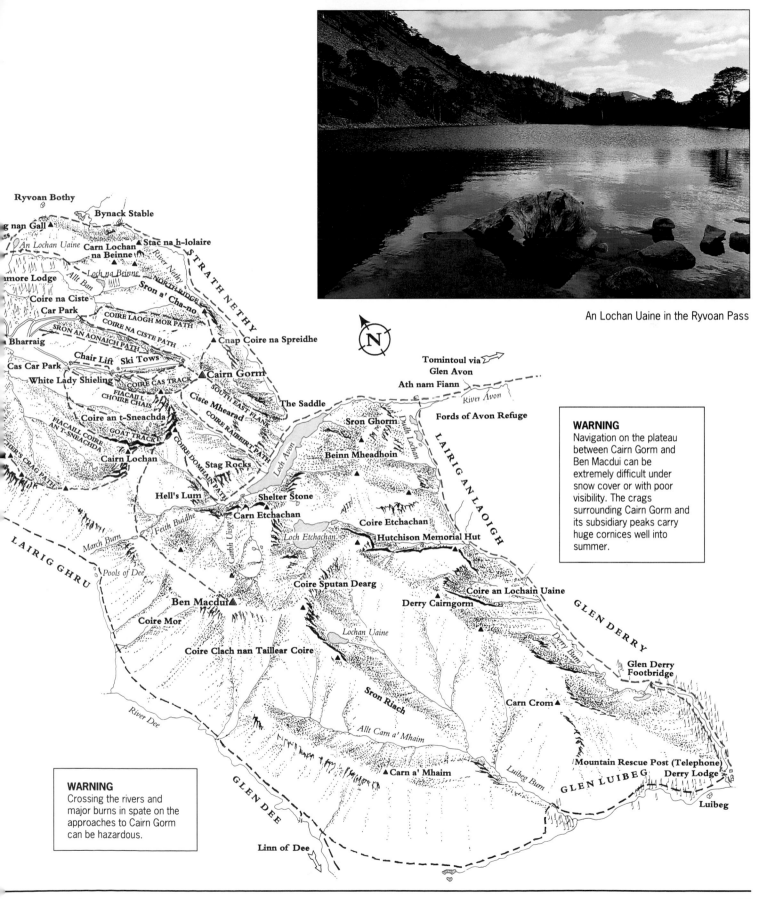

An Lochan Uaine in the Ryvoan Pass

Ryvoan Bothy

Bynack Stable

g nan Gall ▲

Stac na h-Iolaire

An Lochan Uaine

Carn Lochan
na Beinne

River Nethy

S T R A T H   N E T H Y

more Lodge

Loch na Beinne

Allt Ban

Sron a' Cha-no

NORTH RIDGE

Coire na Ciste
Car Park

COIRE LAOGH MOR PATH

COIRE NA CISTE PATH

Cnap Coire na Spreidhe

Bharraig

SRON AN AONAICH PATH

Chair Lift

Ski Tows

Cairn Gorm ▲

Cas Car Park

White Lady Shieling

COIRE CAS TRACK

SOUTH EAST FLANK

The Saddle

Tomintoul via
Glen Avon

Ath nam Fiann

River Avon

Fords of Avon Refuge

FIACAILL
CHOIRE CHAIS

Ciste Mhearad

COIRE RAIBEIRT PATH

Sron Ghorm

Dubh Lochan

WARNING
Navigation on the plateau
between Cairn Gorm and
Ben Macdui can be
extremely difficult under
snow cover or with poor
visibility. The crags
surrounding Cairn Gorm and
its subsidiary peaks carry
huge cornices well into
summer.

Coire an t-Sneachda

FIACAILL COIRE
AN T-SNEACHDA

GOAT TRACK

COIRE DOMHAIN PATH

Beinn Mheadhoin

L A I R I G   A N   L A O I G H

ER'S CRAG PATH

Cairn Lochan ▲

Stag Rocks

Loch Avon

Hell's Lum

Carn Etchachan

Shelter Stone

Feith Buidhe

Garbh Uisge

Coire Etchachan

Hutchison Memorial Hut

Loch Etchachan

LAIRIG GHRU

March Burn

Pools of Dee

Coire Sputan Dearg

Coire an Lochain Uaine

Derry Cairngorm

G L E N   D E R R Y

Ben Macdui ▲

Coire Mor

Lochan Uaine

Derry Burn

Glen Derry
Footbridge

Coire Clach nan Taillear Coire

Sron Riach

Carn Crom ▲

River Dee

Allt Carn a' Mhaim

Luibeg Burn

Mountain Rescue Post (Telephone)

Derry Lodge

GLEN DEE

Carn a' Mhaim ▲

G L E N   L U I B E G

Luibeg

WARNING
Crossing the rivers and
major burns in spate on the
approaches to Cairn Gorm
can be hazardous.

Linn of Dee

Cairn Gorm and Forefinger Pinnacle from the top of Shelter Stone Crag

COIRE NA CISTE PATH

Grade: Easy
Time: 2 hours
Distance: 2.25 miles (3.6km)
Height Gain: 2280ft (695m)
Terrain: Steep narrow corrie, open upper corrie and stony summit
Start: Coire na Ciste Car Park, GR998074

Summary: Coire na Ciste extends directly N from the summit dome of Cairn Gorm. It shares the same fate as Coire Cas as a very popular ski ground. In winter it is generally busy with skiers but in summer it gives a quiet and pleasant walk alongside the Allt na Ciste.

Ascent: From the Coire na Ciste Car Park follow the Allt na Ciste SSE up through the narrow confines of Coire na Ciste to the old path on the east side of Cairn Gorm. Join the path and ascend it SSW to Cairn Gorm.

Descent: Take the old path NNE from the radio relay station to the head of Coire na Ciste. Descend NNW through the corrie to the car park at the bottom chair lift station.

The crags of Coire an Lochain

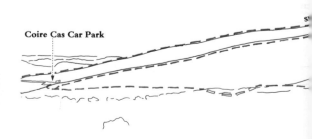

Coire Cas Car Park

NORTH RIDGE

Grade: Intermediate
Time: 3.5–4 hours
Distance: 6.5 miles (10.5km)
Height Gain: 2969ft (905m)
Terrain: Long undulating ridge and stony summit
Variation: The main ridge can also be gained via Coire Laogh Mor starting either at Coire na Ciste Car Park, GR998074, or Glenmore, GR977098.
Start: Glenmore, GR977098

Summary: The long North Ridge of Cairn Gorm runs the length of Strath Nethy. A superb route, it takes in the fine little top of Cnap Coire na Spreidhe then descends the narrow ridge Sron a' Cha-no to the woodland of Glen More.

Ascent: Take the Glenmore Lodge road and follow it E past the lodge, then NE and take the Ryvoan Pass Track. Before An Lochan Uaine turn R and climb the vague path SE below Creag nan Gall. Once through the woodland turn S and follow the vague path to Loch na Beinne. Before the loch swing SE and climb past the woodland enclosure to the shallow col at the foot of the Sron a' Cha-no. Follow the ridge S then SW past Cnap Coire na Spreidhe to join the old path on the east side of Cairn Gorm. Join the path and ascend it SSW to Cairn Gorm.

Descent: Take the old path NNE from the radio relay station to the head of Coire na Ciste. Head NE across the broad col towards Cnap Coire na Spreidhe then swing N and follow the ridge as it descends steadily to the shallow col at the foot of the Sron a' Cha-no. From the col descend past the woodland to the north end of Loch na Beinne and join the vague path which is followed N then NW to join the Ryvoan Pass Track. Turn L and follow it to Glenmore.

Fords of Avon

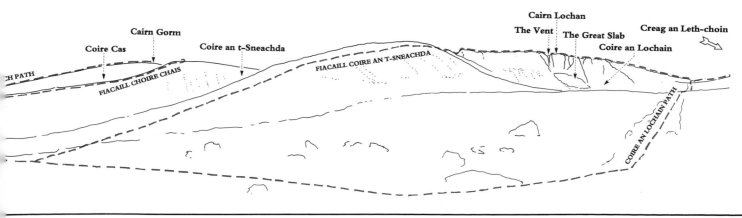

Cairn Gorm and the northern corries from the north

The steep descent from Stob Coire Bhealaich – can be avoided via Coire a' Bhuic

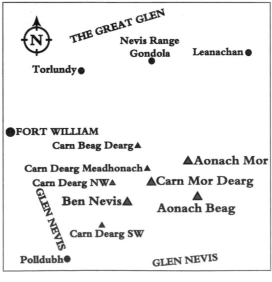

AONACH BEAG
4049FT (1234M)

AONACH BEAG SITS BETWEEN THE MAIN BEN NEVIS range and the peaks of The Grey Corries. Close by to the north is Aonach Mor and to the south is the deep trough of Glen Nevis. Set in such a commanding position amongst such fine peaks and glens Aonach Beag affords superb panoramic views.

The massive and complex An Aghaidh Garbh forms the northeast face of Aonach Beag. From its base extending northeast towards Glen Spean and the Leanachan Forest is An Coire Calma which in turn runs down into Coire an Eoin. Aonach Beag cannot be ascended directly up An Aghaidh Garbh, instead the cols at either end of the crag have to be gained. The combined approach via either of the cols and along the length of the corries is a fine but arduous expedition across terrain which is trackless, rough and unbelievably beautiful.

The southwest side of Aonach Beag is easily accessible from Glen Nevis. Its slopes form a horseshoe around the high hanging corrie of Coire nan Laogh. The northernmost arm (Southwest Ridge) is a high truncated spur which ends abruptly above Coire Giubhsachan. The southern arm is formed by the sharp scree-covered peak Sgurr a' Bhuic.

MAPS
Ordnance Survey: Outdoor Leisure 1: 25000 No 32 (Mountainmaster of Ben Nevis); Landranger 1: 50000 No 41. Tourist Map 1: 63360 Ben Nevis and Glen Coe.

INFORMATION
Tourist Information Centres: Fort William and Spean Bridge.

ACCOMMODATION
Youth Hostels: Glen Nevis.

Hotels and B&B: Fort William, Glen Nevis, Spean Bridge and Roy Bridge.

Camp sites: Glen Nevis, Camaghael, Inverroy and Roy Bridge.

Bothies and Howffs: Steall Hut, GR178684, Glen Nevis – a locked private hut booked through either the Scottish Mountaineering Club or the British Mountaineering Council.

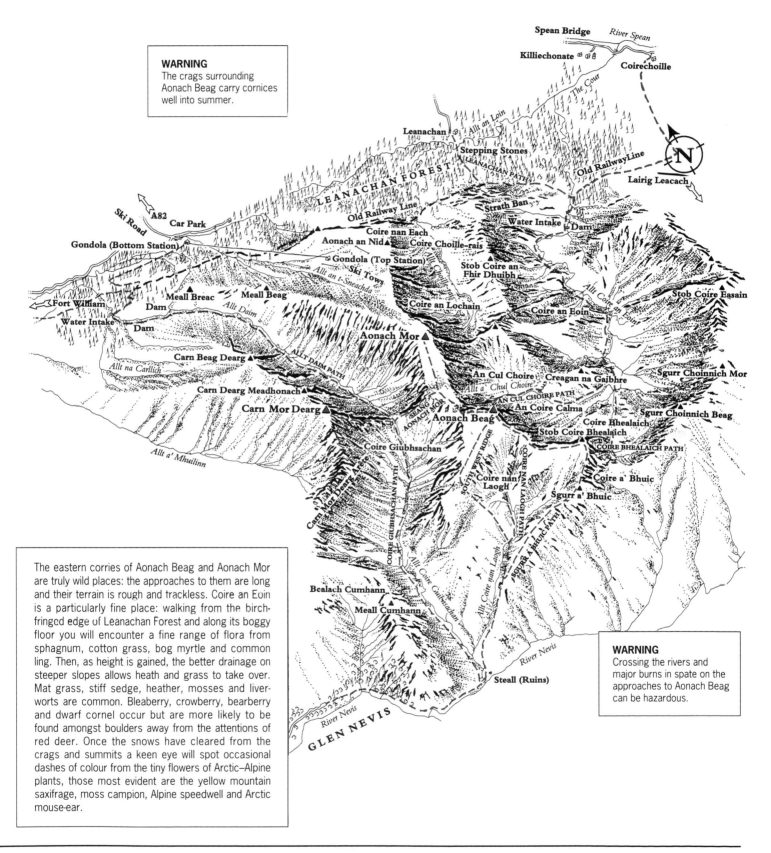

WARNING
The crags surrounding Aonach Beag carry cornices well into summer.

WARNING
Crossing the rivers and major burns in spate on the approaches to Aonach Beag can be hazardous.

The eastern corries of Aonach Beag and Aonach Mor are truly wild places: the approaches to them are long and their terrain is rough and trackless. Coire an Eoin is a particularly fine place: walking from the birch-fringed edge of Leanachan Forest and along its boggy floor you will encounter a fine range of flora from sphagnum, cotton grass, bog myrtle and common ling. Then, as height is gained, the better drainage on steeper slopes allows heath and grass to take over. Mat grass, stiff sedge, heather, mosses and liver-worts are common. Bleaberry, crowberry, bearberry and dwarf cornel occur but are more likely to be found amongst boulders away from the attentions of red deer. Once the snows have cleared from the crags and summits a keen eye will spot occasional dashes of colour from the tiny flowers of Arctic–Alpine plants, those most evident are the yellow mountain saxifrage, moss campion, Alpine speedwell and Arctic mouse-ear.

Aonach Beag (**AB**) from Carn Mor Dearg (**CMD**),
SAM Seang Aonach Mor, **ER** East Ridge,
CG Coire Giubhsachan

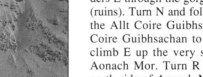

COIRE GIUBHSACHAN PATH

Grade: Strenuous
Time: 3.5 hours
Distance: 4.75 miles (7.6km)
Height Gain: 3704ft (1129m)
Terrain: Narrow wooded gorge, craggy glen, steep loose slope, scree and summit plateau
Start: Glen Nevis Car Park, GR167692

Summary: Climbing steadily alongside the waterslides and waterfalls of the Allt Coire Giubhsachan, the Coire Giubhsachan Path twists its way N to the col on the west side of Aonach Mor. Access to Aonach Beag from the col involves a steep ascent up the Seang Aonach Mor then a walk SW along the main ridge.

Ascent: From the car park follow the path as it meanders E through the gorge to the footbridge by the Steall (ruins). Turn N and follow the path up the west side of the Allt Coire Guibhsachan. Continue N up through Coire Guibhsachan to the col at its head. At the col climb E up the very steep and in parts loose Seang Aonach Mor. Turn R and descend to the col on the north side of Aonach Mor. Cross it and climb the path SE up the scree. As the angle eases turn SSE to the summit of Aonach Beag.

Descent: From the summit descent NNW, then NW following the path down the scree to the col on the north side of Aonach Beag. Cross it and climb NNW to the top of the Seang Aonach Mor (small cairn). Turn W and descend the vague path down the steep and in parts loose slope to the col. Turn S and follow the Allt Coire Giubhsachan down to the footbridge at the Steall (ruins). At the footbridge join the Glen Nevis footpath and follow it W through the gorge to the car park.

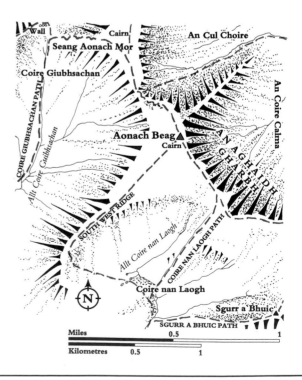

ALLT DAIM PATH

Grade: Strenuous
Time: 4 hours
Distance: 5.5 miles (8.9km)
Height Gain: 3835ft (1169m)
Terrain: Woodland, craggy glen, steep loose slope, scree and summit plateau
Variation: The Allt Daim Path can be gained from the gondola top station via a steep descent from Meall Beag. Can also be started via the course of the old railway line from the A82 at either the Distillery, GR126757, or Golf Course, GR136762.
Start: Gondola Car Park, GR172774

Summary: Climbs steadily along the wild glen occupied by the Allt Daim to the high col between Carn Mor Dearg and the Aonachs massif. A simple direct route but the ascent of Seang Aonach Mor can be problematic especially with snow cover and poor visibility.

Ascent: From the car park head SW then turn S and take the zig-zags up the course of the old narrow-gauge railway. Follow it SW to the water intake, then turn SE and climb alongside the Allt Daim. Continue alongside the Allt Daim to the col, then turn E and climb the very steep and in parts loose Seang Aonach Mor. At the top turn R and descend to the col on the north side of Aonach Mor. Cross it and climb the path SE up the scree. As the angle eases turn SSE to the summit of Aonach Beag.

Descent: From the summit descend NNW, then turn NW following the path down the scree to the col on the north side of Aonach Beag. Cross it and climb NNW to the top of the Seang Aonach Mor (small cairn). Turn W and descend the vague path down the steep and in parts loose slope to the col. Turn N and follow the Allt Daim on its southwest side to the water intake and join the old narrow-gauge railway. Follow its course NE, then take the zig-zags N. At the bottom turn R and head NE to the Gondola Car Park.

AN CUL CHOIRE PATH

Grade: Very strenuous
Time: 4.5–5 hours
Distance: 7 miles (11.3km)
Height Gain: 3688ft (1124m)
Terrain: Forest, rough pathless glen, remote craggy corrie, scree and summit plateau
Variation: Can also be started via the course of the old narrow-gauge railway from either the Gondola Car Park, GR172774, or Coirechoille in the Spean Valley, GR250806.
Start: Leanachan, GR219786

Summary: A long approach via the secretive An Cul Choire. The route climbs through its southwest bay tucked away behind the towering Northeast Ridge of Aonach Beag – which may contain snow even in summer.

Ascent: Follow the forest track SW to a fork. Take the left branch SE over the stepping stones to the building ruins. From the ruins follow the footpath S as it climbs to the course of the old railway line. Turn E and follow its course to the Allt Coire an Eoin Bridge. Cross it and turn R onto the access track; follow it SW to the water intake. Follow the Allt Coire an Eoin SW, S, then SW through the pathless wilds of Coire an Eoin to the mouth of An Cul Choire. Enter the corrie then climb the southwest bay to the col between Aonach Mor and Aonach Beag. Turn L and climb the path SE up the scree. As the angle eases turn SSE onto the summit of Aonach Beag.

Descent: From the summit descend NNW, turn NW following the path down the scree to the col on the north side of Aonach Beag. Descend the steep bay NE into An Cul Choire. Cross the corrie floor then follow the Allt Coire an Eoin NE, N then NE through Coire an Eoin to the water intake. Take the access track NE down to the old railway line then follow its course W to the top of the Leanachan Path. Turn L and follow it past the ruins and over the stepping stones to the public road.

Aonach Beag from the east face of Aonach Mor

COIRE NAN LAOGH PATH

SOUTH WEST RIDGE

GLEN NEVIS

Coire nan Laogh

Meall Cumhann

SGURR A BHUIC PATH

Sgurr a' Bhuic

Steall

Stob Coire Bhealaich

Carn Mor Dearg Arête

COIRE GHRUISACHAN PATH

Carn Mor Dearg

Coire a' Bhuic

Aonach Beag

SEANG AONACH MOR

Sgurr Choinnich Beag

Carn Dearg Meadhonach

Coire Bhealaich

AN GUL CHOIRE PATH

Aonach Mor

Sgurr Choinnich Mor

An Coire Calma

Carn Beag Dearg

THE GREY CORRIES

COIRE BHEALAICH PATH

Allt a' Chul Choire

Stob an Cul Choire

ALLT DAIM PATH

Stob Coire Easain

Stob Coire an Fhir Dhuibh

Breac Lach

Creagan na Gaibhre

Coire an Lochain

Ski Tows

Chair Lift

Allt an t-Sneachda

Coire an Eoin

Coire Choille-rais

Gondola (Top Station)

Meall Beag

Meall Breac

Water Intake

Aonach an Nid

Allt Choille-rais

Coire nan Each

River

N

Strath Ban

Gondola (Bottom Station)

Intake

Pipe Line

Tom na Sroine

Car Park

Ski Road

Old Railway Line

LEANACHAN FOREST

Allt an Loin

Stepping Stones

Leanachan

Lairig Leacach

Tom Liath

Steall Footbridge

Golf Course

Glen Nevis

W

A82

Coirechoille

Railway Station

Spean Bridge

The Cour

Cour Bridge

Killiechonate

River Spean

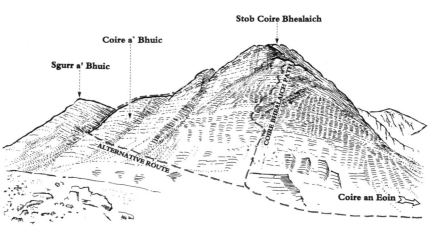

The Mamores from Coire nan Laogh

COIRE BHEALAICH PATH

Grade: Very strenuous
Time: 4.5–5 hours
Distance: 7.5 miles (12km)
Height Gain: 3688ft (1124m)
Terrain: Forest, rough pathless glen, remote rocky corrie, very steep loose slope, exposed ridge and summit plateau
Variation: The steep slope below Stob Coire Bhealaich can be avoided by making a diagonal traverse across Coire a' Bhuic to or from the col on the northeast side of Sgurr a' Bhuic. Can also be started via the course of the old narrow-gauge railway from either the Gondola car park GR172774, or Coirechoille in the Spean Valley, GR250807.
Start: Leanachan, GR219786

Summary: Aonach Beag drops away dramatically on its east side. The link between it and the peaks of The Grey Corries is via the big descent to the broad col above Coire Bhealaich. Approaching Coire Bhealaich along Coire an Eoin from Leanachan gives a long diverse walk with the added spice of some exposed scrambling to finish.

Ascent: Follow the forest track SW to a fork. Take the left branch SE over the stepping stones to the building ruins. From the ruins follow the footpath S as it climbs to the course of the old railway line. Turn E and follow its course to the Allt Coire an Eoin Bridge. Cross it and turn R onto the access track; follow it SW to the water intake. Follow the Allt Coire an Eoin SW, S, then SW through the pathless wilds of Coire an Eoin to the mouth of An Coire Calma. Head S up through the corrie to the col at the head of Coire Bhealaich. From the col either climb the steep tortuous path W to Stob Coire Bhealaich or traverse SW through Coire a' Bhuic to the col then NNE to Stob Coire Bhealaich. Head W then NW along the main ridge to Aonach Beag.

Descent: Head SE then E down the main ridge to Stob Coire Bhealaich. Turn SSW and descend to the col on the north side of Sgurr a' Bhuic. Traverse NE through Coire a' Bhuic to the broad col above Coire Bhealaich. Descend N through Coire Bhealaich then An Coire Calma to the Allt Coire an Eoin. Follow it NE, N then NE through Coire an Eoin to the water intake. Take the access track NE down to the old railway line then follow its course W to the top of the Leanachan path. Turn L and follow it past the ruins and over the stepping stones to the public road.

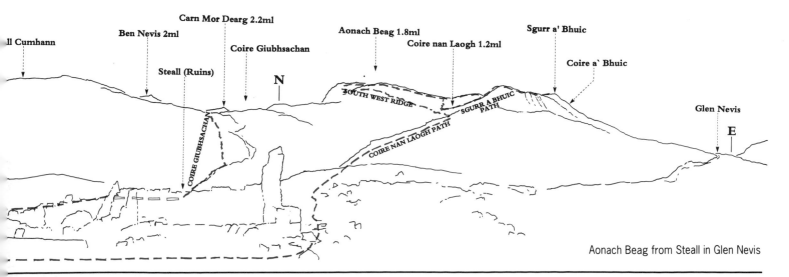

Aonach Beag from Steall in Glen Nevis

SGURR A' BHUIC PATH

Grade: Strenuous
Time: 3.5–4 hours
Distance: 4.5 miles (7.2km)
Height Gain: 3802ft (1159m)
Terrain: Narrow wooded gorge, steep rocky slope, scree-strewn ridge, exposed ridges and summit plateau
Variation: An alternative line lies through Coire nan Laogh.
Start: Glen Nevis Car Park, GR168692

Summary: Climbs the ridge on the south side of Coire nan Laogh via the shapely peak Sgurr a' Bhuic to join the main ridge of Aonach Beag at Stob Coire Bhealaich.

Ascent: From the car park follow the path as it meanders E through the gorge to the footbridge by the Steall (ruins). Cross it and climb NE alongside the Allt Coire nan Laogh then climb the west ridge of Sgurr a' Bhuic. From the summit descend N to the col at the head of Coire a' Bhuic then climb NNE to Stob Coire Bhealaich. Head W then NW along the main ridge to Aonach Beag.

Descent: Head SE then E down the main ridge to Stob Coire Bhealaich. Turn SSW and descend to the col on the north side of Sgurr a' Bhuic. Climb S to the summit of Sgurr a' Bhuic then descend the steep ridge W to Coire nan Laogh. From the corrie head SW down the southeast side of the Allt Coire nan Laogh to the footbridge at the Steall (ruins). Cross it and follow the Glen Nevis footpath W through the gorge to the car park.

Aonach Beag's summit cairn

SOUTHWEST RIDGE

Grade: Strenuous
Time: 3–3.5 hours
Distance: 3.75 miles (6km)
Height Gain: 3589ft (1094m)
Terrain: Narrow wooded gorge, steep rocky slope, rocky corrie, steep ridge and summit plateau
Start: Glen Nevis Car Park, GR168692

Summary: Climbs the long arm of Aonach Beag's southwest ridge. With steep ground on both sides the traverse of this ridge requires careful navigation in poor weather. The most direct route from Glen Nevis.

Ascent: From the car park follow the path as it meanders E through the gorge to the footbridge by the Steall (ruins). Cross it and climb NE alongside the Allt Coire nan Laogh, then turn NW and cross the corrie floor to the slope on the southeast side of the southwest ridge. Climb the slope to the crest of the ridge then turn NE and follow it to the summit of Aonach Mor.

Descent: Head SW down the crest of the ridge then turn SE (taking care to avoid its steep truncated end) and descend steeply into Coire nan Laogh. Cross the corrie then head SW down the southeast side of the Allt Coire nan Laogh to the footbridge at the Steall (ruins). Cross it and follow the Glen Nevis footpath W through the gorge to the car park.

Sgurr a' Bhuic from Stob Coire Bhealaich

Water intake on the Allt Coire an Eoin, GR227758. Part of the Lochaber Water Power Scheme this small dam feeds supplementary water into an underground tunnel which drains water from Loch Treig and carries it to the power station at the aluminium works at Fort William

Allt Coire Guibhsachan

AONACH MOR LINK

Grade: Intermediate
Time: 0.5 hours
Distance: 1 mile (1.6km)
Height Gain: 427ft (130m)
Terrain: Steep scree-strewn slope, exposed col and broad summit ridge
Start: Aonach Beag, GR197715

Summary: Aonach Beag is separated from Aonach Mor by a narrow col. The walk between the two peaks is simple enough so long as the weather is clear, in mist and with snow cover it can be confusing. Particularly the steep descent to the col from Aonach Beag.

Route: From the summit descend NNW; turn NW following the path down the scree to the col on the north side of Aonach Beag. Cross it and climb the summit plateau N to Aonach Mor.

CARN MOR DEARG LINK

Grade: Strenuous
Time: 1–1.5 hours
Distance: 1.5 miles (2.4km)
Height Gain: 1270ft (387m)
Terrain: Steep loose slope and steep rocky ridge
Start: Aonach Beag, GR197715

Summary: The steep descent down the loose Seang Aonach Mor then the climb up the sweeping East Ridge of Carn Mor Dearg involves a considerable height loss and demands considerable leg work.

Route: From the summit descend NNW, then NW following the path down the scree to the col on the north side of Aonach Beag. Cross the col and climb NNW to the top of the Seang Aonach Mor (small cairn). Turn W and descend the vague path down the steep and in parts loose slope to the col. Head W across the col to climb the long steep East Ridge direct to the summit of Carn Mor Dearg.

The ruined buildings at Steall, GR187688, mark the start of the southern approaches to Aonach Beag

AONACH MOR
4006FT (1221M)

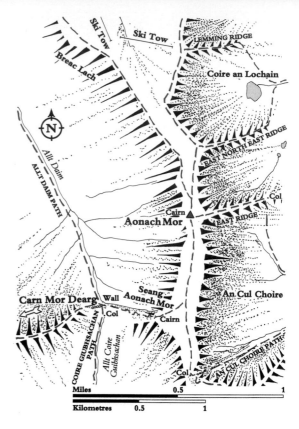

AONACH MOR'S NAME COULD NOT HAVE BEEN more appropriately chosen, it means big-ridged mountain, and it is just that. In profile it has the appearance of a whale-back with a summit plateau which extends for about 0.75 miles (1.2km). To the south the slopes end abruptly at a col adjoining Aonach Beag while to the north the slope falls away steadily to Leanachan Forest. On the east and west are precipitous crags.

Since the completion of the Nevis Range ski grounds with gondola cable car and constructed paths, access to the northern side of Aonach Mor has become considerably easier. The skiing area occupies almost the whole of the Coire nan Geaddh or corrie of the goose (not named on Ordnance Survey maps), and at either side paths climb the bounding ridges to the summit plateau. These two northern routes are the only easy routes on the mountain.

The western and eastern approaches pass through outstanding scenery and involve long walks and steep ascents. From the Allt Daim or Coire Guibhsachan the only feasible route onto the summit plateau is up the steep loose slope of Seang Aonach Mor. To the east the choice is much wider. Three superb ridges and a corrie head wall can be climbed from the rough and remote corries Coire Choille-rais and Coire an Eoin.

Aonach, Mor (**AM**) from Carn Mor Dearg, **PR** Pinnacle Ridge, **AD** Allt Daim, **ER** East Ridge, **SAM** Seang Aonach Mor

MAPS

Ordnance Survey: Outdoor Leisure 1: 25000 No 32 (Mountainmaster of Ben Nevis); Landranger 1: 50000 No 41; Tourist Map 1: 63360 Ben Nevis and Glen Coe.

INFORMATION

Tourist Information Centres: Fort William and Spean Bridge.

ACCOMMODATION

Youth Hostels: Glen Nevis.

Hotels and B&B: Fort William, Glen Nevis, Spean Bridge and Roy Bridge.

Camp sites: Glen Nevis, Camaghael, Inverroy and Roy Bridge.

Bothies and Howffs: Steall Hut, GR178684, Glen Nevis – a locked private hut booked through either the Scottish Mountaineering Club or the British Mountaineering Council.

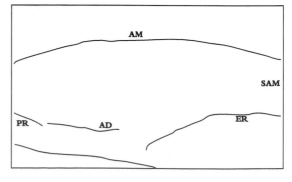

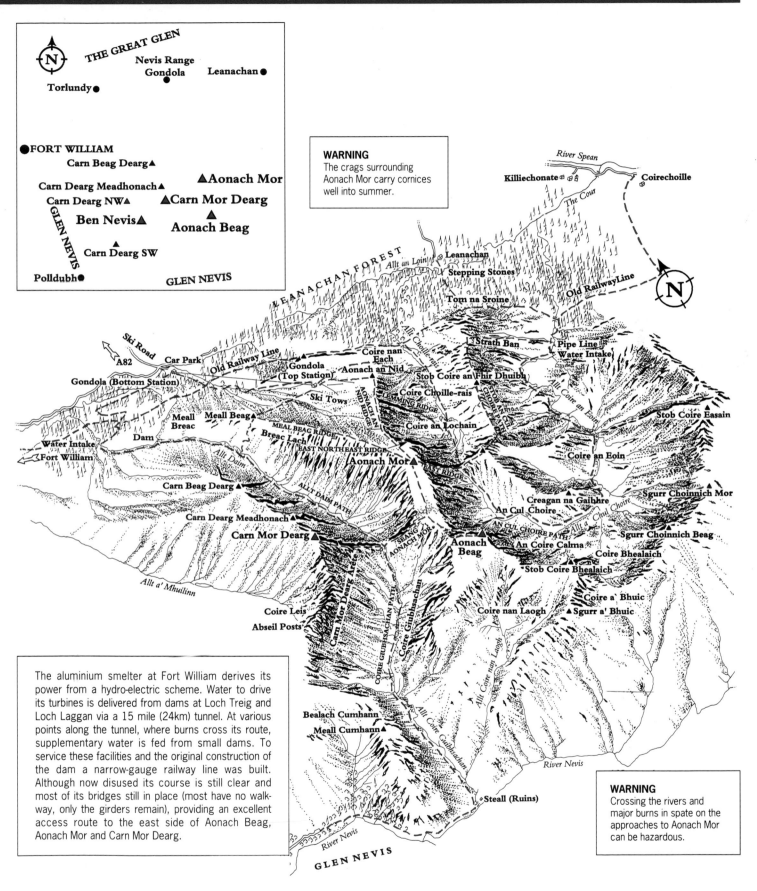

THE GREAT GLEN

Nevis Range
Gondola   Leanachan ●

Torlundy ●

● FORT WILLIAM
    Carn Beag Dearg ▲
    Carn Dearg Meadhonach ▲   ▲ Aonach Mor
    Carn Dearg NW ▲   ▲ Carn Mor Dearg
    Ben Nevis ▲   ▲
                        Aonach Beag
        Carn Dearg SW ▲
Polldubh ●   GLEN NEVIS

WARNING
The crags surrounding Aonach Mor carry cornices well into summer.

The aluminium smelter at Fort William derives its power from a hydro-electric scheme. Water to drive its turbines is delivered from dams at Loch Treig and Loch Laggan via a 15 mile (24km) tunnel. At various points along the tunnel, where burns cross its route, supplementary water is fed from small dams. To service these facilities and the original construction of the dam a narrow-gauge railway line was built. Although now disused its course is still clear and most of its bridges still in place (most have no walkway, only the girders remain), providing an excellent access route to the east side of Aonach Beag, Aonach Mor and Carn Mor Dearg.

WARNING
Crossing the rivers and major burns in spate on the approaches to Aonach Mor can be hazardous.

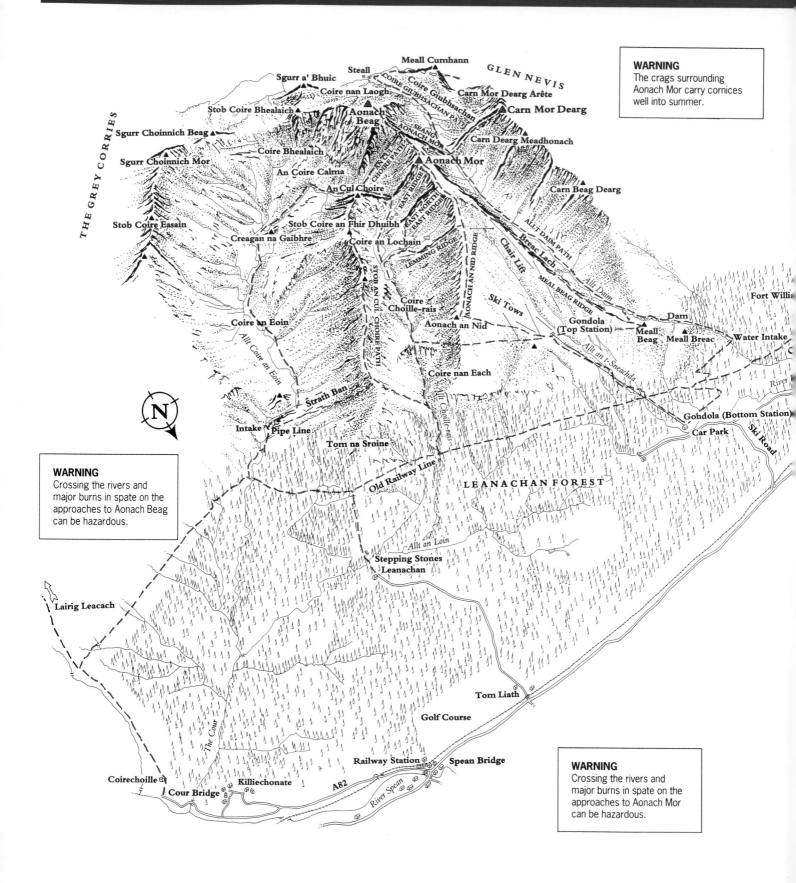

WARNING
The crags surrounding Aonach Mor carry cornices well into summer.

WARNING
Crossing the rivers and major burns in spate on the approaches to Aonach Beag can be hazardous.

WARNING
Crossing the rivers and major burns in spate on the approaches to Aonach Mor can be hazardous.

Aonach Mor's summit cairn

ALLT DAIM PATH

Grade: Strenuous
Time: 4 hours
Distance: 5.75 miles (9.3km)
Height Gain: 3678ft (1121m)
Terrain: Woodland, craggy glen, steep loose slope and broad summit ridge
Variation: The Allt Daim Path can be gained from the gondola top station via a steep descent from Meall Beag. Can also be started via the course of the old railway line from either A82, Distillery, GR126757, or A82, Golf Course, GR136762.
Start: Gondola Car Park, GR172774

Summary: The long west wall of Aonach Mor is a series of steep broken crags. From Allt Daim there are lines up these rocks though they would require the use of ropes. For the walker the only alternative is via Seang Aonach Mor.

Ascent: From the car park head SW then turn S and take the zig-zags up to the course of the old narrow-gauge railway. Follow it SW to the water intake then turn SE and climb alongside the Allt Daim. Continue alongside the Allt Daim to the col, then turn E and climb the very steep and in parts loose Seang Aonach Mor. At the top turn N and climb the summit slopes to Aonach Mor.

Descent: Head S down the summit slopes to the top of the Seang Aonach Mor (small cairn). Turn W and descend the vague path down the steep and in parts loose slope to the col. Turn N and follow the Allt Daim on its southwest side to the water intake and join the old narrow-gauge railway. Follow its course NE then take the zig-zags N. At the bottom turn R and head NE to the Gondola Car Park.

Small cairn which marks the top of Seang Aonach Mor

COIRE GIUBHSACHAN PATH

Grade: Strenuous
Time: 3.5 hours
Distance: 5 miles (8km)
Height Gain: 3547ft (1081m)
Terrain: Narrow wooded gorge, craggy glen, steep loose slope and broad summit ridge
Start: Glen Nevis Car Park, GR167692

Summary: Climbing steadily alongside the waterslides and waterfalls of the Allt Coire Giubhsachan the Coire Giubhsachan Path twists its way N to the col on the west side of Aonach Mor.

Ascent: From the car park follow the path as it meanders E through the gorge to the footbridge by the Steall (ruins). Turn N and follow the path up the west side of the Allt Coire Giubhsachan. Continue N up through Coire Giubhsachan to the col at its head. At the col climb E up the very steep and in parts loose Seang Aonach Mor. At the top turn N and climb the summit slopes to Aonach Mor.

Descent: Head S down the summit slopes to the top of the Seang Aonach Mor (small cairn). Turn W and descend the vague path down the steep and in parts loose slope to the col. Turn S and follow the Allt Coire Giubhsachan down to the footbridge at the Steall (ruins). At the footbridge join the Glen Nevis footpath and follow it W through the gorge to the car park.

MEALL BEAG RIDGE

Grade: Intermediate
Time: 3–3.5 hours
Distance: 4 miles (6.4km)
Height Gain: 3678ft (1121m)
Terrain: Woodland, broad ridge, scree and broad summit ridge
Start: Gondola Car Park, GR172774

Summary: High above the Allt Daim along the top of the steep west face of Aonach Mor the Meall Beag Ridge climbs steadily to the summit plateau.

Ascent: From the car park follow the waymarked path SE up to the gondola top station. Turn W and follow the constructed path to Meall Beag. From the end of the path climb the vague path SE up the broad ridge to the summit plateau.

Descent: Head N then descend NW down the broad ridge to the start of the constructed path at Meall Beag. Take it E to the gondola top station, then descend NW down the waymarked path to the car park.

AONACH AN NID RIDGE

Grade: Intermediate
Time: 3 hours
Distance: 3.5 miles (5.6km)
Height Gain: 3678ft (1121m)
Terrain: Woodland, expansive corrie, steep ridge and broad summit ridge
Start: Gondola Car Park, GR172774

Summary: Extending N from the summit plateau of Aonach Mor the Aonach an Nid Ridge provides a fairly steep but easy approach. From its lofty position it affords superb views over the eastern corries into the Spean Valley.

Ascent: From the car park follow the waymarked path SE to the gondola top station. Turn E and skirt the ski grounds, then head SE to join the broad ridge. Climb S up the ridge to Aonach an Nid after which it becomes more defined. Continue S up the ridge to the summit plateau.

Descent: Head N and descend the ridge to Aonach an Nid. Continue down the ridge as it becomes broader, then swing around to the NW. Skirt the ski grounds and join the constructed path W to the gondola top station. Then descend NW down the waymarked path to the car park.

Cairn on Aonach an Nid

LEMMING RIDGE

Grade: Strenuous (involves some simple scrambling; Grade 1 winter climb)
Time: 3.5–4 hours
Distance: 5.5 miles (8.8km)
Height Gain: 3645ft (1111m)
Terrain: Forest, steep rocky burn, rough remote corrie, steep narrow ridge and broad summit ridge
Variation: Can also be started via the course of the old narrow-gauge railway from either the Gondola Car Park, GR172774, or Coirechoille in the Spean Valley, GR250807. Coire Choille-rais can be gained from the gondola top station via a descent into Coire nan Each.
Start: Leanachan, GR219786

Summary: Coire an Lochain is the beautiful high corrie on the east side of Aonach Mor; bounding its northern edge is Lemming Ridge. It provides a short simple scramble – useful as a route down into the remote Coire Choille-rais.

Ascent: Follow the forest track SW to a fork. Take the left branch SE over the stepping stones to the ruined buildings. From the ruins follow the footpath S as it climbs to the course of the old railway line. Turn R onto it and follow it W over the Allt Choille-rais Bridge to a forest track on the left. Take this as it climbs round to the water intake. From the intake follow the Allt Choille-rais as it climbs steeply S then W into Coire an Lochain. Climb N from the Lochain to the foot of Lemming Ridge then climb its crest W onto the summit plateau. Head S around the edge of the crags to the summit of Aonach Mor.

Descent: Head N around the edge of the crags to the top of Lemming Ridge (close to the top ski tow). Descend its steep crest E into Coire an Lochain then turn N and descend the length of Coire Choille-rais to the water intake. Take the access track down to the course of the old railway line. Join it and follow it E to the top of the Leanachan Path. Turn L onto it and follow it past the ruins and over the stepping stones to the public road.

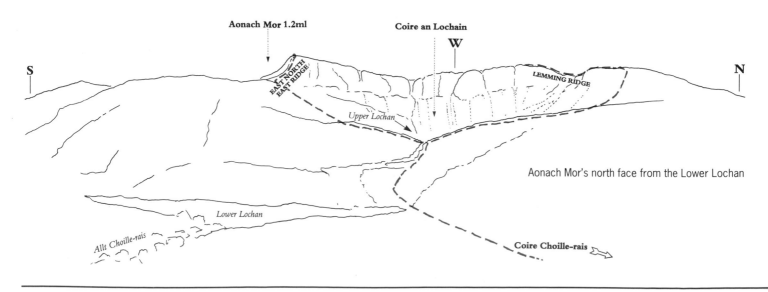

Aonach Mor's north face from the Lower Lochan

EAST-NORTHEAST RIDGE

Grade: Strenuous (Grade 1 scramble: Grade 1 winter route)
Time: 3.5–4 hours
Distance: 5.25 miles (8.4km)
Height Gain: 3645ft (1111m)
Terrain: Forest, steep rocky burn, rough remote corrie, steep narrow ridge and broad summit ridge
Variation: Can also be started via the course of the old narrow-gauge railway from either the Gondola Car Park, GR172774, or Coirechoille in the Spean Valley, GR250807. Coire Choille-rais can be gained from the gondola top station via a descent into Coire nan Each.
Start: Leanachan, GR219786

Summary: Bounding the south side of Coire an Lochain the East-Northeast Ridge of Aonach Mor is longer and slightly harder than its near neighbour, Lemming Ridge. The ridge steepens as height is gained and the final section is poised high above the corrie floor.

Ascent: Follow the forest track SW to a fork. Take the left branch SE over the stepping stones to the ruined buildings. From the ruins follow the footpath S as it climbs to the course of the old railway line. Turn R onto it and follow it W over the Allt Choille-rais Bridge to a forest track on the left. Take this as it climbs round to the water intake. From the intake follow the Allt Choille-rais as it climbs steeply S then W into Coire an Lochain. Climb S from the Lochain to the foot of the East-Northeast Ridge then climb its crest W onto the summit plateau. Head S around the edge of the crags to the summit of Aonach Mor.

EAST RIDGE

Grade: Very strenuous (Grade 1 scramble; Grade 1 winter climb)
Time: 4.5–5 hours
Distance: 7 miles (11.3km)
Height Gain: 3645ft (1111m)
Terrain: Forest, rough pathless glen, remote craggy corrie, narrow rocky ridge and broad summit ridge
Variation: Can also be started via the course of the old narrow-gauge railway from either the Gondola Car Park, GR172774, or Coirechoille in the Spean Valley, GR250807. Coire Choille-rais can be gained from the gondola top station via a descent into Coire nan Each.
Start: Leanachan, GR219786

Summary: Directly below the summit of Aonach Mor the East Ridge climbs onto the summit plateau from the exposed col at the head of An Cul Choire. The approach to it is long up the pathless wilderness of the beautiful Coire an Eoin.

Ascent: Follow the forest track SW to a fork. Take the left branch SE over the stepping stones to the building ruins. From the ruins follow the footpath S as it climbs to the course of the old railway line. Turn E and follow its course to the Allt Coire an Eoin Bridge. Cross it and turn R onto the access track; follow it SW to the water intake. Follow the Allt Coire an Eoin SW, S, then SW through the pathless wilds of Coire an Eoin to the mouth of An Cul Choire. Climb the corrie NE to the col at its head. Then turn L and climb the crest of the East Ridge to the summit of Aonach Mor.

The Gondola top station

STOB AN CUL CHOIRE PATH

Grade: Very strenuous
Time: 4.5 hours
Distance: 5.75 miles (9.3km)
Height Gain: 4006ft (1221m)
Terrain: Forest, steep rocky slope, long narrow ridge, narrow rocky ridge and broad summit ridge
Variation: The northern end of the main ridge can be gained from Coire Choille-rais. Can also be started via the course of the old narrow-gauge railway from either the Gondola Car Park, GR172774, or Coirechoille in the Spean Valley, GR250807.
Start: Leanachan, GR219786

Summary: Situated between two of Scotland's wildest corries the long northern ridge of Stob an Cul Choire gives a particularly fine approach to the eastern side of Aonach Mor.

Ascent: Follow the forest track SW to a fork. Take the left branch SE over the stepping stones to the building ruins. From the ruins follow the footpath S as it climbs to the course of the old railway line. Turn E and follow its course to the Allt Coire an Eoin Bridge. Cross it and turn R onto the access track; follow it SW to the water intake. Climb the hillside E from the intake to the broad ridge at Tom na Sroine then climb S to the unnamed top. Continue S down the ridge to Stob Coire an Fhir Dhuibh then follow it as it swings round to the SW to gain Stob an Cul Choire. Descend W to the col, cross it, and climb the crest of the East Ridge to the summit of Aonach Mor.

AONACH BEAG LINK

Grade: Intermediate
Time: 0.5 hours
Distance: 1 mile (1.6km)
Height Gain: 475ft (145m)
Terrain: Broad summit ridge, exposed col and steep scree-strewn slopes
Start: Aonach Mor, GR194729

Summary: Aonach Mor is separated from Aonach Beag by a narrow col. The walk between the two peaks is simple enough so long as the weather is clear, in mist and with snow cover it can be confusing.

Route: Head S down the summit plateau to the narrow col. Cross it and climb the path SE up the scree. As the angle eases turn SSE to the summit of Aonach Beag.

CARN MOR DEARG LINK

Grade: Strenuous
Time: 1–1.5 hours
Distance: 1.5 miles (2.4km)
Height Gain: 1270ft (387m)
Terrain: Steep loose slope and steep rocky ridge
Start: Aonach Mor, GR194729

Summary: The steep descent down the loose Seang Aonach Mor then the climb up the sweeping East Ridge of Carn Mor Dearg involves a considerable height loss and demands a great deal of leg work.

Route: Head S down the summit slopes to the top of the Seang Aonach Mor (small cairn). Turn W and descend the vague path down the steep and in parts loose slope to the col. Head W across the col and climb the long steep East Ridge direct to the summit of Carn Mor Dearg.

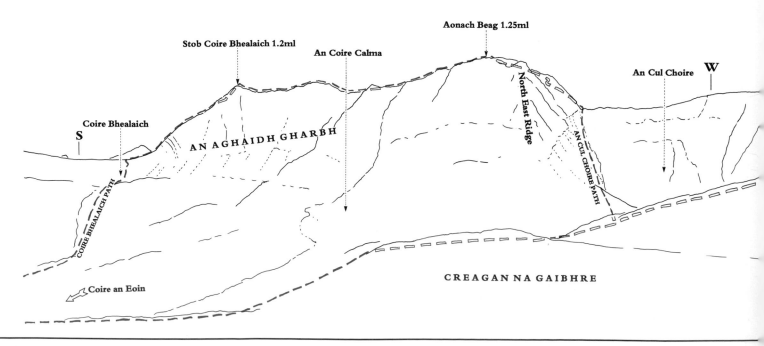

The steep section of the East Ridge

AN CUL CHOIRE PATH

Grade: Very strenuous
Time: 4.5–5 hours
Distance: 7.25 miles (11.7km)
Height Gain: 3645ft (1111m)
Terrain: Forest, rough pathless glen, remote craggy corrie and broad summit ridge
Variation: Can also be started via the course of the old narrow-gauge railway from either the Gondola Car Park, GR172774, or Coirechoille in the Spean Valley, GR250807.
Start: Leanachan, GR219786

Summary: Beside the towering Northeast Ridge of Aonach Beag the head of An Cul Choire cuts back deeply into the Aonachs massif. Snowbound until after the first half of the summer it provides the easiest route to Aonach Mor from Coire an Eoin.

Ascent: Follow the forest track SW to a fork. Take the left branch SE over the stepping stones to the building ruins. From the ruins follow the footpath S as it climbs to the course of the old railway line. Turn E and follow its course to the Allt Coire an Eoin Bridge. Cross it and turn R onto the access track which is followed SW to the water intake. Follow the Allt Coire an Eoin SW, S, then SW through the pathless wilds of Coire an Eoin to the mouth of An Cul Choire. Enter the corrie then climb the southwest bay to the col between Aonach Mor and Aonach Beag. Turn R and climb N across the summit plateau to Aonach Mor.

Descent: Head S across the summit plateau to the col between Aonach Mor and Aonach Beag. Descend the steep bay NE into An Cul Choire. Cross the corrie floor then follow the Allt Coire an Eoin NE, N then NE through Coire an Eoin to the water intake. Take the access track NE down to the old railway line then follow its course W to the top of the Leanachan path. Turn L onto it and follow it past the ruins and over the stepping stones to the public road.

Aonach Mor **Stob an Cul Choire**

STOB AN CUL CHOIRE PATH

EAST RIDGE

Aonach Mor and Aonach Beag from Creagan na Gaibhre

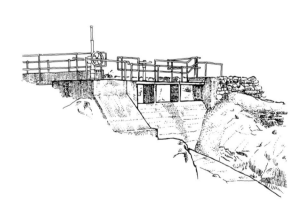

Water intake on the Allt Choille-rais, GR204767. Part of the Lochaber Water Power Scheme this small dam feeds supplementary water into an underground tunnel which drains water from Loch Treig and carries it to the power station at the aluminium works at Fort William

CARN MOR DEARG
4003FT (1220M)

CARN MOR DEARG'S SIMPLE ELEGANT LINES tend to be overshadowed by the close proximity of Ben Nevis. The two peaks may share the same cirque at the head of the Allt a' Mhuilinn around which they are linked by the magnificent knife-edge of the Carn Mor Dearg Arête, but they are completely different. Carn Mor Dearg is formed of a uniform granite from which it gets its red hue while Ben Nevis is the product of a complex series of geological events including volcanic activity, cauldron subsidence and glacial erosion. This gives each of them a totally different shape.

Carn Mor Dearg forms a long high ridge running northwest between the Allt a' Mhuilinn and the Allt Daim. The Allt a' Mhuilinn side is a long unbroken slope with few features save drainage gullies and a liberal covering of scree. The Allt Daim side is much more interesting: cut into by steep-sided corries it has three fine ridges each of which makes an excellent route. The East Ridge is the most popular of the three as it affords direct access to Glen Giubhsachan and is a through route to Aonach Mor and Aonach Beag. For quality, though, Pinnacle Ridge is best, giving easy but exciting scrambling.

MAPS
Ordnance Survey: Outdoor Leisure 1: 25000 No 32 (Mountainmaster of Ben Nevis); Landranger 1: 50000 No 41; Tourist Map 1: 63360 Ben Nevis and Glen Coe.

INFORMATION
Tourist Information Centre: Fort William.

ACCOMMODATION
Youth Hostels: Glen Nevis.

Hotels and B&B: Fort William and Glen Nevis.

Camp sites: Glen Nevis and Camaghael.

Bothies and Howffs: There is a shelter in Coire Leis (GR173714), but it is for emergencies and should not be used for planned overnight stays. The CIC Hut (GR168722) alongside the Allt a' Mhuilinn and the Steall Hut (GR178684) in Glen Nevis are locked private huts and need to be booked through either the Scottish Mountaineering Club or the British Mountaineering Council.

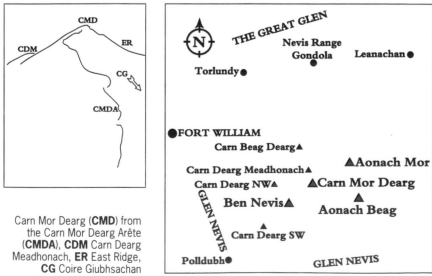

Carn Mor Dearg (**CMD**) from the Carn Mor Dearg Arête (**CMDA**), **CDM** Carn Dearg Meadhonach, **ER** East Ridge, **CG** Coire Giubhsachan

CARN MOR DEARG ARÊTE

Grade: Very strenuous
Time: 2.5–3 hours
Distance: 2.5 miles (4km)
Height Gain: 3806ft (1160m)
Terrain: Steep grassy slope, rock outcrops, steep boulders and rocky arête
Variation: Bealach Cumhann can also be gained from Steall via the lower reaches of Coire Giubhsachan.
Start: Glen Nevis Car Park, GR167692

Summary: Sickle-shaped ridge around the head of Coire Leis linking Carn Mor Dearg with Ben Nevis. A truly classic route; the crossing of the Carn Mor Dearg is a justifiably popular undertaking that combines exciting walking with a magnificent situation. It is usual to complete it as a round but it is equally worthwhile as a direct approach to Carn Mor Dearg.

Ascent: From the car park traverse NE up to the Bealach Cumhann. From the Bealach climb the ridge NW then NNE past the top of Sloc nan Uan to the sign at the top of the Abseil Posts. This is the start of the Carn Mor Dearg Arête. Follow its crest NE then climb N direct to the summit of Carn Mor Dearg.

Descent: Descend steeply S onto the Carn Mor Dearg Arête and follow its crest around to the SW to the Abseil Posts at the head of Coire Leis. From the sign at the top of the posts descend steeply SSW to the head of Sloc nan Uan then SE down the steep ridge to Bealach Cumhann. In poor visibility and under snow cover this route cannot be recommended as a descent route

NORTHWEST FLANK

Grade: Intermediate
Time: 3.5 hours
Distance: 4.5 miles (7.2km)
Height Gain: 4071ft (1241m)
Terrain: Woodland, moorland, steep grassy slope, scree and narrow summit ridge
Start: A82, Distillery, GR126757, or A82, Golf Course, GR136762

Summary: A featureless rounded slope which provides a simple and direct route. Useful as a descent to the Allt a' Mhuilinn.

Ascent: From the A82 gain the water intake on the Allt a' Mhuilinn via the path from either the Distillery or the Golf Course. Head up the Allt a' Mhuilinn on the northeast side then turn SE and climb the steep rounded ridge SE to Carn Beag Dearg. Turn SSE and follow the fine ridge over Carn Beag Meadhonach to Carn Mor Dearg.

Descent: Head NNW down the ridge over Carn Dearg Meadhonach to Carn Beag Dearg. Turn NW and descend the steep rounded ridge NW to the Allt a' Mhuilinn. Follow the path on its northeast side to the intake. Cross the Allt a' Mhuilinn and take either the Distillery path or the Golf Course path down to the A82.

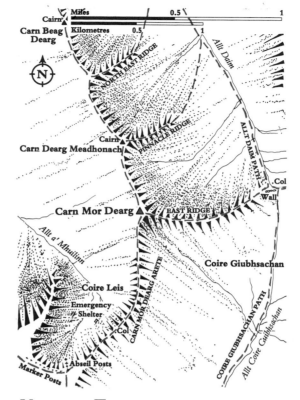

The summit of Carn Mor Dearg provides the best views of the impressive northeast face of Ben Nevis

NORTH FLANK

Grade: Intermediate
Time: 3.5 hours
Distance: 4.75 miles (7.6km)
Height Gain: 3770ft (1149m)
Terrain: Woodland, steep grassy slope, scree and narrow summit ridge
Variation: Can also be started via the course of the old railway line from either A82, Distillery, GR126757, or A82, Golf Course, GR136762.
Start: Gondola Car Park, GR172774

Summary: A featureless rounded slope which provides a simple and direct route. Useful as a descent to the Allt Daim.

Ascent: From the car park head SW then turn S and take the zig-zags up to the course of the old narrow-gauge railway. Follow it SW to the water intake then turn SE and climb alongside the Allt Daim. At the second dam turn S and climb the steep rounded ridge direct to Carn Beag Dearg. From the cairn head SSE and follow the fine ridge over Carn Beag Meadhonach to Carn Mor Dearg.

Descent: Head NNW down the ridge over Carn Dearg Meadhonach to Carn Beag Dearg. From the cairn descend the steep rounded ridge N to the Allt Daim. Follow it on its southwest side to the water intake and join the old narrow-gauge railway. Follow its course NE then take the zig-zags N. At the bottom turn R and head NE to the Gondola Car Park.

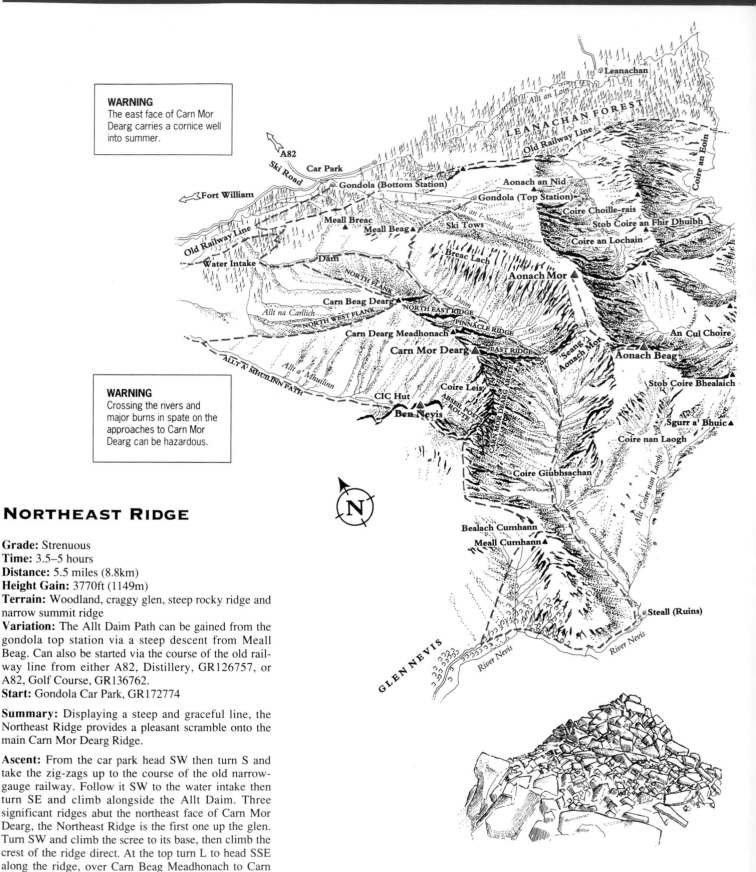

WARNING
The east face of Carn Mor Dearg carries a cornice well into summer.

WARNING
Crossing the rivers and major burns in spate on the approaches to Carn Mor Dearg can be hazardous.

NORTHEAST RIDGE

Grade: Strenuous
Time: 3.5–5 hours
Distance: 5.5 miles (8.8km)
Height Gain: 3770ft (1149m)
Terrain: Woodland, craggy glen, steep rocky ridge and narrow summit ridge
Variation: The Allt Daim Path can be gained from the gondola top station via a steep descent from Meall Beag. Can also be started via the course of the old railway line from either A82, Distillery, GR126757, or A82, Golf Course, GR136762.
Start: Gondola Car Park, GR172774

Summary: Displaying a steep and graceful line, the Northeast Ridge provides a pleasant scramble onto the main Carn Mor Dearg Ridge.

Ascent: From the car park head SW then turn S and take the zig-zags up to the course of the old narrow-gauge railway. Follow it SW to the water intake then turn SE and climb alongside the Allt Daim. Three significant ridges abut the northeast face of Carn Mor Dearg, the Northeast Ridge is the first one up the glen. Turn SW and climb the scree to its base, then climb the crest of the ridge direct. At the top turn L to head SSE along the ridge, over Carn Beag Meadhonach to Carn Mor Dearg.

Carn Mor Dearg's summit cairn

PINNACLE RIDGE

Grade: Strenuous (Grade 1 scramble; Grade 2 winter climb)
Time: 3.5–4 hours
Distance: 5.5 miles (8.8km)
Height Gain: 3770ft (1149m)
Terrain: Woodland, craggy glen, steep rocky ridge and narrow summit ridge
Variation: The Allt Daim Path can be gained from the gondola top station via a steep descent from Meall Beag. Can also be started via the course of the old railway line from either A82, Distillery, GR126757, or A82, Golf Course, GR136762.
Start: Gondola Car Park, GR172774

Summary: From the Allt Daim the most striking feature on the northeast face of Carn Mor Dearg is the Pinnacle Ridge. It climbs steeply up the side of the glen to the minor peak Carn Dearg Meadhonach. From below it looks quite daunting but once established on its crest it proves to be an uncomplicated scramble. The most exciting line follows the crest throughout.

Ascent: From the car park head SW then turn S and take the zig-zags up to the course of the old narrow-gauge railway. Follow it SW to the water intake then turn SE and climb alongside the Allt Daim. Pinnacle Ridge's distinct bump is clearly visible from the glen. Once below it turn SW and climb the scree to its base, then climb the crest of the ridge direct. At the top turn L and head SSE along the ridge to Carn Mor Dearg.

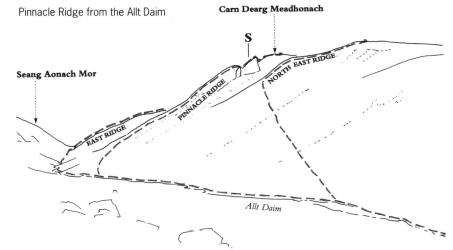

Pinnacle Ridge from the Allt Daim

Steall footbridge crosses the Allt Coire Giubhsachan near the ruins at Steall, GR186687

Carn Mor Dearg and Ben Nevis from Carn Dearg Meadhonach

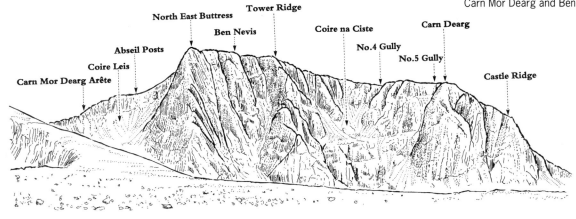

Carn Mor Dearg provides the best view of the northeast face of Ben Nevis

WARNING
Crossing the rivers and major burns in spate on the approaches to Carn Mor Dearg can be hazardous.

WARNING
The east face of Carn Mor Dearg carries a cornice well into summer.

Northeast Face of Ben Nevis from Carn Mor Dearg

AONACHS LINK

Grade: Strenuous
Time: 1–1.5 hours
Distance: 1 mile (1.6km)
Height Gain: 1017ft (310m)
Terrain: Steep loose slope and steep rocky ridge
Start: Carn Mor Dearg, GR177722

Summary: The steep descent down the sweeping East Ridge then the steep loose ascent up the Seang Aonach Mor involves a considerable height loss and demands a fair amount of leg work.

Route: Descend steeply E down the narrow ridge to the col at the head of Coire Giubhsachan. Cross the col and climb E up the very steep and in parts loose Seang Aonach Mor. At the top either head N for Aonach Mor or head S then SE for Aonach Beag.

EAST RIDGE

Grade: Strenuous
Time: 3.5 hours
Distance: 4.5 miles (7.2km)
Height Gain: 3543ft (1080m)
Terrain: Narrow wooded gorge, craggy glen and steep rocky ridge
Variation: Access to the base of East Ridge can be gained along the Allt Daim.
Start: Glen Nevis Car Park, GR168692

Summary: Coire Giubhsachan and the headwaters of the Allt Daim are separated by a high col. Sweeping down to it from Carn Mor Dearg is the beautiful curve of the East Ridge. A perfect adjunct to the Carn Mor Dearg Arête it makes Carn Mor Dearg appear a true Alpine-like giant when viewed from the south.

Ascent: From the car park follow the path as it meanders E through the gorge to the footbridge by the Steall (ruins). Turn N and follow the path up the west side of the Allt Coire Giubhsachan. Continue N up through Coire Giubhsachan to the col at its head. At the col turn W and climb the long steep East Ridge direct to the summit of Carn Mor Dearg.

Descent: Descend steeply E down the narrow ridge to the col at the head of Coire Giubhsachan. Turn S and follow the Allt Coire Giubhsachan down to the footbridge at the Steall (ruins). At the footbridge join the Glen Nevis footpath and follow it W through the gorge to the car park.

BEN NEVIS LINK

Grade: Strenuous
Time: 1–1.5 hours
Distance: 1.5 miles (2.4km)
Height Gain: 938ft (286m)
Terrain: Rocky arête and steep boulder-strewn ridge
Start: Carn Mor Dearg, GR177722

Summary: Follows the Carn Mor Dearg Arête then climbs the southeast shoulder of Ben Nevis.

Route: Descend steeply S onto the Carn Mor Dearg Arête and follow its crest around to the SW to the Abseil Posts at the head of Coire Leis. From the sign at the top of the posts head W and climb the steep path by the marker posts which swings NW onto the summit plateau.

Carn Beag Dearg summit cairn

WALES'S 3000FT MOUNTAINS

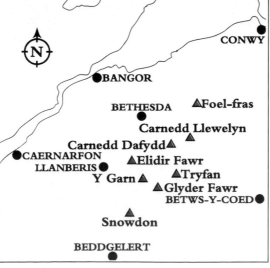

Snowdon (**S**) from Plas y Brenin.
LM Llynnau Mymbyr, **YL** Y
Lliwedd, **YW** Yr Wyddfa, **CG**
Crib Goch, **CyD** Crib Y Ddysgl
(*Trail Walker*/Bob Atkins)

WALES HAS FIFTEEN SUMMITS over 3000ft, eight of which can clearly be defined as separate mountains. They lie between the Conwy Valley and the coast within the Snowdonia National Park, and are conveniently situated in three distinct but compact groups.

Each of the three groups is clearly defined geographically, being separated from its adjacent group by a major valley. To the south of the Llanberis Pass, Snowdon's sprawling bulk provides routes with a fitting mountaineering flavour. In the middle, between the Llanberis Pass and the Ogwen Valley, the four peaks of the Glyders massif – Glyder Fawr, Y Garn, Elidir Fawr and Tryfan – offer steep but short routes with a predominance of fine scrambles. The northern group containing Carnedd Llewelyn, Carnedd Dafydd and Foel-fras forms a high extensive plateau with rounded undulating ridges and impressive hidden crags.

SNOWDON
(YR WYDDFA)
3560FT (1085M)

CRIB Y DDYSGL
3494FT (1065M)

CRIB GOCH
3028FT (923M)

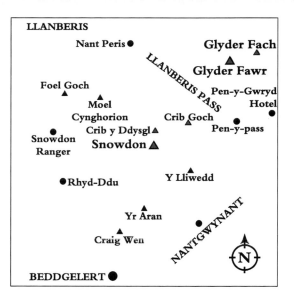

ON VIEWING SNOWDON there can be no doubt of its status as the highest peak in Wales. Majestic and refined, the impressive proportions of its pyramidal lines are instantly recognisable. Often described as having five ridges and five cwms in a star-like symmetry, this description is apt but only tells half the story. Its ridges have numerous spurs and crags while its corries are twisted and multi-levelled, reflecting past glacial activity. By anybody's standards Snowdon is a very complex mountain.

Snowdon's influence is massive; it covers an area greater than the Glyders and comparable to the whole of the Carneddau. The northeast side is a continual line of crags forming a steep wall above Llanberis Pass. To the south the slopes are less dour but only marginally less steep. They extend to Beddgelert and are bounded to the southwest by Nant Colwyn and to the southeast by the lovely wooded Nantgwynant.

The roll call of names of Snowdon's crags and ridges is intertwined with the history of Welsh mountaineering. From the early days of rock-climbing on Y Lliwedd's Alpine-like north face to the modern-day test pieces on Clogwyn Du'r Arddu's blank walls and from the highway-like Llanberis Path to the teetering exposure of the scramble over Crib Goch's fine pinnacles, Snowdon provides adventure for all who venture onto it.

Sadly for such a fine mountain, Snowdon has not remained inviolate to less altruistic human activities. In the depths of Cwm Glaslyn are the remains of copper mines and a series of constructed paths; blighting Cwm Dyli are the bold lines of hydro-electric water pipes and climbing the Northwest Ridge is the Snowdon Mountain Railway. All of these projects have or have had their supporters to present a strong case for their existence – but most people must surely feel that Snowdon would be better without them.

MAPS
Ordnance Survey: Outdoor Leisure 1: 25000 No 17; Landranger 1: 50000 No 115.

Harvey Mountain Maps: Snowdonia West 1: 40000.

INFORMATION
Tourist Information Centres: Bangor; Beddgelert; Caernarfon; Llanberis; Betws-y-Coed.

ACCOMMODATION
Youth Hostels: Nant y Betws: *Snowdon Ranger*; Llanberis; Llanberis Pass: *Peny-y-pass*; Capel Curig; Nantgwynant: *Bryn Gwynant*.

Hotels and B&B: Beddgelert; Rhyd-Ddu; Betws Garmon; Llanberis; Nant Peris; Capel Curig; Nantgwynant.

Camp sites: Beddgelert; Rhyd-Ddu; Betws Garmon; Llanberis Pass: *Nant Peris, Gwastadnant*; Capel Curig; Nantgwynant.

Snowdon from Y Garn

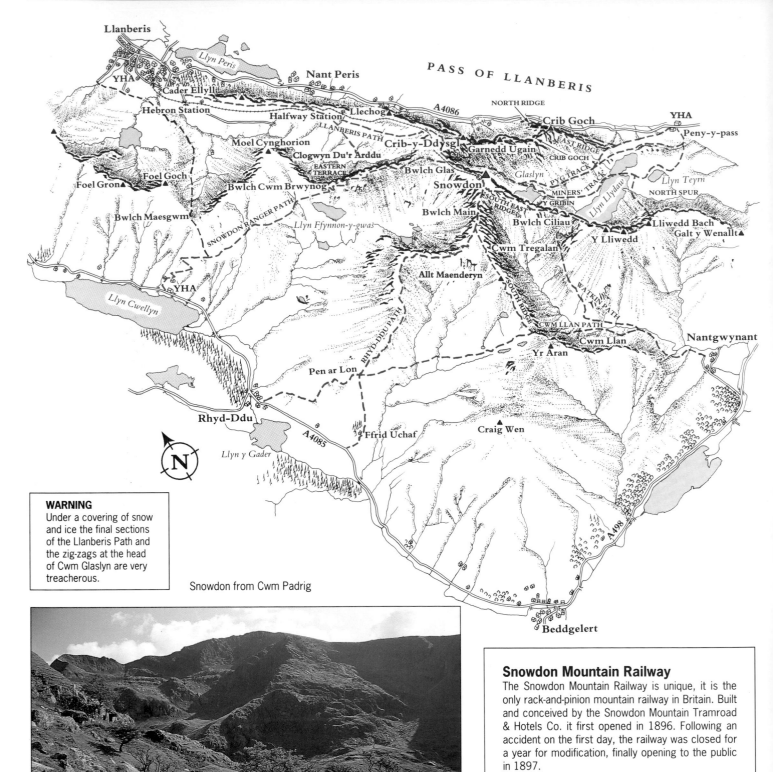

Llanberis
Llyn Peris
YHA
Cader Ellyll
Nant Peris
PASS OF LLANBERIS
A4086
NORTH RIDGE
Hebron Station
Halfway Station
Llechog
Crib Goch
YHA
Peny-y-pass
LLANBERIS PATH
Moel Cynghorion
Crib-y-Ddysgl
Garnedd Ugain
EAST RIDGE
Clogwyn Du'r Arddu
CRIB GOCH
EASTERN TERRACE
Bwlch Glas
PYG TRACK
Glaslyn
Foel Gron
Foel Goch
Snowdon
Llyn Teyrn
Bwlch Cwm Brwynog
MINERS' TRACK
Llyn Llydaw
NORTH SPUR
Y GRIBIN
Bwlch Maesgwm
Bwlch Main
SOUTH EAST RIDGE
Bwlch Ciliau
Lliwedd Bach
SNOWDON RANGER PATH
Llyn Ffynnon-y-gwas
Cwm Tregalan
Y Lliwedd
Galt y Wenallt
WATKIN PATH
Allt Maenderyn
YHA
SOUTH RIDGE
Llyn Cwellyn
CWM LLAN PATH
Cwm Llan
Nantgwynant
RHYD-DDU PATH
Yr Aran
Pen ar Lon
Rhyd-Ddu
A4085
Craig Wen
Ffrid Uchaf
Llyn y Gader
N
A498
Beddgelert

WARNING
Under a covering of snow and ice the final sections of the Llanberis Path and the zig-zags at the head of Cwm Glaslyn are very treacherous.

Snowdon from Cwm Padrig

Snowdon Mountain Railway

The Snowdon Mountain Railway is unique, it is the only rack-and-pinion mountain railway in Britain. Built and conceived by the Snowdon Mountain Tramroad & Hotels Co. it first opened in 1896. Following an accident on the first day, the railway was closed for a year for modification, finally opening to the public in 1897.

The track climbs Snowdon's long and easy-angled Northwest Ridge from Llanberis to the Summit Station which lies on the west side of the summit. The total ascent is 3140ft (957m) which is gained in just under 5 miles (8km). Trains usually run from the middle of March until the beginning of November – snow and wind permitting.

SOUTH RIDGE

Grade: Intermediate
Time: 2.5–3 hours
Distance: 4 miles (6.4km)
Height Gain: 2920ft (890m)
Terrain: Moorland, exposed col and long narrow ridge
Variation: Can also be started from Nantgwynant, GR627505, via Cwm Llan and from the A4085 near Ffridd Uchaf, GR576515.
Start: Rhyd-Ddu, GR569528

Summary: An enjoyable and straightforward approach along a fine airy ridge. Strangely, the South Ridge does not see as much traffic as the other routes on the south side of Snowdon despite the fact that it is more entertaining.

Ascent: From Rhyd-Ddu take the bridleway E to the junction at Pen ar Lon. Continue E straight across the junction and climb to Bwlch Cwm Llan. Turn N at the col and climb straight up the crest of the South Ridge. At Bwlch Main the path meets the Rhyd-Ddu bridleway. Join it and follow it NE along the narrow ridge over the exposed Bwlch Main and up to Snowdon's summit.

Descent: From the south end of the Summit Station drop SE down the scree then the narrow ridge to Bwlch Main. Cross the exposed col SE to a split in the bridleway. Take the left branch (path) and follow it S down the crest of the South Ridge to Bwlch Cwm Llan. At the col turn R and make the steady descent W to Rhyd-Ddu.

RHYD-DDU PATH

Grade: Intermediate
Time: 2.5–3 hours
Distance: 3.75 miles (6km)
Height Gain: 2920ft (890m)
Terrain: Moorland, steep rocky slopes and long narrow ridge
Variation: Can also be started from the A4085 near Ffridd Uchaf, GR576515.
Start: Rhyd-Ddu, GR569528

Summary: Climbs an easy course across the mouth of the featureless Cwm Caregog then circles the impressive cliffs of Cwm Clogwyn.

Ascent: From Rhyd-Ddu take the bridleway E to the junction at Pen ar Lon. Take the left turn and follow the Rhyd-Ddu Path (bridleway) NE up the rounded slopes of Llechog. On Llechog the bridleway swings SE then NE around the head of Cwm Clogwyn to Bwlch Main. Continue NE over Bwlch Main and climb the crest of the ridge to Snowdon's summit.

Descent: From the south end of the Summit Station drop SE down the scree then the narrow ridge to Bwlch Main. Cross the exposed col SE to a split in the bridleway. Take the right branch (Rhyd-Ddu Path) and follow it SW then NW around the head of Cwm Clogwyn. Once past Llechog the bridleway swings SW and descends to the junction at Pen ar Lon. At the junction turn R and follow the bridleway down to Rhyd-Ddu.

Crib Goch from Garnedd Ugain

Summit trig point – Snowdon (Yr Wyddfa)

SNOWDON RANGER PATH

Grade: Intermediate
Time: 3 hours
Distance: 4 miles (6.4km)
Height Gain: 3064ft (934m)
Terrain: Steep pasture, huge open corrie, exposed col, narrow ridge and broad summit ridge
Variation: The lower section of the Snowdon Ranger Path can be accessed from Llanberis via the long Maesgwm bridleway – useful for completing a circuit of Snowdon.
Start: Alongside the Snowdon Ranger Youth Hostel, GR565551

Summary: The Snowdon Ranger path derives its name from the old inn at its start (now a youth hostel) which was run by the mountain guide, John Morton. He used to take clients up Snowdon along the course of the present-day bridleway, which is generally regarded as the oldest route to the summit. Originally used as a pony route, its course zig-zags steadily up the feature-less west side of Snowdon.

Ascent: From the A4085 take the bridleway on the northwest side of the youth hostel and follow it as it zig-zags NE up the steep pasture. At the top of the zig-zags the bridleway turns E; continue along it as it traverses the slopes of Cwm Treweunydd to Bwlch Cwm Brwynog. From the col the bridleway steepens and is followed ESE up the side of Snowdon's West-northwest Ridge. At the top of the ridge the gradient eases and the bridleway turns SE to join the Llanberis Path (bridleway) alongside the mountain railway. At the junction turn S and follow the course of the railway to the summit.

Descent: Follow the course of the railway line N to the fork in the bridleway at Bwlch Glas. Take the L fork and follow it WNW to Bwlch Cwm Brwynog. From the south side of the col the bridleway swings W; continue along it across the slopes of Cwm Treweunydd to the top of the zig-zags. Descend the zig-zags SW to the A4085 at the side of the youth hostel.

> **WARNING**
> Under a covering of snow and ice the final sections of the Llanberis Path and the zig-zags at the head of Cwm Glaslyn are very treacherous.

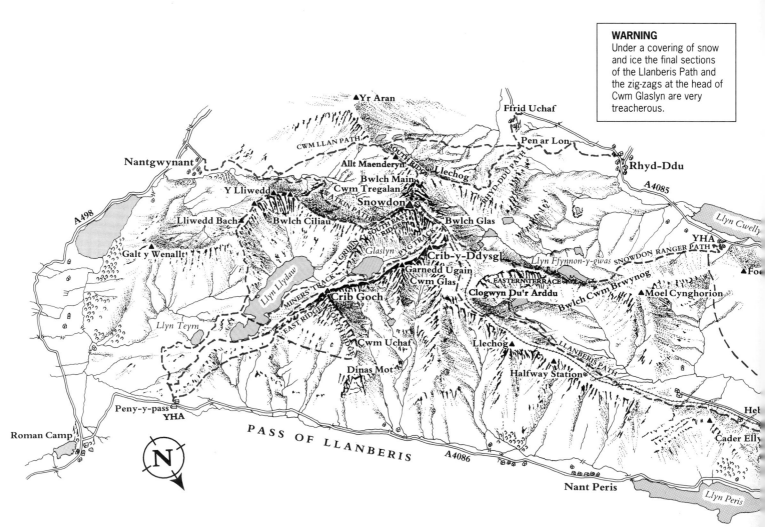

EASTERN TERRACE
(CLOGWYN DU'R ARDDU)

Grade: Strenuous (Grade 1 scramble)
Time: 3–3.5 hours
Distance: 4 miles (6.4km)
Height Gain: 2772ft (845m)
Terrain: Open valley, high craggy corrie, rock buttresses, narrow ridge and broad summit ridge
Variation: The Western Terrace of Clogwyn Du'r Arddu provides a slightly harder (Grade 2 scramble) alternative route.
Start: Cader Ellyll to the north of Llanberis, GR582589

Summary: One of the most impressive pieces of rock in Wales, the steep cliffs of Clogwyn Du'r Arddu have been a major forcing ground for rock-climbing standards. The Eastern Terrace follows a diagonal weakness between East and West Buttresses and is used as a descent route by climbers. As a scrambling route its course offers an exciting way of taking a close look at these awe-inspiring cliffs.

Ascent: From the minor road at Cader Ellyll take the Llanberis Path (bridleway) SE to the Halfway House. Leave the bridleway and contour the slopes S to Llyn Du'r Arddu. Walk around the lake, and once on the south side climb up to the base of the East Buttress. To the left of the base of the crags gain the ramp which is followed R onto the Eastern Terrace proper. Ascend the ramp turning the difficult section by the zig-zags to the upper scree slope (avoiding dislodging stones) which is climbed to the top of the cliffs. Head S across the grass to join the Snowdon Ranger Path (bridleway). Turn L onto it and follow it ESE up the side of Snowdon's West-northwest Ridge. At the top of the ridge the gradient eases and the bridleway turns SE to join the Llanberis Path (bridleway) alongside the mountain railway. At the junction turn S and follow the course of the railway to the summit.

LLANBERIS PATH

Grade: Easy
Time: 3 hours
Distance: 3.75 miles (6km)
Height Gain: 2772ft (845m)
Terrain: Open valley, high craggy corrie, high mountain ridge and broad summit ridge
Start: Cader Ellyll to the north of Llanberis, GR582589

Summary: Gains height steadily along the west side of Snowdon's long Northwest Ridge roughly following the course of the Snowdon Mountain Railway. In summer the distracting presence of trains and the throngs of tourists greatly detract from the quality of the otherwise pleasant route – best left until the winter months when a little of its former tranquillity returns.

Ascent: From the minor road at Cader Ellyll take the Llanberis Path (bridleway) SE past the Halfway House and on towards Clogwyn Station. After the bridleway has passed beneath the railway line it starts to swing S up onto the summit slopes of Crib y Ddysgl. Continue generally S across the slopes of Crib y Ddysgl to Bwlch Glas, then make the final ascent SSE to the summit of Snowdon.

Descent: From the Summit Station take the bridleway NNW to Bwlch Glas. From Bwlch Glas the bridleway descends N then NNE and finally NNW across the summit slopes of Crib y Ddysgl to the bridge beneath the railway line. Once past the bridge the bridleway swings NW and is followed down the side of the Northwest Ridge to the minor road at Cader Ellyll.

Crib Goch from Cwm Padrig

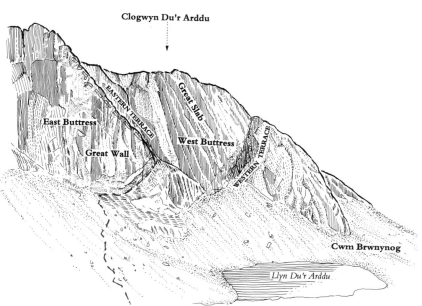

Clogwyn Du'r Arddu

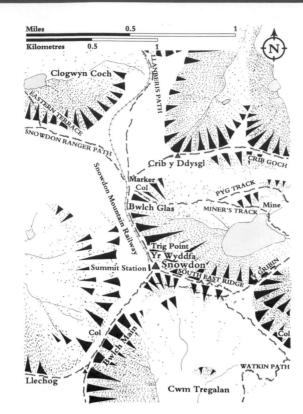

CRIB GOCH

Grade: Strenuous (Grade 1 scramble; Grade 1 winter climb)
Time: 3–3.5 hours
Distance: 4 miles (6.4km)
Height Gain: 2802ft (854m)
Terrain: Rocky slopes, craggy mountainside, rocky arête, pinnacles, exposed col, high mountain ridge and broad summit ridge

Variation: Crib Goch can also be gained by the North Ridge (Grade 1 scramble; Grade 1 winter climb) which offers a quieter alternative to the usual East Ridge approach. To gain the North Ridge start from Pen-y-pass (GR647557) and follow the Pyg Track W before leaving it to contour NE around Cwm Beudy Mawr to the shoulder above Dinas Mot. From the shoulder climb the crest of the ridge S to Crib Goch.
Start: Pen-y-pass, GR647557

Summary: A fine undulating arête high above magnificent mountain scenery, the passage through which involves exciting scrambling. Arguably the best mountain route in Wales.

Ascent: From Peny-y-pass take the Pyg Track WSW to Bwlch y Moch. Cross Bwlch y Moch and climb the well-worn East Ridge to the exposed summit of Crib Goch. From the summit of Crib Goch follow the crest of the ridge WSW then weave a route through the pinnacles to make the descent to Bwlch Coch. Cross the col and climb directly W up the steepening ridge to the summit of Crib y Ddysgl. From the summit trig point make the slight descent SW to join the Llanberis Path (bridleway) which is then taken S and SSE to the summit of Snowdon.

Descent: from the Summit Station take the bridleway NNW to Bwlch Glas. Head N across Bwlch Glas then immediately swing R and take the path NE to the summit of Crib y Ddysgl. From the trig point descend E and make the steep scramble down the crest of the ridge to Bwlch Coch. From the col follow the path E that weaves its way through the pinnacles and heads ENE onto the summit of Crib Goch. From the summit scramble E down the very steep ridge to the easier ground of Bwlch y Moch. From Bwlch y Moch join the Pyg Track and take it ENE to Pen-y-pass.

The pinnacles of Crib Goch from Bwlch Coch

Summit trig point – Crib y Ddysgl

Snowdon from Glyder Fawr

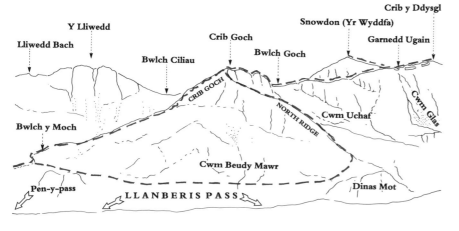

PYG TRACK

Grade: Intermediate
Time: 2.5–3 hours
Distance: 3.25 miles (5.2km)
Height Gain: 2381ft (725m)
Terrain: Rocky slopes, craggy corries, steep head wall, exposed col and broad summit ridge
Start: Pen-y-pass, GR647557

Summary: Skirts the southern slopes of Crib Goch high above the beautiful waters of Llyn Llydaw and Glaslyn. The over-zealous techniques used to reconstruct the zig-zag path below Bwlch Glas tend to detract from the wild setting through which the Pyg Track passes.

Ascent: From Pen-y-pass take the Pyg Track WSW to Bwlch y Moch. Cross Bwlch y Moch and continue WSW then W as the path skirts across the southern slopes of Crib Goch to a junction with the Miners' Track high above Glaslyn. From the junction climb the steep zig-zags W up the head wall to Bwlch Glas. At Bwlch Glas the path joins the Llanberis Path (bridleway) which is taken S then SSE to Snowdon's summit.

Descent: From the Summit Station take the bridleway NNW to Bwlch Glas. At the stone marker turn E and descend the zig-zags towards Glaslyn. Midway down the corrie head wall the path splits. Take the left fork (the right-hand fork is the Miners' Track) and follow it E then ENE across the southern slopes of Crib Goch to Bwlch y Moch. Continue generally ENE across Bwlch y Moch and then make the final descent to Pen-y-pass.

Descending the East Ridge of Crib Goch

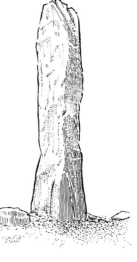

Marker stone at Blwch Glas to the north of Snowdon's summit, GR608549.
Marks the top of the zig-zags and the descent to Glaslyn (Pyg Track and Miners' Track)

127

THE MINERS' TRACK

Grade: Intermediate
Time: 2.5–3 hours
Distance: 4 miles (6.4km)
Height Gain: 2381ft (725m)
Terrain: Rocky slopes, craggy corries, steep head wall, exposed col and broad summit ridge
Start: Pen-y-pass, GR647557

Summary: Originally an access track to the mines, the Miners' Track climbs an easy gradient to Llyn Llydaw and then on to Glaslyn after which it joins the Pyg Track and climbs the constructed zig-zags to Bwlch Glas. As with the Pyg Track it suffers from over-zealous path construction techniques – but these are more than compensated by the fine views of Y Lliwedd and the crags of Clogwyn y Garnedd.

Ascent: From Pen-y-pass take the Miners' Track (access track) S, W then SW to Llyn Llydaw. Cross Llyn Llydaw NW via the Causeway then follow the track SW around the lake then W up to Glaslyn. Head NW around the lake and then make the steep ascent to the junction with the Pyg Track. From the junction climb the steep zig-zags W up the head wall to Bwlch Glas. At Bwlch Glas the path joins the Llanberis Path (bridleway) which is taken S then SSE to Snowdon's summit.

Descent: From the Summit Station take the bridleway NNW to Bwlch Glas. At the stone marker turn E and descend the zig-zags towards Glaslyn. Midway down the corrie head wall the path splits. Take the right-hand fork (the left fork is the Pyg Track) and follow it SE down the steep slope to Glaslyn. From Glaslyn follow the good track E to Llyn Llydaw then NE around the lake to the Causeway. Cross it and follow the track generally NE to Pen-y-pass.

Y GRIBIN

Grade: Strenuous (Grade 1 scramble; Grade 1 winter climb)
Time: 3–3.5 hours
Distance: 4 miles (6.4 km)
Height Gain: 2381ft (725m)
Terrain: Rocky slopes, craggy corries, steep rocky ridge and scree-covered ridge
Start: Pen-y-pass, GR647557

Summary: Y Gribin is the pronounced spur that extends NE from Snowdon's Southeast Ridge. It climbs high above Glaslyn and offers a short but exciting scramble.

Ascent: From Pen-y-pass take the Miners' Track (access track) S, W then SW to Llyn Llydaw. Cross Llyn Llydaw NW via the Causeway then follow the track SW around the lake then W up to Glaslyn. Cross the Afon Glaslyn and climb the grass-and-rocks slope SW on the shallow col. From the col climb the crest of the ridge SW onto the levelling on the Southeast Ridge of Snowdon. Once on the Southeast Ridge either descend slightly SW to join the Watkin Path W then NE to the summit or climb directly (NW) up the more exciting crest of the Southeast Ridge.

Snowdon from Cwm Padrig

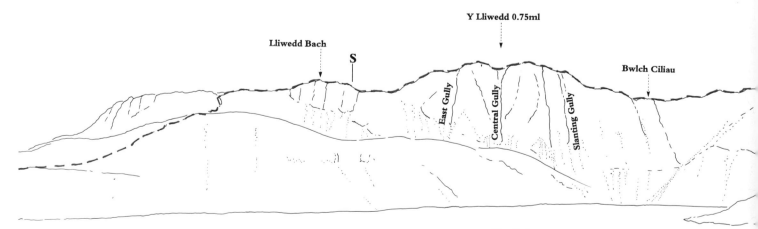

Snowdon from the side of Llyn Llydaw

SOUTHEAST RIDGE

Grade: Strenuous
Time: 3–3.5 hours
Distance: 4 miles (6.4km)
Height Gain: 2871ft (875m)
Terrain: Rocky slopes, craggy corries, steep rounded ridge, narrow rocky summit, steep rocky ridge, exposed col and scree-covered ridge
Start: Pen-y-pass, GR647557

Summary: Snowdon's Southeast Ridge, although a little broken in parts, provides a superb high-level link with Y Lliwedd. Most people complete a traverse of its length as part of the classic 'Snowdon Horseshoe' usually in descent. As an ascent route its qualities are equally good, particularly for the views of Snowdon's summit pyramid.

Ascent: From Pen-y-pass take the Miners' Track (access track) S, W then SW to Llyn Llydaw. Before the Causeway turn L off the track and follow the path which climbs the steep rounded ridge SSW towards Lliwedd Bach. Climb onto the Northeast Ridge of Y Lliwedd and follow it SW over Lliwedd Bach then W to Y Lliwedd. From the summit descend NW down the steep ridge (this involves some simple scrambling) to Bwlch Ciliau. Cross the col then follow the Watkin Path NW to a levelling. As the Southeast Ridge starts to rear-up leave the Watkin Path and climb the crest of the ridge NW to Snowdon's summit.

Descent: From the trig point descend the scree then the crest of the Southeast Ridge down to the levelling. Join the Watkin Path for a short distance to Bwlch Ciliau. Cross the col and climb SE up the rocky ridge to Y Lliwedd. Head E then NE from the summit of Y Lliwedd to Lliwedd Bach. Continue NE a short distance down the ridge until it is possible to take the narrow path NNE down the steep rounded ridge to Llyn Llydaw. At the side of the lake join the Miners' Track and follow it generally NE to Pen-y-pass.

WATKIN PATH

Grade: Intermediate
Time: 3.5 hours
Distance: 4 miles (6.4km)
Height Gain: 3373ft (1028m)
Terrain: Woodland, huge crag-ringed corrie, steep head wall, exposed col and scree-covered ridge
Start: Nantgwynant, GR627505

Summary: The product of a dedication by Sir Edward Watkin and opened by Gladstone on 13 September 1892, the Watkin Path climbs a logical route up the head wall of the wild and lovely Cwm Llan.

Ascent: From the A498 at Nantgwynant take the lane N to the start of the Watkin Path on the left. Join the path and follow it as it weaves its way NW over a bridge and past the Gladstone Rock into Cwm Llan. Through the spoil heaps at the abandoned quarries the path turns NE then N and climbs the steep head wall to Bwlch Ciliau. Once on the col turn NW and follow the Watkin Path NW then W across the south side of Snowdon's summit pyramid. As the Southwest Ridge is gained turn NE and make the final short ascent to the Summit Station.

Descent: From the Summit Station descend the Southwest Ridge a short distance then turn sharp L and descend E down the zig-zags of the Watkin Path. Past the zig-zags continue E to the levelling at the base of the Southeast Ridge, then head SE to Bwlch Ciliau. At the col turn SW then S down the steep head wall of Cwm Llan. Follow the path through the old workings then turn SE along the Watkin Path down through Cwm Llan to join the access lane which is followed the short distance S to the A498 at Nantgwynant.

The Snowdon Massif from Plas y Brenin
(*Trail Walker*/Bob Atkins)

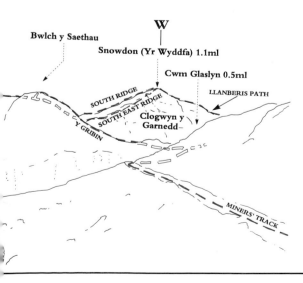

CARNEDD LLEWELYN 3484FT (1062M)

FOEL GRACH 3202FT (976M)

YR ELEN 3156FT (962M)

GARNEDD UCHAF 3038FT (926M)

CARNEDD LLEWELYN, THE SECOND-HIGHEST peak in Wales, lies at the very heart of the Carneddau. It acts as a hub for the whole massif, radiating a series of complex ridges and subsidiary tops. Characterised by rounded summit ridges which form an extensive plateau and by steep crags hidden on the surrounding flanks Carnedd Llewelyn has the added edge of being remote. Whether approaching from the Conwy Valley, the Ogwen Valley, Bethesda or Aber, your route will involve either crossing a subsidiary top or a complex valley approach.

To the northwest of Carnedd Llewelyn's summit dome along a narrow ridge lies the shapely Yr Elen. Three of the four Bethesda approaches climb this subsidiary top first, the other follows the steep course of the Nant Fach out of Cwm Llafar. Of the three routes up Yr Elen the Northeast Ridge is the most exciting, climbing a very steep line high above the remote waters of Ffynnon Caseg.

Carnedd Llewelyn has a wealth of long meandering routes which are excellent for long days when time is not a problem and plenty of diversions can be made to explore quiet corners. Fitting the bill perfectly are the Cwm Eigiau Path and the Cwm Goch Path; each has its own hidden secrets which reward those who are prepared to spend time searching them out. As could be expected with such a major peak Carnedd Llewelyn has its fair share of cliffs – these in the main occur on the Conwy Valley side. To the east of the subsidiary top Foel Grach lie the cliffs of Craig y Dulyn and Craig-fawr; between them a steep spur provides an adventurous route which is worth climbing after exploring their dark corries. Further south on the southeast side of Carnedd Llewelyn itself is Craig yr Ysfa. This extensive crag always seems dark and forbidding but in its time has produced some classic rock climbs. The most notable feature on it is the wide gully at its centre – Amphitheatre Gully – which, surprisingly for such an intimidating line, produces a scramble.

> **WARNING**
> Navigation on the main Carneddau ridge can be extremely difficult if the route is obliterated with fresh snow or visibility is poor.

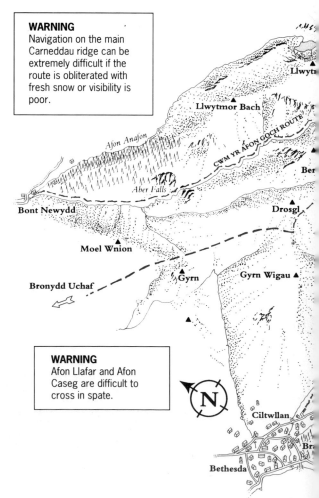

> **WARNING**
> Afon Llafar and Afon Caseg are difficult to cross in spate.

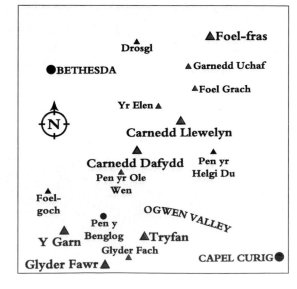

Carnedd Llewelyn (**CL**) from Yr Elen. **CC** Cwm Caseg. **FC** Ffynnon Caseg

MAPS

Ordnance Survey: Outdoor Leisure 1: 25000 No 17; Landranger 1: 50000 No 115.

Harvey Mountain Maps: Snowdonia South 1: 40000.

INFORMATION

Tourist Information Centres: Bangor; Beddgelert; Caernarfon; Llanberis; Betws-y-Coed.

ACCOMMODATION

Youth Hostels: Nant y Betws: *Snowdon Ranger*; Llanberis; Llanberis Pass: *Pen-y-pass*; Capel Curig; Nantgwynant: *Bryn Gwynant*.

Hotels and B&B: Beddgelert; Rhyd-Ddu; Betws Garmon; Llanberis; Nant Peris; Capel Curig; Nantgwynant.

Camp sites: Beddgelert; Betws Garmon; Llanberis; Llanberis Pass: *Nant Peris, Gwastadnant*; Capel Curig; Nantgwynant.

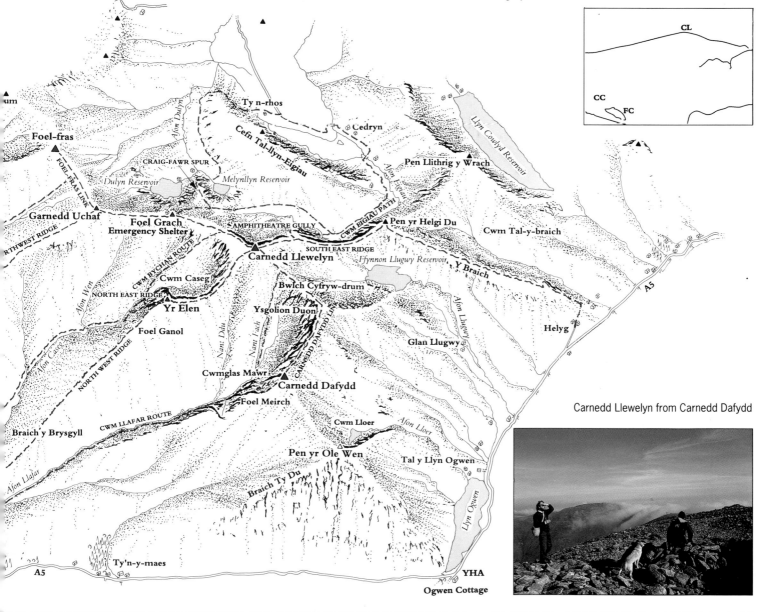

Carnedd Llewelyn from Carnedd Dafydd

SOUTHEAST RIDGE

Grade: Intermediate
Time: 2.5–3 hours
Distance: 3.75 miles (6km)
Height Gain: 2566ft (782m)
Terrain: Major valley, steep ridge, narrow col, high mountain ridge and exposed summit
Variation: The col on the northwest side of Pen yr Helgi-Du can also be gained by taking the access road to Ffynnon Llugwy Reservoir (a popular approach), then climbing the steep head wall of the corrie – start at the side of the A5, GR688602.
Start: A5 near Helyg, GR691602

Summary: The long Southeast Ridge of Carnedd Llewelyn extends to the satellite peak, Pen yr Helgi-Du. An enjoyable way of gaining it from the Ogwen Valley is along the rounded grassy ridge Y Braich.

Ascent: From the A5 at Helyg take the bridleway E then the path NE up to the footbridge over the leat at the base of Y Braich. Cross the bridge and climb the crest of Y Braich N to the summit of Pen yr Helgi-Du. Descend NW to the Bwlch Eryl Farchog. Cross the col and then climb the crest of the Southeast Ridge generally NW to the summit of Carnedd Llewelyn.

Descent: Head ESE to start then descend SE down the crest of the Southeast Ridge to Bwlch Eryl Farchog. Cross the narrow col and make the ascent SE to the summit of Pen yr Helgi-Du. From the summit descend S down the crest of Y Braich to the footbridge over the leat. Cross it and follow the path SW then the bridleway W to the A5 at Helyg.

NORTHWEST RIDGE

(YR ELEN)

Grade: Intermediate
Time: 2.5–3 hours
Distance: 3.75 miles (6km)
Height Gain: 2851ft (869m)
Terrain: Pasture, moorland, long grassy ridge, exposed summit, exposed col and rounded summit ridge
Variation: An alternative route is via the steep northern spur of the Northwest Ridge starting from the banks of Afon Caseg at GR668666.
Start: Ciltwllan on the east side of Bethesda, GR637663

Summary: A simple ridge line to the fine subsidiary top Yr Elen. Set between two beautiful corries this route is best left for a descent at the end of the day when low-angled sunlight will show the surrounding scenery at its most magnificent.

Ascent: Take the access track E then NW as it winds its way round to the pumping station. Pass the pumping station and turn E along the track. Follow it to the intake gate then take the vague path SE to the Afon Caseg. Cross the Afon Caseg (difficult in spate) and then climb steadily SSE to the broad shoulder at the base of the Northwest Ridge. Turn ESE and climb the

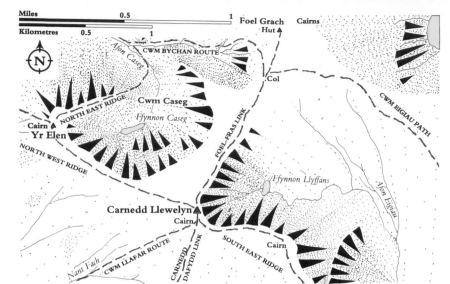

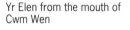

Yr Elen from the mouth of Cwm Wen

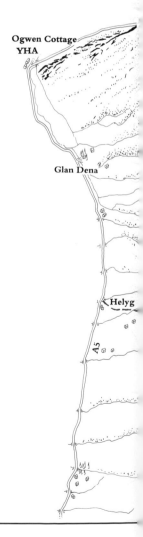

crest of the ridge to Foel Ganol. Pass Foel Ganol then turn SE up the ridge proper and climb the crest to Yr Elen. From the summit skirt SE down to a narrow col. Cross it and climb SE up the crest of the ridge to Carnedd Llewelyn.

Descent: Head NW down the crest of the ridge to the col on the southeast side of Yr Elen. Skirt NW from the col to the summit of Yr Elen. Continue NW over the summit and descend the crest of the steep ridge to Foel Ganol. Descend WNW past Foel Ganol and down the crest of the ridge until the gradient eases at its base. Turn NNE and follow the vague path to the Afon Caseg. Cross the Afon Caseg (difficult in spate) then head NW to join the access track. Take it W to the pumping station then turn SE along it and finally W to Ciltwllan.

CARNEDD DAFYDD LINK

Grade: Easy
Time: 1 hour
Distance: 2 miles (3.2km)
Height Gain: 358ft (109m)
Terrain: High mountain ridge and exposed summit
Start: Carnedd Llewelyn, GR683645

Summary: Simple high-level ridge walk around the edge of Cwm Llafar.

Route: Descend SE down the rounded ridge to Bwlch Cyfryw-drum. Cross the col and continue along the main ridge path as it swings SW then W skirting the top of Ysgolion Duon to the summit of Carnedd Dafydd.

Summit cairn – Carnedd Llewelyn

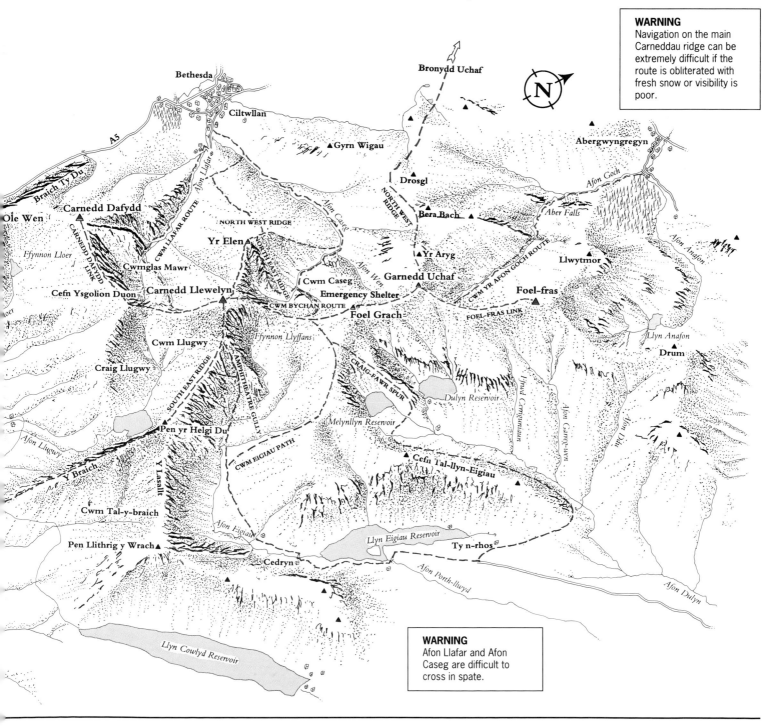

Bethesda
Ciltwllan
Bronydd Uchaf
Abergwyngregyn
Braich Ty Du
Gyrn Wigau
Drosgl
Carnedd Dafydd
Ole Wen
NORTH WEST RIDGE
Bera Bach
Aber Falls
Ffynnon Lloer
Yr Elen
Afon Goch
Llwytmor
Afon Anafon
Cwmglas Mawr
Yr Aryg
Garnedd Uchaf
Foel-fras
Cefn Ysgolion Duon
Carnedd Llewelyn
Cwm Caseg
Emergency Shelter
CWM YR AFON GOCH ROUTE
Llyn Anafon
CWM BYCHAN ROUTE
Foel Grach
FOEL-FRAS LINK
Drum
Cwm Llugwy
Ffynnon Llyffans
Craig Llugwy
CRAIG-FAWR SPUR
Dulyn Reservoir
Afon Carreg-wen
Pen yr Helgi Du
Melynllyn Reservoir
Afon Llugwy
Y Braich
Y Lasallt
CWM EIGIAU PATH
Cefn Tal-llyn-Eigiau
Afon Ddu
Cwm Tal-y-braich
Afon Eigiau
Pen Llithrig y Wrach
Llyn Eigiau Reservoir
Ty n-rhos
Cedryn
Afon Porth-llwyd
Afon Dulyn
Llyn Cowlyd Reservoir

Yr Elen from Garnedd Uchaf
(John Gillham)

NORTHEAST RIDGE
(YR ELEN)

Grade: Strenuous
Time: 3–3.5 hours
Distance: 4.75 miles (7.6km)
Height Gain: 2851ft (869m)
Terrain: Pasture, moorland, steep-sided valley, high remote corrie, steep narrow ridge, exposed summit, exposed col and rounded summit ridge
Start: Ciltwllan on the east side of Bethesda, GR637663

Summary: Tucked away on the north side of Yr Elen the Northeast Ridge climbs a steep uncompromising route above the wild Cwm Caseg. A real hidden gem, this route is one of the finest approaches to Carnedd Llewelyn.

Ascent: Take the access track E then NW as it winds its way round to the pumping station. Pass the pumping station and turn E along the track. After the settlement remains the track becomes less distinct. Roughly follow the course of the Afon Caseg E then SE to the mouth of Cwm Caseg. Turn SW and climb the very steep slope then the narrow ridge directly to the summit of Yr Elen. From the summit skirt SE down to a narrow col. Cross it and climb SE up the crest of the ridge to Carnedd Llewelyn.

Descent: Head NW down the crest of the ridge to the col on the southeast side of Yr Elen. Skirt NW from the col to the summit of Yr Elen. Descend the very steep narrow ridge and slope NE to the mouth of Cwm Caseg. Cross the Afon Caseg and roughly follow its north side NW then W to pick up the access track at the settlement remains. Take it W to the pumping station, then turn SE along it and finally W to Ciltwllan.

CWM LLAFAR ROUTE

Grade: Intermediate
Time: 2.5–3 hours
Distance: 4 miles (6.4km)
Height Gain: 2680ft (817m)
Terrain: Steep pasture, steep-sided valley, high remote corrie, high mountain ridge and exposed summit
Start: Gwernydd on the southeast side of Bethesda, GR637660

Summary: Gains the southern side of Carnedd Llewelyn along the length of Cwm Llafar and up the course of the fast-flowing Nant Fach. The lower half of this lonely valley is open and quite pleasant but the upper half is of a completely different nature – ringed by the dark cliffs of Ysgolion Duon it is an intimidating place.

Ascent: Cross the Afon Llafar then follow the path S then SE past the waterworks. Continue SE along the path past the old dam and along the side of the Afon Llafar to the entrance to Cwmglas Bach. Continue SE a short distance, then at the mouth of Cwmglas Mawr turn ENE and climb the steepening slopes alongside Nant Fach to Bwlch Cyfryw-drum. On the col turn L and climb NE up the rounded ridge to the summit of Carnedd Llewelyn.

Descent: Descend SW down the rounded ridge to Bwlch Cyfryw-drum. At the col turn and descend the steep slope alongside Nant Fach SW, W then WSW to the mouth of Cwmglas Mawr. Head NW and pick up the Cwm Llafar Path which is followed NW past the the old dam, past the waterworks then over the Afon Llafar to the road head.

Looking up into Cwm Bychan and Cwm Caseg from the Afon Caseg below Carreg y Gath

NORTHWEST RIDGE (GARNEDD UCHAF)

Grade: Easy
Time: 4 hours
Distance: 6.25 miles (10km)
Height Gain: 3123ft (952m)
Terrain: Pasture, moorland, long rounded ridge and high mountain ridge
Variation: The middle section of the Northwest Ridge can be gained via intersecting the northerly spur occupied by the minor tops, Bera Mawr and Bera Bach. Start from Bont Newydd on the Aber road (GR662720). Take the Aber Falls Path S past the falls then SE to the foot of the spur in Cwm yr Afon Goch. Climb the crest and join the Northwest Ridge Path on the south side of Bera Bach.
Start: Bronydd Isaf (T-junction on minor road), GR624704

Summary: A long, meandering route over moorland and up a gentle, grassy ridge to gain the subsidiary top, Garnedd Uchaf, on the north side of Carnedd Llewelyn.

Ascent: From the minor road take the path which winds steadily SE up through pasture and under the power lines. Once on the open hillside continue generally SE till the path splits. Take the left branch and continue SE along it and through the low col between Moel Wnion and Gyrn to join the Northwest Ridge by skirting around the south side of Drosgl. Skirt the south side of Bera Bach then climb the rounded crest of the ridge SE to Garnedd Uchaf. Head S along the main ridge path over Foel Grach then SSW to Carnedd Llewelyn.

Descent: Head NNE along the main ridge path then trend N over Foel Grach and continue to Garnedd Uchaf. Make the steady descent NW along the rounded crest of the ridge then trend W to skirt Bera Bach and Drosgl. Turn NNW around Drosgl then descend NW to the broad col between Moel Wnion and Gyrn. From the col continue the steady descent NW under the power lines and down through pasture to the minor road at Bronydd Isaf.

FOEL-FRAS LINK

Grade: Easy
Time: 1–1.5 hours
Distance: 3 miles (4.8km)
Height Gain: 416ft (127m)
Terrain: High mountain ridge
Start: Carnedd Llewelyn, GR683645

Summary: In good conditions a pleasant stroll along an undulating ridge with fine panoramic views. In poor visibility and with snow cover it can be a nightmare as the featureless terrain makes navigation difficult.

Route: Head NNE along the main ridge path then trend N over Foel Grach and continue to Garnedd Uchaf. From the summit descend NE to the col at the head of Cwm yr Afon Goch. From the col continue NE climbing the rounded ridge to Foel-fras.

CWM BYCHAN ROUTE

Grade: Intermediate
Time: 3 hours
Distance: 4.5 miles (7.2km)
Height Gain: 2664ft (812m)
Terrain: Pasture, moorland, steep-sided valley, high remote corrie and rounded summit ridge
Start: Ciltwllan on the east side of Bethesda, GR637663

Summary: Follows the course of the Afon Caseg then gains the north side of Carnedd Llewelyn via the lonely Cwm Bychan.

Ascent: Take the access track E then NW as it winds its way round to the pumping station. Pass the pumping station and turn E along the track. After the settlement remains the track becomes less distinct. Roughly follow the course of the Afon Caseg E then SE to the mouth of Cwm Bychan. Climb E up through the corrie, then on the final slopes trend SE to join the main ridge path at the broad col on the northeast side of Carnedd Llewelyn. Head SW up the path to the summit.

Descent: Head NE along the main ridge path then NW across the broad col and descend into Cwm Bychan. Trend W down through the corrie to gain the north side of the Afon Caseg. Roughly follow its north side NW then W to pick up the access track at the settlement remains. Take it W to the pumping station then turn SE along it and finally W to Ciltwllan.

Springs in Cwm Caseg

Emergency mountain refuge on the north side of Foel Grach's summit GR689659. Single room split into two providing simple emergency accommodation

Cwm yr Afon Goch Route

Grade: Easy
Time: 3.5–4 hours
Distance: 5.5 miles (8.8km)
Height Gain: 3484ft (1062m)
Terrain: Wooded valley, crags and scree, steep-sided valley, grassy head wall and high mountain ridge
Start: Bont Newydd on the Aber road, GR662720

Summary: An interesting route, it samples classic Carneddau scenery. Starting with the delights of the Aber Falls then the remoteness of Cwm yr Afon Goch and finishing with the high exposed slopes of the main ridge.

Ascent: Take the Aber Falls Path SSE, follow it across the Afon Rhaeadr-fawr and then to a fork (past the power lines). Take the left branch and follow it as it climbs up through woodland then trends S across scree to the top of Aber Falls. Follow the southwest bank of the Afon Goch generally SE into Cwm yr Afon Goch. Continue SE up the corrie head wall to the col on the northeast side of Garnedd Uchaf. Join the main ridge path and take it SW up onto Garnedd Uchaf. From the summit turn S along the main ridge path over Foel Grach then SSW to Carnedd Llewelyn.

Descent: Head NNE along the main ridge path then trend N over Foel Grach and continue to Garnedd Uchaf. From the summit descend NE to the col at the head of Cwm yr Afon Goch. Descend NW down the head wall then follow the southwest bank of the Afon Goch generally NW to the top of Aber Falls. Take the path N down the scree and then NNW through woodland. Once out of the woodland join the Aber Falls Path and take it NNW over the Afon Rhaeadr-fawr to the road at Bont Newydd.

Craig-Fawr Spur

Grade: Strenuous (can attain a Grade 1 scramble depending on the line followed)
Time: 3 hours
Distance: 4.25 miles (6.8km)
Height Gain: 2398ft (731m)
Terrain: Moorland, open valley, craggy corrie, steep spur, craggy head wall and high mountain ridge
Start: Cwm Eigiau Car Park, GR732663

Summary: The north side of the subsidiary top Foel Grach is occupied by two secluded corries. Between their steep craggy head walls a steep spur extends east – this is the Craig-fawr Spur. Its base can be reached easily via the Melynllyn Reservoir access track from where it gives a steep but exciting route onto the main ridge.

Ascent: At the northeast end of the car park take the Melynllyn Reservoir access track NW. It climbs around the flanks of Clogwynyreryr and is then followed SW then NW to the outlet stream. Cross the Afon Melynllyn then climb the steep slope NW onto the Craig-fawr Spur. Follow the crest of the spur SW then climb the head wall to join the Cwm Eigiau Path on the east side of Foel Grach. Trend SW and gain the main ridge path which is followed to the summit of Carnedd Llewelyn.

Pen yr Helgi Du and Craig yr Ysfa from Cwm Eigiau

Craig yr Ysfa and Carnedd Llewelyn from Cwm Eigiau

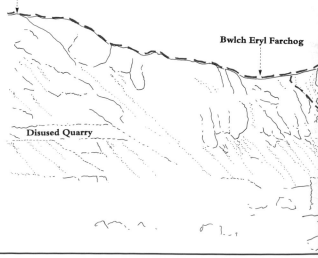

Pen yr Helgi Du 0.5ml

Bwlch Eryl Farchog

Disused Quarry

CWM EIGIAU PATH

Grade: Easy
Time: 3–3.5 hours
Distance: 5.5 miles (8.8km)
Height Gain: 2398ft (731m)
Terrain: Moorland, steep-sided valley, craggy corrie, grassy spur and high mountain ridge
Start: Cwm Eigiau Car Park, GR732663

Summary: Long steady approach from the Conway Valley side of the Carneddau via the cold depths of Cwm Eigiau. At the head of Cwm Eigiau the impressive cliffs of Craig yr Ysfa can be viewed in all their glory.

Ascent: From the car park follow the access track SW to the old dam. Cross the Afon Porth-llwyd then follow the rough track SSW then SW up into Cwm Eigiau. At the old quarry tips and buildings take the vague path NW, N then NW as it climbs up onto the east flank of Foel Grach. Turn SW and climb to the col on the south side of Foel Grach. From the col join the main ridge path and take it SSW to Carnedd Llewelyn.

Descent: Head NNE along the main ridge path to the col on the north side of Carnedd Llewelyn. From the col descend NE to join the Cwm Eigiau Path on the east flank of Foel Grach (the path is vague and can be difficult to locate in poor visibility). Once on it take it SE, S and then SE to the old quarry tips and buildings in Cwm Eigiau. Join the access track and take it E then NE around Cwm Eigiau to the old dam. Cross the Afon Porth-llwyd and head NE along the access track to the car park at the road head.

AMPHITHEATRE GULLY

Grade: Very strenuous (Grade 2 scramble; Grade 1/2 winter climb)
Time: 3 hours
Distance: 4.5 miles (7.2km)
Height Gain: 2398ft (731m)
Terrain: Moorland, steep-sided valley, craggy corrie, steep gully, narrow ridge and exposed summit
Variation: If on approaching the entrance to Amphitheatre Gully the route looks too difficult, the Southeast Ridge above can be gained via a traverse S around the base of Craig yr Ysfa.
Start: Cwm Eigiau Car Park, GR732663

Summary: Although rather forbidding, Amphitheatre Gully makes an exciting scramble. The technical difficulties are fewer than would appear from below – the main problems are psychological from exposure and from the foreboding atmosphere.

Ascent: From the car park follow the access track SW to the old dam. Cross the Afon Porth-llwyd then follow the rough track SSW then SW up into Cwm Eigiau. At the old quarry tips and buildings head WNW across the corrie floor, then up the scree to the entrance to Amphitheatre Gully (widest of the gullies on the crag). Climb the gully bed to the steepening which is turned on the right. Above the difficult middle section the gradient begins to ease as a series of zig-zags give access to the upper exit slopes. Gain the Southeast Ridge and follow it generally NW to the summit of Carnedd Llewelyn.

Craig yr Ysfa from the head of Cwm Eigiau

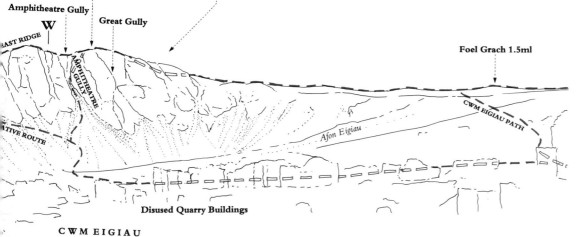

CARNEDD DAFYDD
3425FT (1044M)

PEN YR OLE WEN
3209FT (978M)

CARNEDD DAFYDD'S PRESENCE IS big and dramatic. Rearing up from the shores of Llyn Ogwen its south face dominates the entire length of the north side of the Ogwen Valley. To the west it extends two long ridges which cast their influence for over three miles to the outskirts of Bethesda. Most dramatic of all are the formidable cliffs of Ysgolion Duon, presenting a long north wall which in aspect and character has more in common with the great cliffs of the Scottish Highlands than its more moderate neighbours.

The plateau-like ridge which links the peaks and tops of the Carneddau can be very misleading. Its undulating form tends to give the impression of rounded rolling mountains, and while this is true for the ridge lines the vast amount of rock to be found on the flanks is often overlooked.

The most direct route to the blasted summit of Carnedd Dafydd is from Pen y Benglog (Ogwen Cottage) via the very steep South Ridge of the subsidiary top Pen yr Ole Wen. This popular and rather joyless approach can only really be recommended for its views along the Ogwen Valley and towards the Glyders Massif. The East Ridge of Pen yr Ole Wen and the Craig-Llugwy Spur are far more interesting and do not involve as much hard work. From Bethesda either the Northwest Ridge or the Braich Ty Du follow pleasant courses which have the distinct advantage of being quiet.

The classic route to Carnedd Dafydd has to be the Llech Ddu Spur. Climbing from the depths of Cwmglas Bach this steep truncated spur is a sheep among wolves. It offers a fine scramble in the shadow of the huge towering cliffs of Ysgolion Duon – ground which is the preserve of roped parties.

MAPS
Ordnance Survey: Outdoor Leisure 1: 25000 No 17; Landranger 1: 50000 No 115.

Harvey Mountain Maps: Snowdonia South 1: 40000.

INFORMATION
Tourist Information Centres: Bangor; Beddgelert; Caernarfon; Llanberis; Bangor; Betws-y-Coed.

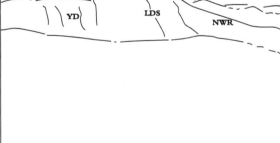

Carnedd Dafydd (**CD**) and the cliffs of Ysgolion Duon (**YD**) from Carnedd Llewelyn. **LDS** Llech Ddu Spur, **NWR** Northwest Ridge

ACCOMMODATION
Youth Hostels: Nant y Betws: *Snowdon Ranger*; Llanberis; Llanberis Pass: *Pen-y-pass*; Capel Curig; Nantgwynant: *Bryn Gwynant*.

Hotels and B&B: Beddgelert; Rhyd-Ddu; Betws Garmon; Llanberis; Nant Peris; Capel Curig; Nantgwynant.

Camp sites: Beddgelert; Betws Garmon; Llanberis; Llanberis Pass: *Nant Peris, Gwastadnant*; Capel Curig; Nantgwynant.

SOUTH RIDGE

Grade: Strenuous
Time: 2–2.5 hours
Distance: 2 miles (3.2km)
Height Gain: 2572ft (784m)
Terrain: Steep rocky ridge, high mountain ridge and exposed summit
Start: Ogwen Cottage (Pen y Benglog), GR650603

Summary: A steep approach to Carnedd Dafydd from the Ogwen Valley via the subsidiary top Pen yr Ole Wen.

Ascent: Cross the Afon Ogwen via the A5 road bridge and take the vague path E to the base of the ridge. Make the short scramble onto the ridge proper. Follow the crest NNE as it climbs unremittingly to the summit of Pen yr Ole Wen. From the summit cairn continue NNE then trend NE around the head of Cwm Lloer and climb the summit slopes to Carnedd Dafydd.

Descent: Head SW then SSW around the head of Cwm Lloer to the summit of Pen yr Ole Wen. From the summit cairn descend the steep rocky ridge SSW to the Afon Ogwen. Head W and cross the river via the A5 road bridge.

Pen yr Ole Wen and Carnedd Dafydd from Y Garn

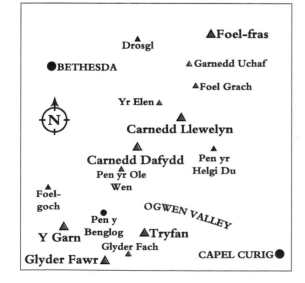

BRAICH TY DU

Grade: Easy
Time: 3 hours
Distance: 4.25 miles (6.8km)
Height Gain: 2900ft (884m)
Terrain: Steep pasture, long rounded ridge, high mountain ridge and exposed summit
Start: Braichmelyn on the south side of Bethesda, GR627659

Summary: A long steady approach up the featureless northwest limb of the subsidiary top Pen yr Ole Wen. Useful as a descent route to Bethesda.

Ascent: Take the lane S then the path SE as it meanders up through the steep pasture on to northeast slopes of Carnedd Dafydd. Once onto open mountainside trend SSE and cross the Afon Berthen to gain the Braich Ty Du proper. Ascend it S then SE to the summit of Pen yr Ole Wen. From the summit cairn continue NNE then trend NE around the head of Cwm Lloer and climb the summit slopes to Carnedd Dafydd.

Descent: Head SW then SSW around the head of Cwm Lloer to the summit of Pen yr Ole Wen. From the summit cairn descend NW along the Braich Ty Du trending N at the bottom to cross the Afon Berthen. Once across contour NNW to join the footpath that meanders NW down to Braichmelyn.

NORTHWEST RIDGE

Grade: Easy
Time: 2.5 hours
Distance: 2.75 miles (4.4km)
Height Gain: 2621ft (799m)
Terrain: Steep pasture, moorland, rounded ridge, steep grassy slopes and exposed summit
Start: Gwernydd on the southeast side of Bethesda, GR637660

Summary: A direct approach to Carnedd Dafydd from Bethesda. Mostly across featureless and uninteresting ground – the only distraction being the views down into Cwm Llafar. Better saved as a descent route.

Ascent: Cross the Afon Llafar then follow the path S then SE past the waterworks. Continue SE along the path until the old dam is reached. Leave the side of the Afon Llafar and climb SE up Mynydd Du onto the Northwest Ridge which is followed around the edge of Cwmglas Bach to the summit of Carnedd Dafydd.

Descent: Head NW down the steep slope, around the edge of Cwmglas Bach and down the crest of Mynydd Du. At the old dam join the Cwm Llafar Path and take it NW down past the waterworks then over the Afon Llafar to the road head.

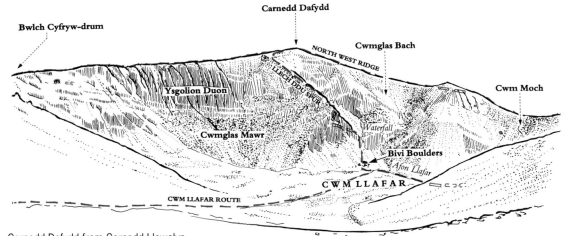

Carnedd Dafydd from Carnedd Llewelyn

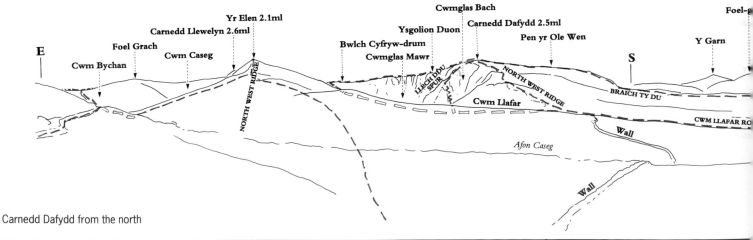

Carnedd Dafydd from the north

LLECH DDU SPUR

Grade: Strenuous (Grade 1 scramble; Grade 1 winter climb)
Time: 2.5–3 hours
Distance: 3.25 miles (5.2km)
Height Gain: 2621ft (799m)
Terrain: Steep pasture, steep-sided valley, complex corrie system, truncated spur and boulder-strewn summit slope
Start: Gwernydd on the southeast side of Bethesda, GR637660

Summary: The Llech Ddu Spur provides a superb scrambling route to the summit dome of Carnedd Dafydd between the complex corrie system of Cwmglas Bach and the dark forbidding cliffs of Ysgolion Duon. For a route set amongst such awesome surroundings the scrambling encountered on the Llech Ddu Spur is surprisingly easy.

Ascent: Cross the Afon Llafar then follow the path S then SE past the waterworks. Continue SE along the path past the old dam and along the side of the Afon Llafar to the boulders at the entrance to Cwmglas Bach. From the boulders head S into the corrie then turn E and climb up the west flank of the Llech Ddu Spur. On reaching the crest turn S and follow it as it steepens to abut the summit slopes. Climb these SW to Carnedd Dafydd's summit.

Bivi boulder, Cwmglas Bach GR664636. Built-up cave beneath boulder – not very appealing as very popular with sheep!

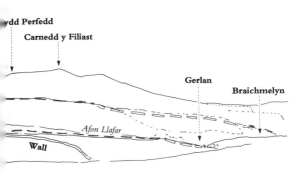

CARNEDD LLEWELYN LINK

Grade: Easy
Time: 1 hour
Distance: 2 miles (3.2km)
Height Gain: 384ft (117m)
Terrain: High mountain ridge and exposed summit
Start: Carnedd Dafydd, GR662631

Summary: Simple high-level ridge walk around the edge of Cwm Llafar.

Route: Take the main ridge path E then NE to Bwlch Cyfryw-drum. Cross the col and continue NE up the rounded ridge to the summit of Carnedd Llewelyn.

On the Llech Ddu Spur

Summit cairn – Carnedd Dafydd

CWM LLAFAR ROUTE

Grade: Intermediate
Time: 3 hours
Distance: 5 miles (8km)
Height Gain: 2621ft (799m)
Terrain: Steep pasture, steep-sided valley, high remote corrie, high mountain ridge and exposed summit
Start: Gwernydd on the southeast side of Bethesda, GR637660

Summary: Gains the eastern side of Carnedd Dafydd along the length of Cwm Llafar and up the course of the fast-flowing Nant Fach. The lower half of this lonely valley is open and quite pleasant but the upper half is of a completely different nature. Ringed by the dark cliffs of Ysgolion Duon it is an intimidating place.

Ascent: Cross the Afon Llafar then follow the path S then SE past the waterworks. Continue SE along the path past the old dam and along the side of the Afon Llafar to the entrance to Cwmglas Bach. Continue SE a short distance, then at the mouth of Cwmglas Mawr, turn ENE and climb the steepening slopes alongside Nant Fach to Bwlch Cyfryw-drum. On the col turn R and follow the main ridge path SW then W to the summit of Carnedd Dafydd.

Descent: Take the main ridge path E then NE to Bwlch Cyfryw-drum. At the col turn L and descend the steep slope alongside Nant Fach NW, W then WNW to the mouth of Cwmglas Mawr. Head NW and pick up the Cwm Llafar Path which is followed NW past the old dam, past the waterworks then over the Afon Llafar to the road head.

EAST RIDGE

Grade: Intermediate
Time: 2.5 hours
Distance: 2.75 miles (4.4km)
Height Gain: 2572ft (784m)
Terrain: Major valley, steep ridge, high mountain ridge and exposed summit
Start: A5 at Glan Dena, GR668605

Summary: The East Ridge of Pen yr Ole Wen separates the wild craggy Cwm Lloer from the Ogwen Valley. It climbs a logical and pleasing line which gains height quickly, and as most people tend to head for its more prominent neighbour, the South Ridge, you are likely to have it to yourself.

Ascent: Take the path N past Glan Dena and follow it as it meanders up the hillside along the course of the Afon Lloer. As the path starts to turn into Cwm Lloer turn W and climb the crest of the East Ridge to the summit of Pen yr Ole Wen. From the summit cairn turn NNE then trend NE around the head of Cwm Lloer and climb the summit slopes to Carnedd Dafydd.

Descent: Head SW then SSW around the head of Cwm Lloer to the summit of Pen yr Ole Wen. From the summit cairn descend E down the crest of the steep rocky ridge. At the bottom pick up the Cwm Lloer Path and follow it down alongside the Afon Lloer to the A5 at Glan Dena.

The Northwest Ridge of Carnedd Dafydd

The Northwest Ridge of Carnedd Dafydd revealed by clearing mist from the summit. Note the 'Brocken Spectre' – a phenomenon seen when a person's shadow is cast onto the mist

WARNING
Navigation on the main Carneddau ridge can be extremely difficult if the route is obliterated with fresh snow or visibility is poor.

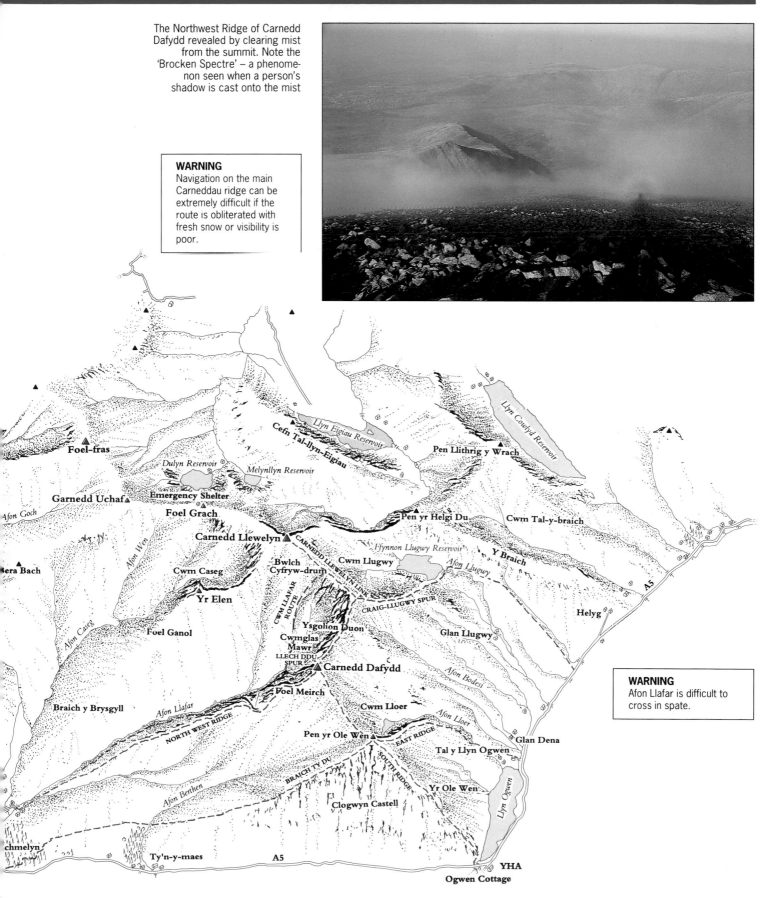

Foel-fras

Llyn Eigiau Reservoir

Cefn Tal-llyn-Eigiau

Pen Llithrig y Wrach

Llyn Cowlyd Reservoir

Dulyn Reservoir

Melynllyn Reservoir

Garnedd Uchaf

Emergency Shelter

Afon Goch

Foel Grach

Pen yr Helgi Du

Cwm Tal-y-braich

Afon Wen

Carnedd Llewelyn

CARNEDD LLEWELYN LINK ROUTE

Ffynnon Llugwy Reservoir

Y Braich

era Bach

Cwm Caseg

Bwlch Cyfryw-drum

Cwm Llugwy

Afon Llugwy

A5

Yr Elen

CWM LLAFAR ROUTE

CRAIG-LLUGWY SPUR

Helyg

Afon Caseg

Foel Ganol

Ysgolion Duon

Glan Llugwy

Cwmglas Mawr

LLECH DDU SPUR

Carnedd Dafydd

Afon Bodesi

Braich y Brysgyll

Foel Meirch

Afon Llafar

NORTH WEST RIDGE

Cwm Lloer

Afon Lloer

Glan Dena

WARNING
Afon Llafar is difficult to cross in spate.

Pen yr Ole Wen

EAST RIDGE

Tal y Llyn Ogwen

BRAICH TY DU

SOUTH RIDGE

Afon Berthen

Yr Ole Wen

Llyn Ogwen

Clogwyn Castell

chmelyn

Ty'n-y-maes

A5

YHA
Ogwen Cottage

Craig-Llugwy Spur

Grade: Intermediate
Time: 2.5–3 hours
Distance: 4 miles (6.4km)
Height Gain: 2474ft (754m)
Terrain: Major valley, high corrie, steep ridge, high mountain ridge and exposed summit
Start: A5 at the start of the reservoir access road, GR688603

Summary: The Craig-Llugwy Spur provides an adventurous and quiet route onto the eastern side of Carnedd Dafydd. Above the Ffynnon Llugwy Reservoir the views south to Tryfan and the Glyders are truly magnificent.

Ascent: Follow the access road NE then NW to the reservoir. Cross the Afon Llugwy then climb NW up the crest of the Craig-Llugwy Spur. At the top join the main ridge path and take it W as it skirts around the top of Ysgolion Duon to the summit of Carnedd Dafydd.

Descent: Skirt E around the top of Ysgolion Duon, then at the head of Cwm Llugwy turn SE then ESE and descend the crest of the Craig-Llugwy Spur. At the bottom cross the Afon Llugwy and join the reservoir access road which is followed SE then SW down to the A5.

WARNING
Afon Llafar is difficult to cross in spate.

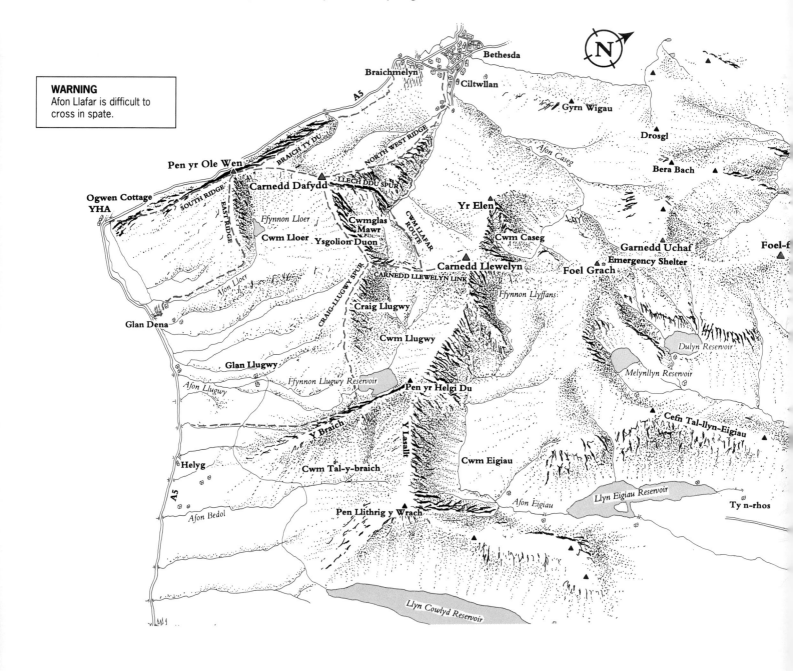

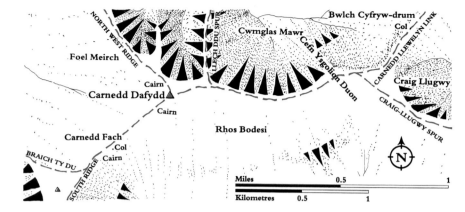

Carnedd Dafydd from Cwm Llafar with the Llech Ddu Spur in sunlight on the left

GLYDER FAWR 3278FT (999M)

GLYDER FACH 3261FT (994M)

GLYDER FAWR IS THE MAJOR PEAK of the Glyders Massif. It occupies a central position between the Ogwen Valley to the north and the Llanberis Pass to the south. Falling into the Llanberis Pass its slopes for the most part are convex and feature-less, the only significant crags lying at their base. To the north the story is reversed, the slopes are concave with deeply indented corries ringed by crags and ridges forming a significant wall at the top.

The north-facing crags and ridges of the Glyders are justifiably famous. They run the entire length of the Ogwen Valley in a complex series of hanging corries at varying levels. The crags, in particular those of Cwm Idwal, give a good selection of middle-grade climbs – a walk past the base of Idwal Slabs in the the summer months will usually see climbers queueing to get onto climbs. Walkers, with good reason, head for Bristly Ridge and Y Gribin Ridge. The best way to tackle these two fine ridges is by ascending Bristly Ridge, the harder of the two, then descending Y Gribin Ridge. This fine round can be completed without too much effort and takes in some superb scrambling set against a backdrop of ever-changing scenery.

Surprisingly for such a popular mountain with easy access it is not difficult to find solitude on Glyder Fawr. Once away from the wide paths of Cwm Idwal and Cwm Bochlwyd you can usually avoid other people until the main ridge is gained, particularly if you aim for the more secluded corries such as Cwm Cneifion or Cwm Tryfan.

Having been less affected by glaciation the southern slopes of the Glyders look rather bland; only from Pont y Gromlech in the Llanberis Pass do they display any dramatic features – in the shape of the crags of Dinas y Gromlech, Garreg Wastad and Clogwyn y Grochan. Above this line of crags most features are lost by the effect of perspective foreshortening. The routes on this side of the Glyders require a certain amount of foresight to embark upon because not until you are established on them do their qualities become apparent. They each provide interesting going at some point, but their real value lies in their unrivalled views of Snowdon.

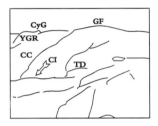

Glyders from Y Garn. **GF** Glyder Fach, **CyG** Castell y Gwynt, **YGR** Y Gribin Ridge, **CC** Cwm Cneifion, **CI** Cwm Idwal, **TD** Twll Du

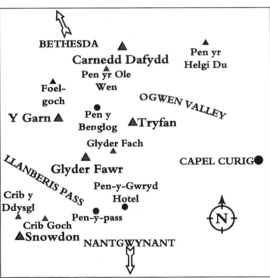

MAPS
Ordnance Survey: Outdoor Leisure 1: 25000 No 17; Landranger 1: 50000 No 115.

INFORMATION
Tourist Information Centres: Caernarfon; Llanberis; Betws-y-Coed; Bangor.

ACCOMMODATION
Youth Hostels: Llanberis Pass: *Pen-y-pass*; Llanberis; Ogwen Valley: *Idwal Cottage*; Capel Curig.

Hotels and B&B: Nantgwryd: *Pen-y-Gwryd Hotel*; Nant Peris; Llanberis; Bethesda; Ogwen Valley; Capel Curig.

Camp sites: Llanberis Pass: *Nant Peris, Gwastadnant*; Llanberis: *Deiniolen*; Bethesda: *Ogwen Bank*; Ogwen Valley: *Gwern Gof Uchaf*; Capel Curig.

Glyder Fawr – summit rocks

SOUTH RIDGE

Grade: Intermediate
Time: 2 hours
Distance: 1.75 miles (2.8km)
Height Gain: 2098ft (640m)
Terrain: Low rocky ridge, shallow col, broad steep ridge, rock outcrops and rocky summit
Variation: The main ridge can also be gained from Cwmffynnon.
Start: Pen-y-pass, GR647557

Summary: Viewed from Pen-y-pass the South Ridge of Glyder Fawr looks like a bit of a slog and a little unappealing. However, this view is misleading for although it is steep the walking is always interesting and the views are magnificent – particularly looking down Llanberis Pass.

Ascent: Leave the A4086 on the left side of the youth hostel and climb the path as it zig-zags NE onto the low spur. On the spur turn R and climb the South Ridge first NW then N and finally NE onto the summit slopes of Glyder Fawr.

Descent: From the summit rocks head SW down to the top of the South Ridge (this can be difficult in poor visibility as the ridge is rounded and difficult to identify) then turn S to descend the ridge. Midway down the ridge crags fringe its west side, these are avoided by turning SE and heading straight down towards the low spur on the north side of Pen-y-pass. From the crest of the spur turn R and zig-zag SW down to the A4086.

> **WARNING**
> In poor visibility or under snow cover the descents N from the main Glyders ridge to the Ogwen Valley can be difficult to locate.

The highest peaks of Wales support numerous Arctic–Alpine plants. These remnants of the ice age survive in some of the most exposed locations on summits and along high ridges. Most common are purple mountain saxifrage, moss campion, woolly-hair moss and dwarf willow. Not so common is the Snowdon lily: this only occurs in Snowdonia, most notably amongst the cliffs and rocks of Twll Du (the Devil's Kitchen).

Castell y Gwnt (Castle of the Winds) on the west side of Glyder Fach's summit

Y GARN LINK

Grade: Easy
Time: 1 hour
Distance: 1.5 miles (2.4km)
Height Gain: 774ft (236m)
Terrain: High mountain ridge and mountain lake
Start: Glyder Fawr, GR642579

Summary: The ridge between Glyder Fawr and Y Garn involves a fair amount of height loss with the dip down to the broad col occupied by Llyn y Cwn. The paths are good though and the views excellent – particularly down into Cwm Clyd from the final ascent to Y Garn.

Route: Head NW then N down the steep slopes to Llyn y Cwn. At the north end of the lake cross the outlet stream and take the path that forks R (not the Twll Du Path – that descends NE) and climbs N up the broad stony slopes of Y Garn. The path climbs to the lip of the crags of Cwm Clyd then turns NW to make the final ascent to Y Garn's distinct summit. There are two paths above the lip of Cwm Clyd: under snow cover, or for those who do not appreciate exposure, the higher of the two would be a better choice.

LLYN Y CWN PATH

Grade: Easy
Time: 2.5 hours
Distance: 2.5 miles (4km)
Height Gain: 2864ft (873m)
Terrain: Steep pasture, steep open corrie, mountain lake, scree, rock outcrops and rocky summit
Start: A4086 near Gwastadnant, GR615576

Summary: A pleasant approach via the beautifully situated Llyn y Cwn on the northwest side of Glyder Fawr. The path up through Cwm Padrig is fairly steep but easy to follow.

Ascent: From the A4086 take the track then path NE to the side of the Afon Las. Continue NE up the path as it climbs alongside the course of the Afon Las detouring slightly E to avoid the crags by the waterfalls to arrive at the broad col occupied by Llyn y Cwn. Walk around the north end of Llyn y Cwn to the main Glyders ridge path. Join it and follow it S then SE as it ascends the steep slopes of Glyder Fawr's summit dome.

Descent: Head NW then N down the steep slopes to Llyn y Cwn. At the north end of the lake cross the outlet stream and take the path that forks L then descends SW alongside the Afon Las into Cwm Padrig. In Cwm Padrig the path detours slightly S then W to avoid the crags adjacent to the waterfalls. Once past the waterfalls continue SW on the good path alongside the Afon Las to join the track to the A4086.

Tryfan and the Glyders from Y Garn

Glyder Fawr from Cwm Idwal

TWLL DU (DEVIL'S KITCHEN) PATH

Grade: Strenuous
Time: 2.5 hours
Distance: 2.5 miles (4km)
Height Gain: 2260ft (689m)
Terrain: Broad craggy corrie, mountain lake, scree, crags, stony col, rock outcrops and rocky summit
Start: Ogwen Cottage (Pen y Benglog), GR650603

Summary: The head of Cwm Idwal is ringed by a series of high towering crags. The likelihood of a walkers' route ascending these great buttresses seems remote, but across the flank of the darkest of these cliffs, Twll Du, is a narrow winding path. It is a handy route to the west side of the main Glyders ridge and passes by some awesome rock architecture.

Ascent: From Ogwen Cottage take the Cwm Idwal Path SE then SW to Llyn Idwal. Take the path on the east side of the lake and follow it S past the base of Idwal Slabs then W up the scree path towards Twll Du. At the base of Twll Du, amongst the boulders, the path swings S and climbs a vague ramp line before turning SW up an open groove. Ascend the groove to reach the broad col occupied by Lyn y Cwn and join the main Glyders ridge path. Turn L onto it and follow it S then SE as it ascends the steep slopes of Glyder Fawr's summit dome.

Descent: Head NW then N down the steep slopes towards Llyn y Cwn. At the east end of the lake descend NE down the Twll Du Path. It enters an open groove and is followed to the top of a vague ramp line. Descend N down the ramp then at the base of Twll Du follow the scree path as it swings around to the E past Idwal Slabs. Head N and make the steady descent to the north end of Llyn Idwal. Join the Ogwen Cottage Path and follow it NE then NW to the buildings and car park at Ogwen Cottage.

CWM CNEIFION ROUTE

Grade: Strenuous (Grade 1 scramble)
Time: 2.5–3 hours
Distance: 2.5 miles (4km)
Height Gain: 2260ft (689m)
Terrain: Broad craggy corrie, mountain lake, steep rocky slope, remote corrie, exposed spur and stony summit slopes
Start: Ogwen Cottage (Pen y Benglog), GR650603

Summary: High up on the south side of Cwm Idwal the hanging corrie Cwm Cneifion provides a wonderfully remote route to the north slopes of Glyder Fawr. The going is adventurous and involves some simple scrambling – the terrain can be confusing so for a first ascent this route is best attempted when visibility is good.

Ascent: From Ogwen Cottage take the Cwm Idwal Path SE then SW to Llyn Idwal. Take the path on the east side of the lake and follow it S towards the base of Idwal Slabs. Well before the slabs are reached turn L off the path and climb the steep slopes SE up into Cwm Cneifion. Head SSW across the floor of the corrie then swing SW and gain the ridge on the right-hand side of the corrie. Ascend the ridge SSW which leads to Glyder Fawr's summit slopes. Continue SSW across them to the summit rocks.

Cwm Idwal from the foot of the Northeast Ridge (John Gillham)

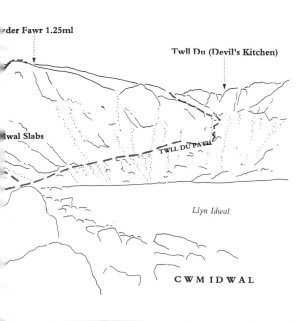

der Fawr 1.25ml

Twll Du (Devil's Kitchen)

Idwal Slabs

TWLL DU PATH

Llyn Idwal

CWM IDWAL

Cairn at the top of Y Gribin Ridge

Y GRIBIN RIDGE

Grade: Strenuous (Grade 1 scramble, Grade 1 winter climb)
Time: 2.5–3 hours
Distance: 2.5 miles (4km)
Height Gain: 2310ft (704m)
Terrain: Rocky slope, craggy corrie, mountain lake, narrow rocky ridge, high mountain ridge and rocky summit
Variation: The base of Y Gribin Ridge can be gained by ascending the steep west side of Cwm Idwal.
Start: Ogwen Cottage (Pen y Benglog), GR650603

Summary: The elegant Y Gribin Ridge attains the main Glyders ridge midway between Glyder Fawr and Glyder Fach. Poised high above the Ogwen Valley between Cwm Cneifion and Cwm Bochlwyd it gains height steadily and finishes suitably with a simple scramble – a classic route.

Ascent: From Ogwen Cottage take the Cwm Idwal Path SE to a fork at the first bend. Take the left branch and continue SE to Cwm Bochlwyd. At the north end of Llyn Bochlwyd turn R and climb the path W onto the base of Y Gribin. On the rounded crest turn S and climb directly up the ridge. The ridge climbs steadily to a shoulder after which it steepens and becomes narrower. Continue S up it, either on the crest or more easily on the west (Cwm Cneifion) side to the main Glyders ridge. Turn R and skirt the top of the Cwm Cneifion crags first SW then WSW to Glyder Fawr's summit rocks.

Descent: Take the main ridge path ENE then leave it and skirt NE around the the top of Cwm Cneifion's crags to the top of Y Gribin Ridge. Scramble N down the ridge either along its crest or more easily on its west (Cwm Cneifion) side. The gradient of the ridge soon eases; continue N down its crest then turn R and descend E to the north end of Llyn Bochlwyd. At the outlet of Nant Bochlwyd turn L and follow the path N then NW down to Ogwen Cottage.

The Cantilever – near the top of Bristly Ridge

BRISTLY RIDGE

Grade: Strenuous (Grade 1 scramble; Grade 1 winter climb)
Time: 3 hours
Distance: 3 miles (4.8km)
Height Gain: 2556ft (779m)
Terrain: Rocky slope, craggy corrie, mountain lake, scree, high col, narrow rocky ridge, high mountain ridge and stony summit slopes
Variation: The difficulties of Bristly Ridge can be avoided by following the scree path on the east side of the ridge.
Start: Ogwen Cottage (Pen y Benglog), GR650603

Summary: Steep and imposing, the pinnacled crest of Bristly Ridge presents a daunting sight. It is justifiably popular as it provides an adventurous scramble and serves as a convenient route onto the east end of the main Glyders ridge. Although it is only a Grade 1 scramble its difficulties should not be underestimated as there are a number of harder alternative lines which are easy to wander on to.

Ascent: From Ogwen Cottage take the Cwm Idwal path SE to a fork at the first bend. Take the left branch and continue SE to Cwm Bochlwyd. Cross the Nant Bochlwyd and climb SE to Bwlch Tryfan. At the col turn R and ascend the scree SW to the mouth of a gully system at the base of Bristly Ridge. Follow the gully, turning the difficult sections on the L, to gain the crest of the ridge via a short traverse R (when wet the gully system can be particularly difficult). Follow the crest over the undulations of the pinnacles (all the steep sections can be avoided) to join the main Glyders ridge on the east side of Glyder Fach. Turn R and follow the main ridge path WSW over Glyder Fach and over Bwlch y Ddwy-Glyder to Glyder Fawr.

Descent: The descent of Bristly Ridge is possible but is best left until experience has been gained with an ascent. An easier descent to Bwlch Tryfan is via the scree path on the east side of Bristly Ridge.

From Glyder Fawr take the main ridge ENE over Glyder Fach. As the main path starts its descent E it splits at a fork. Take the left branch which descends the scree NNE around the east side of Bristly Ridge to Bwlch Tryfan. From the col descend NW and follow the path down to Llyn Bochlwyd. Cross the Nant Bochlwyd and continue NW down to Ogwen Cottage.

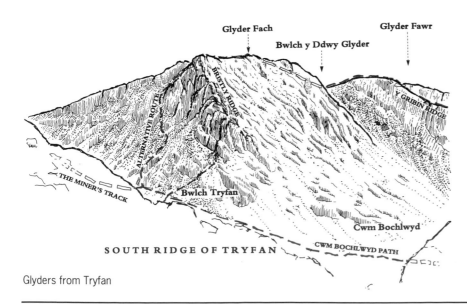

Glyder Fach   Glyder Fawr
Bwlch y Ddwy Glyder
BRISTLY RIDGE
GRIBIN RIDGE
ALTERNATIVE ROUTE
THE MINER'S TRACK
Bwlch Tryfan
Cwm Bochlwyd
CWM BOCHLWYD PATH
SOUTH RIDGE OF TRYFAN

Glyders from Tryfan

TRYFAN LINK

Grade: Strenuous
Time: 1–1.5 hours
Distance: 1.75 miles (2.8km)
Height Gain: 853ft (260m)
Terrain: High mountain ridge, steep scree, high col and rocky ridge
Start: Glyder Fawr, GR642579

Summary: It is usual to climb Tryfan first and then continue on to the main Glyders ridge. Doing it in reverse goes slightly against the grain, particularly in relation to the best of the scrambling, but nevertheless it provides an entertaining outing.

Route: From Glyder Fawr take the main ridge ENE over Glyder Fach. As the main path starts its descent E it splits at a fork. Take the left branch which descends the scree NNE around the east side of Bristly Ridge to Bwlch Tryfan. From the col take the path N up the South Ridge of Tryfan (avoiding the Far South Peak on its west side) and scramble up Tryfan's crest to the summit blocks.

Bristly Ridge (John Gillham)

Tryfan, Glyder Fach and Castell y Gwynt from the top of Y Gribin Ridge

Looking towards Snowdon from Castell y Gwynt.
(*Trail Walker*/Bob Atkins)

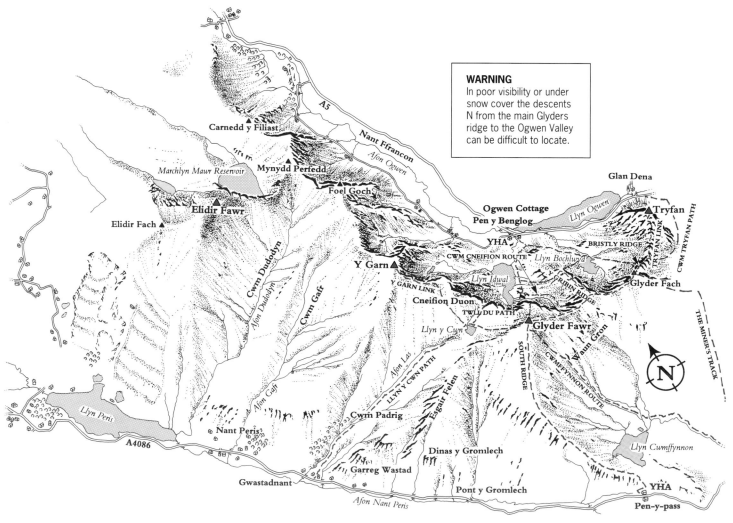

WARNING
In poor visibility or under snow cover the descents N from the main Glyders ridge to the Ogwen Valley can be difficult to locate.

Carnedd y Filiast

Nant Ffrancon

A5

Afon Ogwen

Marchlyn Mawr Reservoir

Mynydd Perfedd

Foel Goch

Glan Dena

Ogwen Cottage
Pen y Benglog

Llyn Ogwen

Tryfan

Elidir Fawr

Elidir Fach

YHA

BRISTLY RIDGE

TRYFAN LINK

CWM TRYFAN PATH

CWM CNEIFION ROUTE

Llyn Bochlwyd

Cwm Dudodyn

Y Garn

Llyn Idwal

CRIBIN RIDGE

Glyder Fach

Afon Dudodyn

Y GARN LINK

Cneifion Duon

TWLL DU PATH

Glyder Fawr

Waun Gron

Cwm Gafr

Llyn y Cŵn

THE MINER'S TRACK

SOUTH RIDGE

CWM MEFYNNON ROUTE

Afon Las

LLYN Y CWN PATH

Afon Gafr

Esgair Felen

Cwm Padrig

Llyn Cumffynnon

Llyn Peris

Nant Peris

Dinas y Gromlech

A4086

Garreg Wastad

YHA

Gwastadnant

Pont y Gromlech

Pen-y-pass

Afon Nant Peris

CWM TRYFAN PATH

Grade: Strenuous
Time: 3 hours
Distance: 3.5 miles (5.6km)
Height Gain: 2569ft (783m)
Terrain: Rough pasture, rough open corrie, scree and boulders, bleak col, high mountain ridge and rocky summit
Start: From the A5 opposite Glan Dena, GR668605

Summary: A rough corrie in the shadow of Tryfan's impressive east face provides a lonely route to the eastern end of the main Glyders ridge.

Ascent: From the A5 take the track E towards Gwern Gof Uchaf. Before the farm turn R and head SW towards Tryfan Bach. Pass below the slabs of Tryfan Bach and continue generally SW to enter the rough bounds of Cwm Tryfan. Follow the narrow path as it works its way to the corrie head to join The Miner's Track. Once on it take it ESE as it climbs to the bleak col at the east side of Glyder Fach. Turn R, off The Miner's Track, and climb W up the moderate grassy slopes to Glyder Fach. Head WSW over the summit of Glyder Fach and over Bwlch y Ddwy-Glyder to Glyder Fawr.

Descent: From Glyder Fawr take the main ridge ENE over Bwlch y Ddwy-Glyder to Glyder Fach then descend E to the bleak col at the head of Cwm Tryfan. Turn L and descend WNW along The Miner's Track into the head of Cwm Tryfan. As The Miner's Track starts to level it forks. Take the right-hand branch and follow it NNE and along the corrie floor to Tryfan Bach. Pass the slabs of Tryfan Bach and head NE towards Gwern Gof Uchaf. Before the farm turn L and take the track W to the A5.

THE MINER'S TRACK

Grade: Easy
Time: 3 hours
Distance: 3.5 miles (5.6km)
Height Gain: 2828ft (862m)
Terrain: Open rocky mountainside, bleak col, high mountain ridge and rocky summit
Start: A4086 near the Pen-y-Gwryd Hotel, GR661559

Summary: Gains the east end of the main Glyders ridge by traversing the gentle southern slopes of Glyder Fach.

Ascent: From the side of the A4086 take the footpath NW to the footbridge. Cross it and follow the path NE as it climbs steadily up the south and east flanks of Glyder Fach. As the crest of the main ridge line is reached the path levels at a bleak col. Turn L and climb W up the moderate grassy slopes to Glyder Fach. Head WSW over the summit of Glyder Fach and over Bwlch y Ddwy-Glyder to Glyder Fawr.

Descent: From Glyder Fawr take the main ridge ENE over Bwlch y Ddwy-Glyder to Glyder Fach then descend E to the bleak col at the head of Cwm Tryfan. Turn R and descend S then SW to the footbridge across the Nant Gwryd. Once across it head SE to the A4086.

CWMFFYNNON ROUTE

Grade: Strenuous
Time: 2.5 hours
Distance: 1.75 miles (2.8km)
Height Gain: 2533ft (772m)
Terrain: Extensive open corrie, steep grass- and heather-covered head wall and stony summit slopes
Start: A4086 near the Pen-y-Gwryd Hotel, GR661559

Summary: Climbs direct to Glyder Fawr from Pen-y-Gwryd via the steep head wall of the wild Cwmffynnon.

Ascent: From the side of the A4086 take the footpath NW to the footbridge. Cross it and follow the Nant Gwryd NW then W into Cwmffynnon. From the corrie floor turn NW again and climb the head wall via the vague gully line (Heather Gully). At the top continue NW up the summit dome to Glyder Fawr.

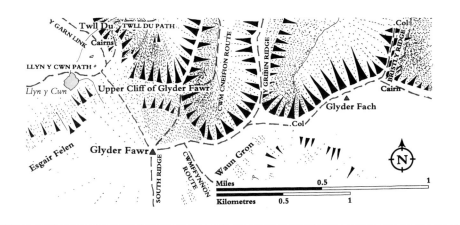

Y GARN
3107FT (947M)

ALTHOUGH CWM IDWAL IS more closely linked to Glyder Fawr, viewed from its wide corrie floor Y Garn looks by far the more prominent of the two peaks. This is due in part to Glyder Fawr's summit dome being hidden by the foreshortening effect of its steep craggy north face but also because Y Garn has such a distinct profile. Elegant and angular with four faces its shape is an almost perfect pyramid. The two Ogwen Valley faces with their colder north and east aspects hold shallow ice-carved corries while on the Llanberis side the south and west faces fall away in long unbroken slopes.

Y Garn's most striking feature is its long Northeast Ridge. It descends towards the mouth of Cwm Idwal between the hanging corries Cwm Cywion and Cwm Clyd. Climbing the spine of this lofty arête is a fine undertaking particularly with a covering of snow when it is endowed with an almost Alpine quality.

The most popular approaches to Y Garn are either along the main ridge or from the Ogwen Valley via the impressive but well-worn Twll Du

Y Garn (**YG**) from the North Ridge of Tryfan. **CI** Cwm Idwal, **EF** Elidir Fawr, **Fg** Foel-goch, **MP** Mynydd Perfedd, **CyF** Carnedd y Filiast

Path. This is predictable because of the popularity of completing the main Glyders ridge and because of the honey-pot attraction of Ogwen Cottage. However, this is rather unfortunate as these two approaches neglect some of Y Garn's finer aspects.

The southern approaches from Nant Peris and the Llanberis Pass provide moderately steep walks, first through pasture and woodland, then through pleasant open corries. Once on the cols expansive views of starkly contrasting terrain open out on either side of Y Garn. The other northern option apart from the Northeast Ridge is the remote and lonely Cwm Cywion. Considering its close proximity to the crowds of Cwm Idwal its pleasant solitude will come as a welcome surprise.

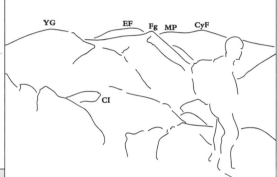

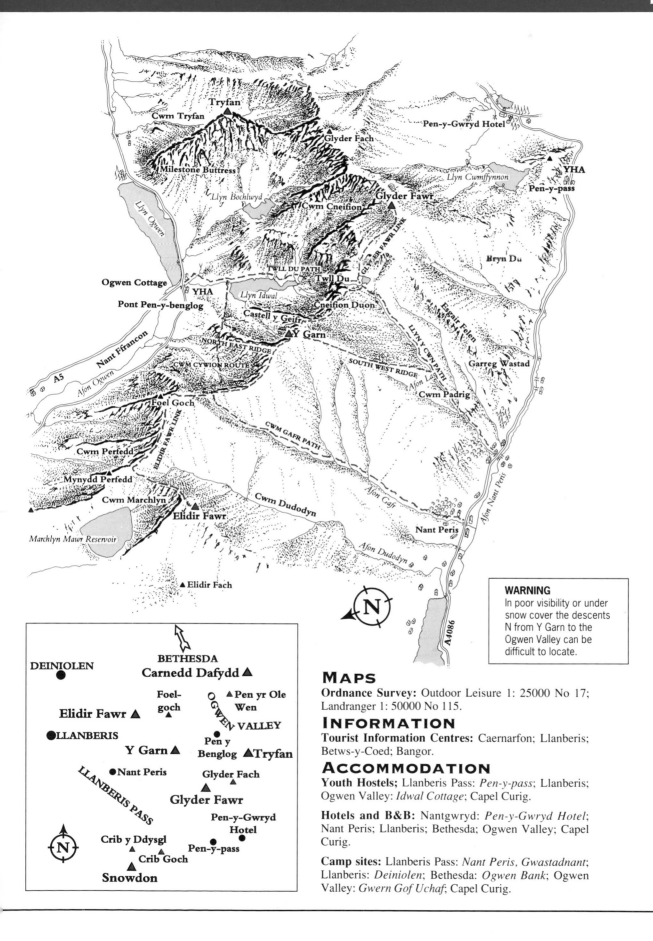

Tryfan
Cwm Tryfan
Pen-y-Gwryd Hotel
Glyder Fach
Milestone Buttress
Llyn Cumffynnon
YHA
Pen-y-pass
Llyn Bochlwyd
Glyder Fawr
Cwm Cneifion
Bryn Du
TWLL DU PATH
Twll Du
Esgair Felen
Ogwen Cottage
YHA
Llyn Idwal
Cneifion Duon
Pont Pen-y-benglog
Castell y Geifr
Y Garn
NORTH EAST RIDGE
Garreg Wastad
Llyn y Cwn Path
Nant Ffrancon
SOUTH WEST RIDGE
A5
Afon Ogwen
CWM CYWION ROUTE
Afon Las
Cwm Padrig
Foel Goch
CWM GAFR PATH
Cwm Perfedd
ELIDIR FAWR LINK
Mynydd Perfedd
Afon Gafr
Cwm Marchlyn
Cwm Dudodyn
Nant Peris
Elidir Fawr
Afon Nant Peris
Marchlyn Mawr Reservoir
Afon Dudodyn
Elidir Fach
A4086

N

DEINIOLEN
BETHESDA
Carnedd Dafydd ▲
Foel-goch
▲Pen yr Ole Wen
Elidir Fawr ▲
OGWEN
●LLANBERIS
VALLEY
Y Garn ▲
Pen y Benglog
▲Tryfan
●Nant Peris
Glyder Fach ▲
LLANBERIS PASS
Glyder Fawr
Pen-y-Gwryd Hotel
N
Crib y Ddysgl ▲
Pen-y-pass ●
Crib Goch ▲
Snowdon

MAPS

Ordnance Survey: Outdoor Leisure 1: 25000 No 17; Landranger 1: 50000 No 115.

INFORMATION

Tourist Information Centres: Caernarfon; Llanberis; Betws-y-Coed; Bangor.

ACCOMMODATION

Youth Hostels; Llanberis Pass: *Pen-y-pass*; Llanberis; Ogwen Valley: *Idwal Cottage*; Capel Curig.

Hotels and B&B: Nantgwryd: *Pen-y-Gwryd Hotel*; Nant Peris; Llanberis; Bethesda; Ogwen Valley; Capel Curig.

Camp sites: Llanberis Pass: *Nant Peris, Gwastadnant*; Llanberis: *Deiniolen*; Bethesda: *Ogwen Bank*; Ogwen Valley: *Gwern Gof Uchaf*; Capel Curig.

Llyn y Cwn Path

Grade: Easy
Time: 2.5 hours
Distance: 2.5 miles (4km)
Height Gain: 2694ft (821m)
Terrain: Steep pasture, steep open corrie, mountain lake, moderate scree-covered slopes and rocky summit
Start: A4086 near Gwastadnant, GR615576

Summary: A pleasant approach via the beautifully situated Llyn y Cwn on the southeast side of Y Garn. The path up through Cwm Padrig is fairly steep but easy to follow.

Ascent: From the A4086 take the track then the path NE to the side of the Afon Las. Continue NE up the path as it climbs alongside the course of the Afon Las, detouring slightly E to avoid the crags by the waterfalls to arrive at a broad col occupied by Llyn y Cwn. Walk to the north end of Llyn y Cwn, then as the path splits take the left fork and follow it N up the broad stony slopes of Y Garn. The path climbs to the lip of the crags of Cwm Clyd then turns NW to make the final ascent to Y Garn's distinct summit. There are two paths above the lip of Cwm Clyd: under snow cover, or for those who do not appreciate exposure, the higher of the two would be a better choice.

Descent: Take the path which descends SE and follow it as it skirts the crags then turns SSE down the broad stony slopes to Llyn y Cwn. At the north end of the lake turn R and follow the path which descends SW alongside the Afon Las into Cwm Padrig. In Cwm Padrig the path detours slightly S then W to avoid the crags adjacent to the waterfalls. Once past the waterfalls continue SW on the good path alongside the Afon Las to join the track to the A4086.

Cwm Gafr Path

Grade: Easy
Time: 2–2.5 hours
Distance: 2 miles (3.2km)
Height Gain: 2739ft (835m)
Terrain: Steep pasture, steep-sided corrie, exposed col, high mountain ridge and rocky summit
Start: Nant Peris, GR606584

Summary: Cwm Gafr is the steep open corrie high above Nant Peris on the west side of Y Garn. The path through it provides the most direct route to Y Garn from Nant Peris.

Ascent: From Nant Peris take the lane (opposite the post office) NE. At the sharp left-hand bend join the Cwm Gafr Path and follow it as it winds E through the buildings then NE up through Cwm Gafr. Near the top of Cwm Gafr turn E and climb to the col on the north side of Y Garn. From the col turn SE and climb the steep summit slopes to Y Garn.

Descent: Head NW from the summit rocks skirting the crags of Cwm Cywion down to the col on the northwest side of Y Garn. From the col descend the steep grassland W to join the vague path on the southeast side of Afon Gafr. Follow the path SE the length of Cwm Gafr, then W as it winds its way through the buildings to the lane. Join the lane and follow it SW a short distance to the A4086 in Nant Peris.

Elidir Fawr Link

Grade: Easy
Time: 1–1.5 hours
Distance: 2.5 miles (4km)
Height Gain: 554ft (169m)
Terrain: High mountain ridge, exposed col and narrow summit ridge
Start: Y Garn, GR631596

Summary: Pleasant high-level walk between two fine mountains. The classic approach to Elidir Fawr when completing the 'Welsh 3000ers'.

Route: Head NW from the summit rocks skirting the crags of Cwm Cywion down to the col on the northwest side of Y Garn. From the col head generally N along the main ridge path then W around the head of Cwm Dudodyn to Bwlch y Marchlyn. From the col climb the steep narrow ridge WSW to the summit of Elidir Fawr.

Llyn y Cwn with Pen yr Ole Wen in the background

Footbridge – Cwm Padrig on the approach to Llyn y Cwn

SOUTHWEST RIDGE

Grade: Easy
Time: 2–2.5 hours
Distance: 1.75 miles (2.8km)
Height Gain: 2694ft (821m)
Terrain: Steep pasture, steep open corrie, mountain lake, scree, rock outcrops and rocky summit
Start: A4086 near Gwastadnant, GR615576

Summary: Useful as a descent, the Southwest Ridge offers a direct route down to the Llanberis side of Y Garn.

Ascent: From the A4086 take the track then path NE to the side of the Afon Las. Continue NE up the path as it climbs alongside the course of the Afon Las, detouring slightly E to avoid the crags by the waterfalls. Once above the waterfalls cross the Afon Las and climb N up the steep slopes onto the rounded crest of the Southwest Ridge. On the ridge climb NW up it to the summit of Y Garn.

WARNING
In poor visibility or under snow cover the descents N from Y Garn to the Ogwen Valley can be difficult to locate.

Descent: Head SW from the summit rocks down the rounded ridge, then turn S and descend the steep slopes into Cwm Padrig. Cross the Afon Las and join the path on the southeast side. Descend the path as it detours slightly S then W to avoid the crags adjacent to the waterfalls. Once past the waterfalls continue SW on the good path alongside the Afon Las to join the track to the A4086.

Y Garn from Elidir Fawr

Summit cairn – Y Garn

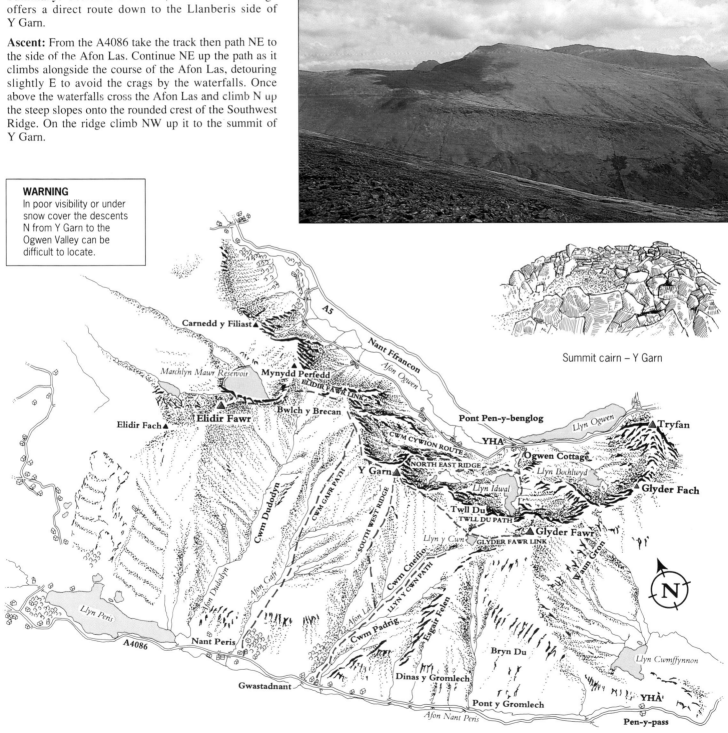

CWM CYWION ROUTE

Grade: Intermediate
Time: 2.5-3 hours
Distance: 2.75 miles (4.4km)
Height Gain: 2238ft (682m)
Terrain: Broad craggy corrie, mountain lake, steep rocky slope, high open corrie, rounded mountain ridge and rocky summit
Start: Ogwen Cottage (Pen y Benglog) GR650603

Summary: The remote and little-visited Cwm Cywion, perched high on the north side of Y Garn, provides a quiet alternative approach away from the crowds found on the more popular Ogwen Valley routes.

Ascent: From Ogwen Cottage take the Cwm Idwal Path SE then SW to Llyn Idwal. Cross the footbridge at the northeast end of the lake and follow the vague path that snakes up to the base of the Northeast Ridge of Y Garn. Before the base of the ridge is reached leave the path and contour round the steep slopes NW into Cwm Cywion. Continue NW up through Cwm Cywion to Llyn Cywion then ascend the head wall, still generally NW, to Bwlch y Cywion. Cross the col and make the short descent to join the path on the southwest side of Foel-goch. Turn L on the path and follow it S then SE to the summit rocks of Y Garn.

Descent: Head NW from the summit rocks skirting the crags of Cwm Cywion down to the col on the northwest side of Y Garn. From the col head generally N along the main ridge path, then on the southwest side of Foel-goch make the short ascent E to Bwlch y Cywion. Cross the col and make the steep descent SE to Llyn Cywion. Continue descending SE through Cwm Cywion and contour around to the bottom of the Northeast Ridge of Y Garn. At the base of the ridge join the vague path and follow it ESE to the footbridge at the northeast end of Llyn Idwal. Cross it and join the Ogwen Cottage Path which is followed NE then NW to the buildings and car park at Ogwen Cottage.

NORTHEAST RIDGE

Grade: Strenuous (Grade 1 scramble)
Time: 2.5 hours
Distance: 2 miles (3.2km)
Height Gain: 2090ft (637m)
Terrain: Broad craggy corrie, mountain lake, steep rocky slope, steep rocky ridge and rocky summit
Start: Ogwen Cottage (Pen y Benglog), GR650603

Summary: A superb knife-edge ridge which rears up steeply from the Ogwen Valley direct to Y Garn's summit rocks.

Ascent: From Ogwen Cottage take the Cwm Idwal Path SE then SW to Llyn Idwal. Cross the footbridge at the northeast end of the lake and follow the vague path which snakes W up the hillside to the base of the Northeast Ridge. Continue along the path as it climbs the crest of the ridge SW to Y Garn's summit ridge. At the top turn L and head S to the summit rocks.

Descent: Head N from the summit rocks to the top of the Northeast Ridge. Descend directly down the crest of the ridge, then at the base follow the vague path that snakes E to the footbridge at the northeast end of Llyn Idwal. Cross it and join the Ogwen Cottage Path which is followed NE then NW to the buildings and car park at Ogwen Cottage.

Y Garn from Foel-goch (Phil Iddon)

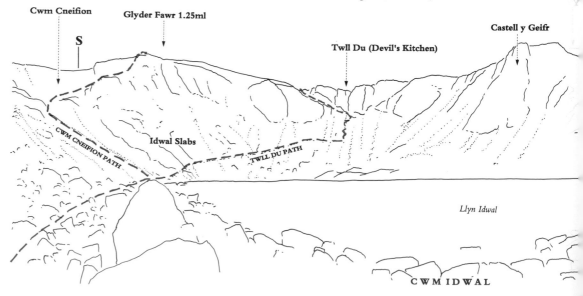

GLYDER FAWR LINK

Grade: Easy
Time: 1 hour
Distance: 1.5 miles (2.4km)
Height Gain: 945ft (288m)
Terrain: High mountain ridge and mountain lake
Start: Y Garn, GR631596

Summary: The ridge between Y Garn and Glyder Fawr involves a fair amount of height loss with the dip down to the broad col occupied by Llyn y Cwn. The paths are good though and the views excellent – particularly of the main Glyders Massif and across Llanberis Pass towards Snowdon.

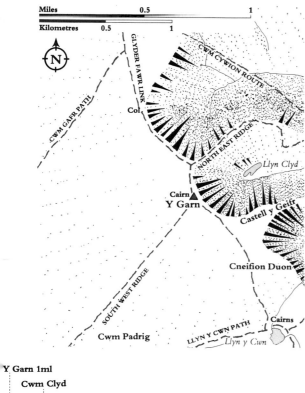

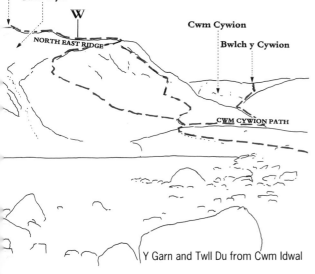

Y Garn and Twll Du from Cwm Idwal

Route: Take the path which descends SE and follow it as it skirts the crags then turns SSE down the broad stony slopes to Llyn y Cwn. At the north end of the lake cross the outlet stream and follow the path ESE then S and finally SE as it ascends the steep slopes of Glyder Fawr's summit dome.

TWLL DU (DEVIL'S KITCHEN) PATH

Grade: Strenuous
Time: 2.5 hours
Distance: 2.75 miles (4.4km)
Height Gain: 2090ft (637m)
Terrain: Broad craggy corrie, mountain lake, moderate scree-covered slopes and rocky summit
Start: Ogwen Cottage (Pen y Benglog), GR650603

Summary: The head of Cwm Idwal is ringed by series of high towering crags. The likelihood of a walkers' route ascending these great buttresses seems remote but across the flank of the darkest of these cliffs, Twll Du, is a narrow winding path. It is a handy route to the broad col on the southwest side of Y Garn.

Ascent: From Ogwen Cottage take the Cwm Idwal Path SE then SW to Llyn Idwal. Take the path on the east side of the lake and follow it S past the base of Idwal Slabs then W up the scree path towards Twll Du. At the base of Twll Du, amongst the boulders, the path swings S and climbs a vague ramp line before turning SW up an open groove. Ascend the groove to reach the broad col occupied by Lyn y Cwn. At the east end of Llyn y Cwn the path splits; take the right-hand branch and follow it WNW over the outlet stream to another fork. Again take the right-hand branch and follow it N up the broad stony slopes of Y Garn. The path climbs to the lip of the crags of Cwm Clyd then turns NW to make the final ascent to Y Garn's distinct summit. There are two paths above the lip of Cwm Clyd: under snow cover, or for those who do not appreciate exposure, the higher of the two would be a better choice.

Descent: Take the path which descends SE and follow it as it skirts the crags then turns SSE down the broad stony slopes to Llyn y Cwn. At the north end of the lake cross the outlet stream and turn ESE to a fork. Take the left branch and descend NE down the Twll Du Path. The path enters an open groove and is followed to the top of a vague ramp line. Descend N down the ramp, then at the base of Twll Du follow the scree path as it swings round to the east and passes the base of Idwal Slabs. Head N and make the steady descent to the north end of Llyn Idwal. Join the Ogwen Cottage Path and follow it NE then NW to the buildings and car park at Ogwen Cottage.

FOEL-FRAS
3091FT (942M)

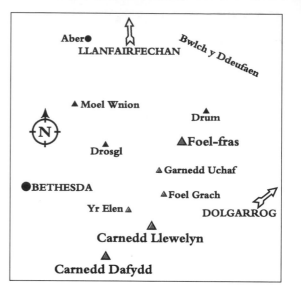

THE SMOOTH ROUNDED FORM OF FOEL-FRAS at the northern end of the Carneddau is a welcome sight for walkers completing the 'Welsh 3000ers'. Its boulder-strewn summit marks the start of the final leg of this long expedition. Any walker thinking they are in for an easy descent though will be in for a little shock, for like the other peaks in the Carneddau, it is a long way from anywhere.

Apart from the dark brooding cliffs of Craig y Dulyn and Craig-fawr the terrain of Foel-fras is of a gentle nature displaying a grandeur derived from subtle changes in shape rather than from individual eye-catching features. On the northwest side, the Aber side, the valleys of the Afon Anafon and Afon Goch are separated by the long ridge of Llwytmor. To the southeast, the Conwy Valley side, grassy slopes fall away steeply, interrupted only by fast-flowing streams and the occasional minor rock outcrop, to the waters of the Afon Dulyn.

For those seeking an adventurous approach to Foel-fras there is really only one alternative: the spur extending east from the subsidiary top Foel Grach. It climbs high between Cwm Dulyn and Craig-fawr and involves some simple scrambling. The other routes up Foel-fras follow uncomplicated lines over ground which requires stamina, rather than agility, and the ability to navigate with few landmarks.

MAPS
Ordnance Survey: Outdoor Leisure 1: 25000 No 17; Landranger 1: 50000 No 115.

INFORMATION
Tourist Information Centres: Llanberis; Bangor; Llanfairfechan; Betws-y-Coed.

ACCOMMODATION
Youth Hostels: Ogwen Valley: *Idwal Cottage*; Rowen: *Rhiw Farm*; Capel Curig.

Hotels and B&B: Capel Curig; Bethesda; Ogwen Valley; Aber; Llanfairfechan; Tal-y-Bont; Betws-y-Coed; Capel Curig.

Camp sites: Capel Curig; Ogwen Valley: *Gwern Gof Uchaf*; Bethesda: *Ogwen Bank*; Betws-y-Coed.

Foel-fras (**Ff**) and Llyn Anafon (**LA**) from Drum (John Gillham)

CARNEDD LLEWELYN LINK

Grade: Easy
Time: 1–1.5 hours
Distance: 3 miles (4.8km)
Height Gain: 738ft (225m)
Terrain: High mountain ridge
Start: Foel-fras, GR696682

Summary: In good conditions a pleasant stroll along an undulating ridge with fine panoramic views. In poor visibility and with snow cover it can be a nightmare as the featureless terrain makes navigation difficult.

Route: Head SSW then SW along the main ridge path to Garnedd Uchaf. From the summit turn S and continue along the main ridge path over Foel Grach then SSW to Carnedd Llewelyn.

The summit of Foel-fras

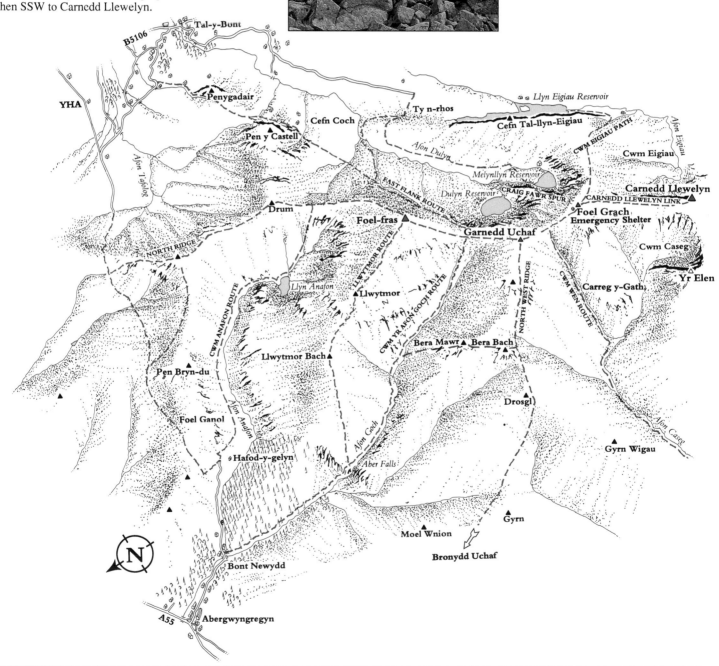

Garnedd Uchaf and Foel-fras
from Yr Elen

CWM WEN ROUTE

Grade: Easy
Time: 3 hours
Distance: 4.75 miles (7.6km)
Height Gain: 2270ft (692m)
Terrain: Pasture, moorland, steep-sided valley, high remote corrie, and high mountain ridge
Start: Ciltwllan on the east side of Bethesda, GR637663

Summary: Follows the course of the Afon Caseg then gains the south side of Foel-fras via the lonely Cwm Wen and the subsidiary top Garnedd Uchaf.

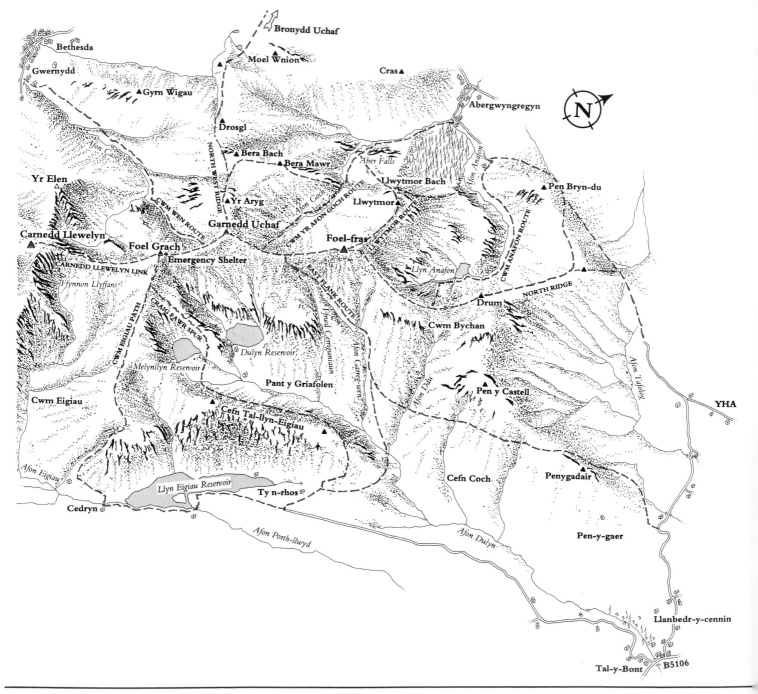

Ascent: Take the access track E then NW as it winds its way round to the pumping station. Pass the pumping station and turn E along the track. After the settlement remains the track becomes less distinct. Roughly follow the course of the Afon Caseg E then SE to the mouth of Cwm Wen. Climb E up through the corrie to join the main ridge path at the broad col on the north side of Foel Grach. Head N along it to Garnedd Uchaf then turn NE and follow the broad ridge, finally trending NNE to the summit of Foel-fras.

Descent: Head SSW then SW along the main ridge path to Garnedd Uchaf. From the summit turn S to the broad col at the head of Cwm Wen. Turn R and descend Cwm Wen to gain the north side of the Afon Caseg. Roughly follow its north side NW then W to pick up the access track at the settlement remains. Take it W to the pumping station, then turn SE along it and finally W to Ciltwllan.

NORTHWEST RIDGE
(GARNEDD UCHAF)

Grade: Easy
Time: 3.5 hours
Distance: 5.75 miles (9.2km)
Height Gain: 2532ft (771m)
Terrain: Pasture, moorland, long rounded ridge and high mountain ridge
Variation: The middle section of the Northwest Ridge can be gained by intersecting the northerly spur occupied by the minor tops Bera Mawr and Bera Bach. Start from Bont Newydd on the Aber road (GR662720). Take the Aber Falls Path S past the falls then SE to the foot of the spur in Cwm yr Afon Goch. Climb the crest direct and join the Northwest Ridge Path on the south side of Bera Bach.
Start: Bronydd Isaf (T-junction on minor road), GR624704

Summary: A long meandering route over moorland and up a gentle, grassy ridge to gain the subsidiary top, Garnedd Uchaf, to the southwest of Foel-fras.

Ascent: From the minor road take the path that winds steadily SE up through pasture and under the power lines. Once on the open hillside continue generally SE till the path splits. Take the left branch and continue SE along it and through the low col between Moel Wnion and Gyrn to join the Northwest Ridge by skirting around the south side of Drosgl. Skirt the south side of Bera Bach then climb the rounded crest of the ridge SE to Garnedd Uchaf. From the summit turn NE and follow the broad ridge NE then NNE to the summit of Foel-fras.

Descent: Head SSW then SW along the main ridge path to Garnedd Uchaf. From the summit turn R and make the steady descent NW along the rounded crest of the ridge then trend W to skirt Bera Bach and Drosgl. Turn NNW around Drosgl then descend NW to the broad col between Moel Wnion and Gyrn. From the col continue the steady descent NW under the power lines and down through pasture to the minor road at Bronydd Isaf.

Foel-fras from Llyn Anafon

Rock outcrop on Yr Aryg on the Northwest Ridge of Garnedd Uchaf

CWM YR AFON GOCH ROUTE

Grade: Easy
Time: 3 hours
Distance: 3.75 miles (6km)
Height Gain: 2828ft (862m)
Terrain: Wooded valley, crags and scree, steep-sided valley, grassy head wall and high mountain ridge
Start: Bont Newydd on the Aber road, GR662720

Summary: An interesting route, it samples classic Carneddau scenery. Starting with the delights of the Aber Falls then the remoteness of Cwm yr Afon Goch and finishing with the high exposed slopes of the main ridge.

Ascent: Take the Aber Falls Path SSE, follow it across the Afon Rhaeadr-fawr and then to a fork (past the power lines). Take the left branch and follow it as it climbs up through woodland then trends S across scree to the top of Aber Falls. Follow the southwest bank of the Afon Goch generally SE into Cwm yr Afon Goch. Continue SE up the corrie head wall to the col on the southwest side of Foel-fras. Turn L and climb the main ridge path NE then NNE to the summit of Foel-fras.

Descent: From the summit descend SSW then SW to the col at the head of Cwm yr Afon Goch. Descend NW down the head wall then follow the southwest bank of the Afon Goch generally NW to the top of Aber Falls. Take the path N down the scree and then NNW through woodland. Once out of the woodland join the Aber Falls Path and take it NNW over the Afon Rhaeadr-fawr to the road at Bont Newydd.

CWM ANAFON ROUTE

Grade: Easy
Time: 2.5–3 hours
Distance: 4 miles (6.4km)
Height Gain: 2434ft (742m)
Terrain: Wooded valley, steep-sided valley, open corrie, steep grassy ridge and exposed summit
Start: Top of the minor road, GR676716

Summary: Straightforward approach via the reservoir access track then up the moderate head wall of Cwm Anafon to the broad col on the northeast side of Foel-fras. A useful descent route – easy to follow if conditions are bad.

Ascent: Follow the minor road ESE as it climbs to the road head above the Afon Anafon then climb the zig-zags E onto the Llyn Anafon Reservoir access track. Join the track and follow it as it winds its way SE to Llyn Anafon. From the reservoir climb steadily SE to Bwlch y Gwryd. Turn R at the col and take the main ridge path as it climbs SW up the curving ridge to Foel-fras's summit.

Descent: Head NE down the curving ridge to Bwlch y Gwryd. At the col turn L and drop down into Cwm Anafon. From the northeast side of Llyn Anafon join the reservoir access track as it winds generally NW down Cwm Anafon. As it contours the steep flanks of Foel Dduarth the track forks. Take the left branch and follow the zig-zags W down to the road head. Join the minor road and follow it WNW down towards Bont Newydd.

EAST FLANK ROUTE

Grade: Easy
Time: 2.5–3 hours
Distance: 4 miles (6.4km)
Height Gain: 1909ft (582m)
Terrain: Steep-sided valley, steep grassy slopes and high mountain ridge
Start: Minor road near Bron-y-Gadair, GR744694

Summary: Ascends the east flank of Foel-fras in a long traverse to gain the main ridge at the col on the southwest side of Foel-fras's summit dome. Generally good going although the top section is a little vague and can be awkward to locate when trying to descend from the main ridge.

Ascent: Follow the track then path SW across the flanks of Penygadir, Pen y Castell and finally Foel-fras to the broad col on the southwest side of Foel-fras. At the col join the main ridge path and take it NE then NNE to the summit of Foel-fras.

Descent: Head SSW then SW down the main ridge path to the col on the southwest side of Foel-fras. At the col turn L (almost doubling back) and follow the vague path (difficult to locate in poor visibility) NE across the flanks of Foel-fras, Pen y Castell and Penygadir to join the minor road.

Foel-fras – summit trig point

NORTH RIDGE

Grade: Easy
Time: 2.5 hours
Distance: 3.75 miles (6km)
Height Gain: 1873ft (571m)
Terrain: Moorland, exposed col, steep grassy ridge and high mountain ridge
Variation: Can also be started by following the Roman Road to Bwlch y Ddeufaen, or the access track to the summit of Drum, from the minor road head, GR676716.
Start: Road head on the east side of Bwlch y Ddeufaen, GR721715

Summary: The Carneddau are generally quieter than the other Snowdonia peaks but no area is more lonely than the northern side of Foel-fras. The route along the North Ridge samples the best of this area and provides a straightforward route with modest height gain.

Ascent: From the road head follow the track (Roman Road) NW to Bwlch y Ddeufaen. Turn L and follow the path SSW up the rounded spur. As the gradient eases head SE then S along the crest of the ridge to Drum. Contine S over Drum to Bwlch Y Gwryd. Cross the col and then climb SW up the curving ridge to Foel-fras's summit.

Descent: Head NE down the curving ridge to Bwlch y Gwryd. Cross the col and follow the main ridge to Drum. Continue N over Drum along the crest of the ridge then swing NW. As the crest of the ridge starts to steepen into a slope turn R and descend the rounded spur NE to Bwlch y Ddeufaen. From the broad col take the track (Roman Road) SE to the road head.

The ascent of Drum from Bwlch y Ddeufaen with views over the Conwy Valley (John Gillham)

Llwytmor Route

Grade: Intermediate
Time: 2.5–3 hours
Distance: 3.75 miles (6km)
Height Gain: 2828ft (862m)
Terrain: Wooded valley, crags and scree, rounded ridge and high mountain ridge
Start: Bont Newydd on the Aber road, GR662720

Summary: Llwytmor occupies a high point on the northwest arm of Foel-fras. Gaining this fine vantage point involves some hard leg-work on the steep slopes above Aber Falls but once they have been negotiated the rest of route follows a pleasant elevated line.

Ascent: Take the Aber Falls Path SSE, follow it across the Afon Rhaeadr-fawr and then to a fork (past the power lines). Take the left branch and follow it as it climbs up through woodland then trends S across scree to the top of Aber Falls. Leave the path and climb the steep slope E onto Llwytmor Bach. Turn SE and climb the steep slope to Llwytmor. Continue SE over the summit and then up the summit slopes of Foel-fras to the trig point on the top.

Descent: From the trig point head NW down the broad ridge to Llwytmor. Continue NW over the summit and descend to Llwytmor Bach. Turn W and drop down the steep slope (avoiding the crags of Marian Rhaeadr-fawr) to join the Cwm yr Afon Goch Path above the Aber Falls. Take the path N down the scree and then NNW through woodland. Once out of the woodland join the Aber Falls Path and take it NNW over the Afon Rhaeadr-fawr to the road at Bont Newydd.

Craig-fawr Spur

Grade: Strenuous (can attain a Grade 1 scramble depending on the line taken)
Time: 3–3.5 hours
Distance: 5 miles (8km)
Height Gain: 2644ft (806m)
Terrain: Moorland, open valley, craggy corrie, steep spur, craggy head wall and high mountain ridge
Start: Cwm Eigiau Car Park, GR732663

Summary: The north side of the subsidiary top, Foel Grach is occupied by two secluded corries. Between their steep craggy head walls a steep spur extends east – this is the Craig-fawr Spur. Its base can be reached easily via the Melynllyn Reservoir access track from where it gives a steep but exciting route onto the main ridge.

Ascent: At the northeast end of the car park take the Melynllyn reservoir access track NW. It climbs around the flanks of Clogwynyreryr and is then followed SW then NW to the outlet stream. Cross the Afon Melynllyn then climb the steep slope NW onto the Craig-fawr Spur. Follow the crest of the spur SW then climb the head wall to join the Cwm Eigiau Path on the east side of Foel Grach. Take it NW to join the main ridge path on the summit of Foel Grach. From Foel Grach head N then NE to Foel-fras.

Cwm Eigiau Path

Grade: Easy
Time: 3.5–4 hours
Distance: 6.5 miles (10.4km)
Height Gain: 2218ft (676m)
Terrain: Moorland, steep-sided valley, craggy corrie, grassy spur and high mountain ridge
Start: Cwm Eigiau Car Park, GR732663

Summary: Long steady approach from the Conwy Valley side of the Carneddau via the cold depths of Cwm Eigiau. At the head of Cwm Eigiau the impressive cliffs of Craig yr Ysfa can be viewed in all their glory.

Ascent: From the car park follow the access track SW to the old dam. Cross the Afon Porth-llwyd then follow the rough track SSW then SW up into Cwm Eigiau. At the old quarry tips and buildings take the vague path NW, N then NW as it climbs across the east flank of Foel Grach to the col on its northeast side. From the col join the main ridge path and follow it NE then NNE to the summit of Foel-fras.

Descent: Head SSW then SW along the main ridge path to the col on the southwest side of Foel-fras. From the col join the Cwm Eigiau Path as it descends SE across the east flank of Foel Grach (the path is vague and can be difficult to locate in poor visibility) then S and finally SE to the old quarry tips and buildings in Cwm Eigiau. Join the access track and take it E then NE around Cwm Eigiau to the old dam. Cross the Afon Porth-llwyd and head NE along the access track to the car park at the road head.

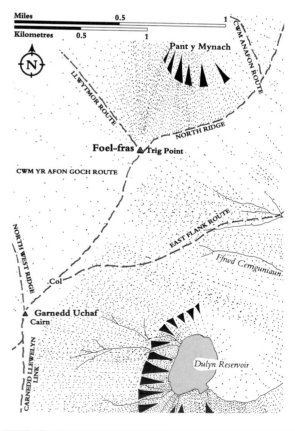

ELIDIR FAWR 3028FT (923M)

ELIDIR FAWR IS THE LAST major peak at the western end of the Glyders Massif. From its summit there is a distinct sense of being between the sea and the mountains. This perhaps comes about because of its position; detached and somewhat out on a limb its main axis lies at right angles to that of its nearest neighbour, Mynydd Perfedd, to which it is connected by the narrow neck of Bwlch y Marchlyn. From the rocky crest of the summit the views are starkly contrasting. To the west you can look out across the roads and towns of coastal plains towards the Menai Straits and to the east across the sharp relief of the Snowdonian mountains.

Sadly the vistas from the summit are not the only contrasts Elidir Fawr displays. The extensive slate quarrying on the west and north flanks have left ugly gaping holes and terraced tips like festering wounds – and if this were not enough of a blight a pumped-storage hydro-electric scheme has been built in chambers in the very heart of the mountain which takes its visual toll from day to day by raising and lowering the dammed Marchlyn Mawr Reservoir. In comparison the wild and lovely Cwm Dudodyn, the summit plateau and the head wall of Cwm Marchlyn, retain a little of the fastness that this once-fine mountain must have previously exhibited throughout.

The standard approach to Elidir Fawr is along the main ridge from Y Garn via Bwlch y Marchlyn, a route popular with walkers completing the 'Welsh 3000ers'. An interesting and quiet variation to this approach and the most direct route from the Ogwen Valley is to gain the main ridge via Cwm Cywion. From the Nant Peris side the two routes from Cwm Duododyn avoid the worst ravages of the quarries and provide steep but entertaining routes. The top section of the South Flank is particularly fine involving simple scrambling along the narrow rocky crest of the summit ridge. Approaches from the north are a little more problematic. Limited access from the Marchlyn Mawr Reservoir means that both the North Flank and the North Ridge have to be started from the north end of the Marchlyn Bach Reservoir. This does not greatly affect the North Ridge but it leads to a rather circuitous start to the North Flank Route.

MAPS
Ordnance Survey: Outdoor Leisure 1: 25000 No 17; Landranger 1: 50000 No 115.

INFORMATION
Tourist Information Centres: Caernarfon; Llanberis; Betws-y-Coed; Bangor.

ACCOMMODATION
Youth Hostels: Llanberis Pass: *Pen-y-pass*; Llanberis; Ogwen Valley: *Idwal Cottage*; Capel Curig.

Hotels and B&B: Nantgwryd: *Pen-y-Gwryd Hotel*; Nant Peris; Llanberis; Bethesda; Ogwen Valley; Capel Curig.

Camp sites: Llanberis Pass: *Nant Peris, Gwastadnant*; Llanberis: *Deiniolen*; Bethesda: *Ogwen Bank*; Ogwen Valley: *Gwern Gof Uchaf*: Capel Curig.

Elidir Fawr (**EF**) from Y Garn.
LP Llyn Peris, **LPa** Llyn Padarn,
SF South Flank

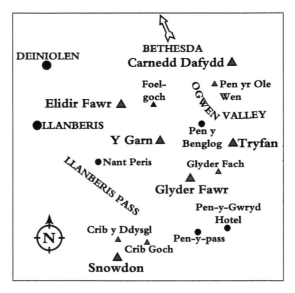

SOUTH FLANK

Grade: Intermediate
Time: 2.5 hours
Distance: 2.25 miles (3.6km)
Height Gain: 2671ft (814m)
Terrain: Steep pasture, steep-sided corrie, rocky ridge and narrow rocky summit
Start: Nant Peris, GR606584

Summary: An unremitting slog from the mouth of Cwm Dudodyn to the southwest end of Elidir Fawr's summit ridge. The final section on the summit ridge is entertaining involving some boulder hopping, but on balance this route probably best serves as a descent.

Ascent: From Nant Peris take the lane (opposite the post office) NE then NW to join a track. Continue generally NW along it as it climbs to the start of the Cwm Dudodyn Path. Follow the path as it zig-zags up to the Afon Dudodyn. The path follows the Afon Dudodyn NE, first on the south bank then over a foot-bridge onto the north bank. Continue along it to the mouth of Cwm Dudodyn proper then make the steep ascent NW up the South Flank. As the summit ridge is reached turn NE. Scramble easily up the crest to the summit cairn and shelter.

Descent: Scramble SW down the narrow crest of the summit ridge. As the angle steepens and the crest becomes less pronounced turn S and descend the steep South Flank to join the Cwm Dudodyn Path. Follow it generally SW alongside the Afon Dudodyn to a foot-bridge. Cross it and head W along the path to the top of a series of zig-zags. Descend the zig-zags and pick up the track then lane down into Nant Peris.

NORTH RIDGE

Grade: Easy
Time: 2 hours
Distance: 2.25 miles (3.6km)
Height Gain: 1972ft (601m)
Terrain: Moorland, rocky corrie, rounded ridge, high open col, scree and narrow summit ridge
Variation: If time allows, a detour up and down the access road to Marchlyn Mawr Reservoir is worth making to view the impressive Cwm Marchlyn.
Start: Talywaen on the east side of Deiniolen, GR594631

Summary: Climbs directly up the rounded North Ridge to the subsidiary peak Elidir Fach then gains Elidir Fawr via the expansive col and scree slopes of Bwlch Melynwyn. Elidir Fach affords panoramic views of the coast.

Ascent: From the road take the Marchlyn Mawr access road (part of the Dinorwig hydro-electric power scheme) ESE to the junction below the Marchlyn Bach Reservoir. Leave the road and ascend the ridge S to Elidir Fach. From the summit of Elidir Fach head SE and cross Bwlch Melynwyn to make the short but steep ascent to the summit ridge of Elidir Fawr. On the ridge turn NE and scramble easily up the crest to the summit cairn and shelter.

Descent: Scramble SW down the narrow crest of the summit ridge. As the angle steepens and the crest becomes less pronounced turn NW and descend the steep slope to Bwlch Melynwyn. Continue NW across the col to Elidir Fach then turn N and descend the North Ridge to the access road junction below the Marchlyn Bach Reservoir. Once on the main access road follow it WNW to the road near Talywaen.

The summit of Elidir Fawr with the Marchlyn Mawr Reservoir on the left

Summit cairn – Elidir Fach

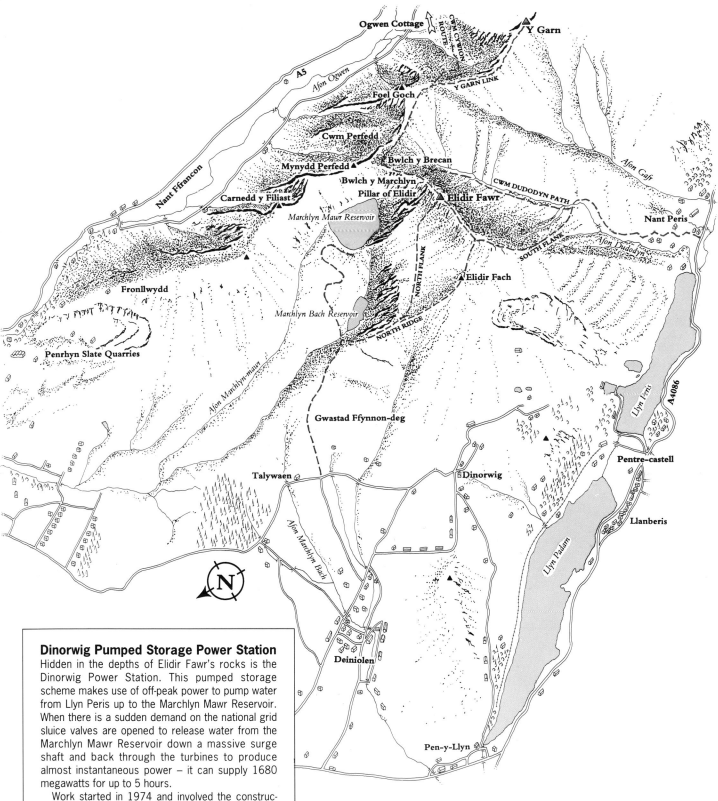

Ogwen Cottage

CWM CYWION ROUTE

A5

Afon Ogwen

Y Garn

Y GARN LINK

Foel Goch

Afon Cafr

Cwm Perfedd

Bwlch y Brecan

Mynydd Perfedd

Bwlch y Marchlyn

CWM DUDODYN PATH

Nant Ffrancon

Carnedd y Filiast

Pillar of Elidir

Elidir Fawr

Nant Peris

Marchlyn Mawr Reservoir

SOUTH FLANK

Afon Dudodyn

NORTH FLANK

Elidir Fach

Fronllwydd

Marchlyn Bach Reservoir

NORTH RIDGE

Afon Marchlyn-mawr

Llyn Peris

A4086

Penrhyn Slate Quarries

Gwastad Ffynnon-deg

Dinorwig

Pentre-castell

Llyn Padarn

Llanberis

Talywaen

Afon Marchlyn Bach

N

Deiniolen

Pen-y-Llyn

Dinorwig Pumped Storage Power Station

Hidden in the depths of Elidir Fawr's rocks is the Dinorwig Power Station. This pumped storage scheme makes use of off-peak power to pump water from Llyn Peris up to the Marchlyn Mawr Reservoir. When there is a sudden demand on the national grid sluice valves are opened to release water from the Marchlyn Mawr Reservoir down a massive surge shaft and back through the turbines to produce almost instantaneous power – it can supply 1680 megawatts for up to 5 hours.

Work started in 1974 and involved the construction of tunnels, machine halls, a massive surge shaft, the upper dam and alterations to Llyn Peris. All this took 10 years with the opening ceremony being carried out by the Prince of Wales in 1984.

Elidir Fawr from the Marchlyn Mawr Reservoir

NORTH FLANK ROUTE

Grade: Intermediate
Time: 2–2.5 hours
Distance: 2.25 miles (3.6km)
Height Gain: 1939ft (591m)
Terrain: Moorland, rocky corrie, rounded ridge, steep scree and narrow summit ridge
Variation: If time allows a detour up and down the access road to Marchlyn Mawr Reservoir is worth making to view the impressive Cwm Marchlyn.
Start: Talywaen on the east side of Deiniolen, GR594631

Summary: Ringed by dark and secretive crags Cwm Marchlyn cuts deeply into the north side of Elidir Fawr. Skirting the top of these crags the North Flank Route works a circuitous but interesting line to Elidir Fawr's rocky summit.

Ascent: From the road take the Marchlyn Mawr access road (part of the Dinorwig hydro-electric power scheme) ESE to the junction below the Marchlyn Bach Reservoir. Leave the road and ascend the ridge S to Elidir Fach. As the angle of the ridge eases at a shallow shoulder contour SE then E towards the edge of the crags of Cwm Marchlyn. Before the edge is reached turn S (in mist or snow this can be difficult to judge – better to err on the cautious side and turn early) and climb the steep scree-covered slopes to Elidir Fawr's summit ridge. On the ridge turn SW and follow the crest to the summit cairn and shelter.

Descent: Head NE along the summit ridge then turn N and descend the steep scree, skirting the top of Cwm Marchlyn's head wall (in mist or snow this can be difficult to judge – better to err on the cautious side and descend from Elidir Fawr's summit NW past Bwlch Melynwyn). Before the bottom of the slope is reached contour W then NW to the shallow shoulder on the north side of Elidir Fach. Descend the North Ridge to the access road junction below the Marchlyn Bach Reservoir. Once on the main access road follow it WNW to the road near Talywaen.

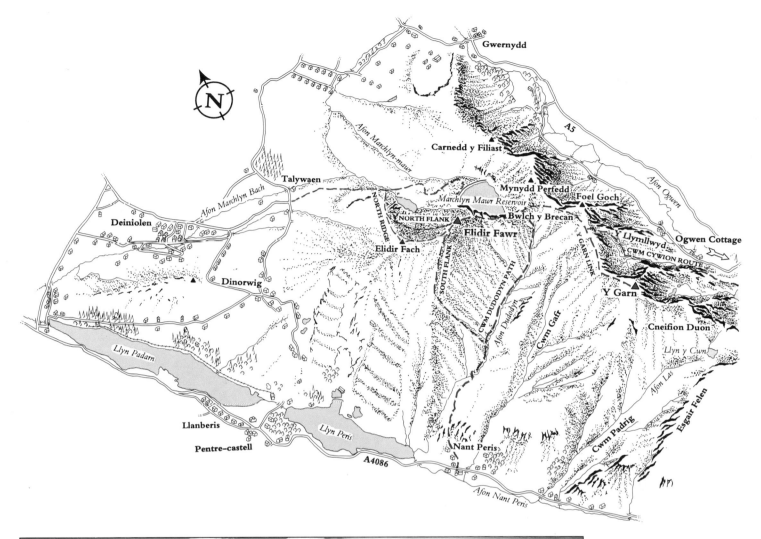

Gwernydd

Afon Marchlyn-mawr

A5

Carnedd y Filiast

Afon Ogwen

Talywaen

Mynydd Perfedd

Foel Goch

Afon Marchlyn Bach

Marchlyn Mawr Reservoir

Bwlch y Brecan

Deiniolen

NORTH FLANK

Elidir Fawr

Y Llymllwyd

Ogwen Cottage

NORTH RIDGE

CWM CYWION ROUTE

Elidir Fach

GARN LINK

Dinorwig

SOUTH FLANK

Y Garn

CWM DUDODYN PATH

Afon Dudodyn

Cwm Gafr

Cneifion Duon

Cwm Padrig

Llyn y Cwn

Llyn Padarn

Afon Las

Esgair Felen

Llanberis

Llyn Peris

Pentre-castell

Nant Peris

A4086

Afon Nant Peris

The North Flank of Elidir Fawr
and the Marchlyn Bach
Reservoir

CWM CYWION ROUTE

Grade: Intermediate
Time: 2.5–3 hours
Distance: 3.5 miles (5.6km)
Height Gain: 2178ft (664m)
Terrain: Broad craggy corrie, mountain lake, steep rocky slope, high open corrie, rounded mountain ridge, exposed col and narrow summit ridge
Start: Ogwen Cottage (Pen y Benglog), GR650603

Summary: The remote and little-visited Cwm Cywion provides a handy approach to Elidir Fawr from the Ogwen Valley.

Ascent: From Ogwen Cottage take the Cwm Idwal Path SE then SW to Llyn Idwal. Cross the footbridge at the northeast end of the lake and follow the vague path which snakes up to the base of the Northeast Ridge of Y Garn. Before the base of the ridge is reached leave the path and contour round the steep slopes NW into Cwm Cywion. Continue NW up through Cwm Cywion to Llyn Cywion then ascend the head wall, still generally NW, to Bwlch y Cywion. Cross the col and make the short descent to join the path on the southwest side of Foel-goch. Turn R and follow it N then W around the head of Cwm Dudodyn to Bwlch y Marchlyn. From the col climb the steep narrow ridge WSW to the summit of Elidir Fawr.

Descent: Descend the path and then the ridge ENE to Bwlch y Marchlyn. Cross the exposed col then contour E then S around the head of Cwm Dudodyn. On the southwest side of the summit slopes of Foel-goch make the short ascent E to Bwlch y Cywion. Cross the col and make the steep descent SE to Llyn Cywion. Continue descending SE through Cwm Cywion and contour around to the bottom of the Northeast Ridge of Y Garn. At the base of the ridge join the vague path and follow it ESE to the footbridge at the northeast end of Llyn Idwal. Cross it and join the Ogwen Cottage Path which is followed NE then NW to the buildings and car park at Ogwen Cottage.

Summit cairn – Elidir Fawr

Y GARN LINK

Grade: Easy
Time: 1–1.5 hours
Distance: 2.5 miles (4km)
Height Gain: 718ft (219m)
Terrain: High mountain ridge, exposed col and narrow summit ridge
Start: Elidir Fawr, GR612613

Summary: Pleasant high-level walk between two fine mountains with excellent views into the more remote corries of the Glyders Massif.

Route: Descend the path and then the ridge ENE down to Bwlch y Marchlyn. Cross the exposed col then contour E then S around the head of Cwm Dudodyn. Past Foel-goch continue generally S to the col on the northwest side of Y Garn. Across the col trend SE and climb the steep summit slopes to Y Garn.

Descending west from the summit of Elidir Fawr
(Phil Iddon/Sheila Iddon)

CWM DUDODYN PATH

Grade: Intermediate
Time: 2.5–3 hours
Distance: 3.25 miles (5.2km)
Height Gain: 2671ft (814m)
Terrain: Steep pasture, steep-sided corrie and narrow rocky summit
Start: Nant Peris, GR606584

Summary: Cwm Dudodyn's southerly aspect and its verdant interior make it an inviting place to explore. Looks can be misleading though, for although it provides a pleasant enough approach to Elidir Fawr it is longer than it would first appear and its head wall is very steep grassland.

Ascent: From Nant Peris take the lane (opposite the post office) NE then NW to join a track. Continue generally NW along it as it climbs to the start of the Cwm Dudodyn Path. Follow the path as it zig-zags up to the Afon Dudodyn. The path follows the Afon Dudodyn NE, first on the south bank then over a footbridge onto the north bank. Continue NE ascending the length of Cwm Dudodyn. At the head of Cwm Dudodyn turn NW and climb the very steep grassy slope to Bwlch y Marchlyn. From the col climb the steep narrow ridge WSW to the summit of Elidir Fawr.

Descent: Descend the path and then the ridge ENE down to Bwlch y Marchlyn. From the col turn SE to descend the steep grassy slope into Cwm Dudodyn. Follow the vague path SW alongside the Afon Dudodyn to a footbridge. Cross it and head W along the path to the top of a series of zig-zags. Descend the zig-zags and pick up the track then the lane down into Nant Peris.

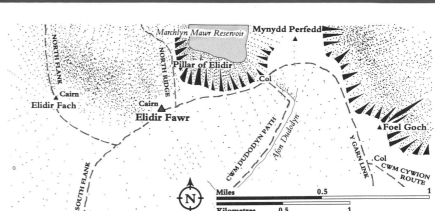

Cwm Dudodyn footbridge

The footbridge over the Afon Dudodyn below the start of the South Flank

TRYFAN
3002FT (915M)

THERE CAN BE FEW MOUNTAINS which more readily fit the description of one of Britain's Highest Peaks than Tryfan. This fine 'shark's fin' of a mountain is separated from its neighbours, the Glyders, by the gulf of Bwlch Tryfan. Displaying nothing but steep crags and ridges from whichever angle it is viewed it epitomises the classic mountain. This is ironic as Tryfan only just scrapes past the magic 3000ft mark.

Set in a high, prominent position between Cwm Tryfan and Cwm Bochlwyd on the south side of the Ogwen Valley it is just possible to view all of Tryfan's facets and features from the valley floor. Because of its open nature Tryfan generates a friendly atmosphere and it is a welcome and familiar sight providing a key landmark when either travelling along the valley road or walking on the surrounding hills.

This friendly face can be a little misleading, however. All the routes cross ground which is rocky and involves sections of scrambling. The classic line on Tryfan, and the classic route of its type in Wales, is the North Ridge. It climbs directly from the A5 by the side of Llyn Ogwen to the summit rocks providing over 3500ft of almost continuous scrambling. For those with a thirst for scrambling, a popular expedition is to ascend the North Ridge then descend the easier South Ridge to Bwlch Tryfan from where an ascent of Bristly Ridge gives access to the Glyders Massif.

Tryfan is not only a popular mountain with walkers; climbers are understandably drawn to its fine crags as well. The two main areas of interest are the slabs of Milestone Buttress at the foot of the North Ridge and the three main buttresses and associated gullies of the east face. Access to the east face is gained along Heather Terrace – a distinct diagonal break which rises steadily from north to south across their base.

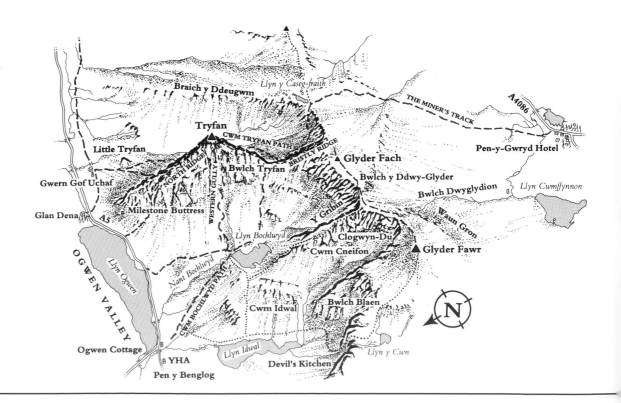

Tryfan (**T**) from the A5.
CT Cwm Tryfan, **SP** South
Peak, **HT** Heather Terrace,
CB Central Buttress, **SG** South
Gully, **NG** North Gully,
NR North Ridge

MAPS

Ordnance Survey: Outdoor Leisure 1: 25000 No 17; Landranger 1: 50000 No 115.

INFORMATION

Tourist Information Centres: Caernarfon; Llanberis; Betws-y-Coed; Bangor.

ACCOMMODATION

Youth Hostels: Llanberis Pass: *Pen-y-pass*; Llanberis; Ogwen Valley: *Idwal Cottage*; Capel Curig.

Hotels and B&B: Nantgwryd: *Pen-y-Gwryd Hotel*; Nant Peris; Llanberis; Bethesda; Ogwen Valley; Capel Curig.

Camp sites: Llanberis Pass: *Nant Peris, Gwastadnant*; Llanberis: *Deiniolen*; Bethesda: *Ogwen Bank*; Ogwen Valley: *Gwern Gof Uchaf*; Capel Curig.

'Adam and Eve'

THE MINER'S TRACK

Grade: Intermediate
Time: 2.5 hours
Distance: 2.5 miles (4km)
Height Gain: 2264ft (690m)
Terrain: Open rocky mountainside, bleak col, scree and boulders, high col, rocky ridge and rocky summit
Start: A4086 near the Pen-y-Gwryd Hotel, GR661559

Summary: Works a devious course around the east flank of Glyder Fach to gain Tryfan's South Ridge via a traverse around the head of Cwm Tryfan. A surprisingly direct route which avoids any major re-ascent crossing the main Glyders ridge.

Ascent: From the side of the A4086 take the footpath NW to the footbridge. Cross it and follow the path NE as it climbs steadily up the south and east flanks of Glyder Fach. As the crest of the main ridge line is reached the path turns N. Follow it across the col to the top of the steep slope at the head of Cwm Tryfan. Drop down the slope and follow the path NW around the head wall to Bwlch Tryfan. From the col take the path N up the South Ridge of Tryfan (avoiding the Far South Peak on its west side) and scramble up Tryfan's crest to the summit blocks.

Descent: From the summit blocks follow the path down the South Ridge (avoiding the Far South Peak on its west side) to Bwlch Tryfan. From the col descend SE and follow The Miner's Track as it skirts around the head of Cwm Tryfan to the bleak col on the east side of Glyder Fach. Descend S then SW from the col to the footbridge across the Nant Gwryd. Once across head SE to the A4086.

'Adam and Eve' – Tryfan's summit rocks

GLYDERS LINK (BRISTLY RIDGE)

Grade: Strenuous or intermediate (Grade 1 scramble; Grade 1 winter climb)
Time: 1–1.5 hours
Distance: 1 mile (1.6km) – to Glyder Fach
Height Gain: 883ft (269m)
Terrain: Rocky ridge, high col, narrow rocky ridge, high mountain ridge and stony summit slopes
Variation: The difficulties of Bristly Ridge can be avoided by following the scree path on the east side of the ridge.
Start: Tryfan's summit, GR664594

Summary: Steep and imposing, the pinnacled crest of Bristly Ridge presents a daunting sight. It is justifiably popular as it provides an adventurous scramble – the most direct link between Tryfan and Glyder Fach. Although it is only a Grade 1 scramble its difficulties should not be underestimated as there are a number of harder alternative lines which are easy to wander onto.

Route: From Tryfan's summit blocks follow the path down the South Ridge (avoiding the Far South Peak on its west side) to Bwlch Tryfan. Cross the col and ascend the scree to the mouth of a gully system at the base of Bristly Ridge. Follow the gully, turning the difficult sections on the L, to gain the crest of the ridge via a short traverse R (when wet the gully system can be particularly difficult). Follow the crest over the undulations of the pinnacles (all the steep sections can be avoided) to join the main Glyders ridge on the east side of Glyder Fach. Turn R and follow the main ridge path WSW over Glyder Fach and over Bwlch y Ddwy-Glyder to Glyder Fawr.

CWM BOCHLWYD PATH

Grade: Intermediate
Time: 2 hours
Distance: 1.75 miles (2.8km)
Height Gain: 2018ft (615m)
Terrain: Rocky slope, broad open corrie, high col, rocky ridge and rocky summit
Variation: Cwm Bochlwyd can also be gained from the A5 via the path that starts at GR658602.
Start: Ogwen Cottage (Pen y Benglog), GR650603

Summary: The path climbing steadily across the floor of Cwm Bochlwyd gives the easiest approach to Tryfan, although the South Ridge section involves some simple scrambling.

Ascent: From Ogwen Cottage take the Cwm Idwal Path SE to a fork at the first bend. Take the left branch and continue SE to Cwm Bochlwyd. Cross the Nant Bochlwyd and climb SE to Bwlch Tryfan. At the col turn L and take the path N up the South Ridge of Tryfan (avoiding the Far South Peak on its west side) and scramble up Tryfan's crest to the summit blocks.

Descent: From the summit blocks follow the path down the South Ridge (avoiding the Far South Peak on its west side) to Bwlch Tryfan. From the col descend NW and follow the path down to Llyn Bochlwyd. Cross the Nant Bochlwyd and continue NW down to Ogwen Cottage.

Overleaf: 'The Cannon', North Ridge of Tryfan with Y Garn in the background
(Peter Hodgkiss)

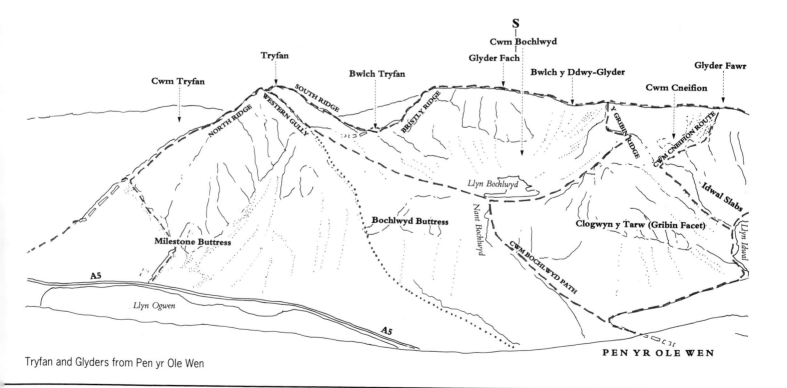

Tryfan and Glyders from Pen yr Ole Wen

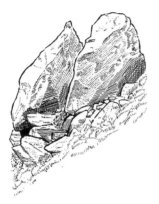

Split block on Heather Terrace that marks the start of Central Buttress

WESTERN GULLY

Grade: Strenuous
Time: 2–2.5 hours
Distance: 1.5 miles (2.4km)
Height Gain: 2018ft (615m)
Terrain: Rocky slope, broad open corrie, broad scree-filled gully and rocky summit
Variation: Cwm Bochlwyd can also be gained from the A5 via the path that starts at GR658602.
Start: Ogwen Cottage (Pen y Benglog), GR650603

Summary: A broad scree-filled gully which climbs directly up the west face of Tryfan. An unremitting slog in ascent, best saved for descent.

Ascent: From Ogwen Cottage take the Cwm Idwal Path SE to a fork at the first bend. Take the left branch and continue SE to Cwm Bochlwyd. Cross the Nant Bochlwyd then climb E directly up the slope to the mouth of Western Gully which is followed to Tryfan's summit slope.

Descent: From the summit blocks head N then turn almost immediately W and descend the path steeply down the scree. Out of the gully and on to the lower slopes keep descending W to the north end of Llyn Bochlwyd. Cross the Nant Bochlwyd and head NW down to Ogwen Cottage.

NORTH RIDGE

Grade: Strenuous (Grade 1 scramble)
Time: 2 hours
Distance: 0.75 miles (1.2km)
Height Gain: 1998ft (609m)
Terrain: Steep craggy ridge
Variation: Via Milestone Buttress (Grade 2/3 scramble).
Start: A5 at the side of Llyn Ogwen, GR663603

Summary: Unremitting line direct from the road to the summit rocks. An entertaining scramble with numerous variations both easy and difficult – a classic route.

Ascent: From the stile on the A5 take the path alongside the wall as it climbs S then SE, to join the North Ridge proper. The ridge is deceptively broad, the most interesting scrambling being found on the crest. Follow the ridge directly over the subsidiary summits to the summit blocks – Adam and Eve.

Descent: Although the North Ridge is used as a descent route it is better to have completed its ascent first. The easiest line is a path running parallel with the ridge a short distance down the east face which can be gained by descending a slab on the east side of the summit blocks.

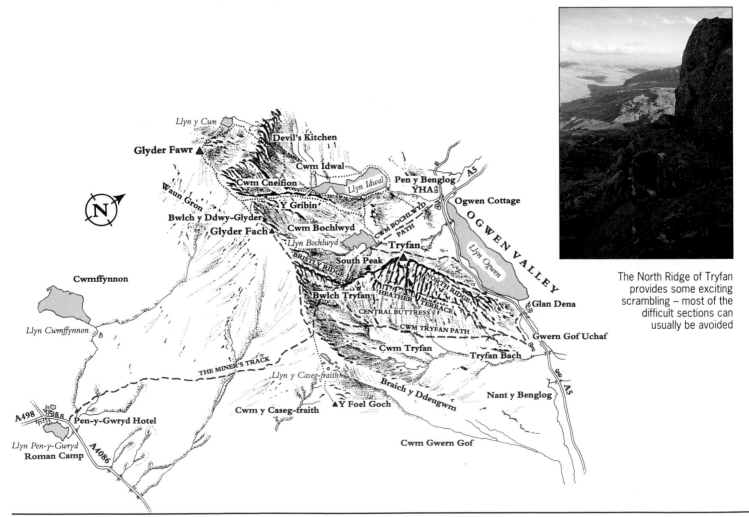

The North Ridge of Tryfan provides some exciting scrambling – most of the difficult sections can usually be avoided

CENTRAL BUTTRESS

Grade: Strenuous (Grade 1 scramble)
Time: 2.5 hours
Distance: 1.5 miles (2.4km)
Height Gain: 1998ft (609m)
Terrain: Rough pasture, steep rock and heather-covered mountainside, steep shallow gully, rock amphitheatre, steep head wall and rocky summit
Variation: The north end of Heather Terrace can be gained from Bwlch Tryfan or via The Miner's Track.
Start: From the A5 opposite Glan Dena, GR668605

Summary: Exploiting the easy sections of Little Gully and North Gully this scramble up Tryfan's Central Buttress makes a superb expedition. The start can be tricky to find but once located the route is easy to follow with short but entertaining technical sections and fine views across the east face.

Ascent: From the A5 take the track E towards Gwern Gof Uchaf. Before the farm turn R and head SW towards Tryfan Bach. Below the slabs of Tryfan Bach turn R and follow the narrow winding path that climbs W then SW to Heather Terrace (avoid the narrower terrace below Heather Terrace – it is easy to confuse the two). Once on Heather Terrace follow it as it climbs steadily SSW across the base of Tryfan's east-face crags. It crosses a number of gully lines which can be confusing; the start of Little Gully is marked by a split block through which Heather Terrace passes (just after crossing the bed of North Gully). Scramble up the ramp on the left side of Little Gully then up its bed to a col. Cross the col and follow the groove system and ledge into the upper reaches of North Gully. Take the zig-zags up the amphitheatre then traverse L across its head, finally climbing the head wall to the summit.

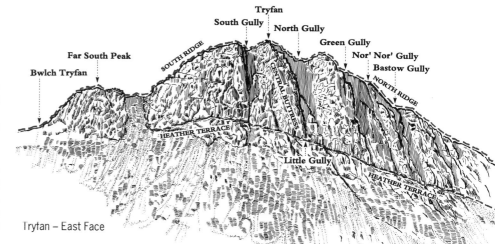

Tryfan – East Face

HEATHER TERRACE

Grade: Intermediate
Time: 2–2.5 hours
Distance: 1.5 miles (2.4km)
Height Gain: 1998ft (609m)
Terrain: Rough pasture, steep rock and heather-covered mountainside, crags, high col, rocky ridge and rocky summit
Variation: The north end of Heather Terrace can also be gained from the A5 by crossing the base of the North Ridge (from the side of Llyn Ogwen, GR663603).
Start: From the A5 opposite Glan Dena, GR668605

Summary: Essentially a climbers' access route to the base of Tryfan's east face it also provides a useful route to or from the South Ridge.

Ascent: From the A5 take the track E towards Gwern Gof Uchaf. Before the farm turn R and head SW towards Tryfan Bach. Below the slabs of Tryfan Bach turn R and follow the narrow winding path that climbs W then SW to Heather Terrace (avoid the narrower terrace below Heather Terrace – it is easy to confuse the two). Once on Heather Terrace follow it as it climbs steadily SSW across the base of Tryfan's east-face crags and then climbs W up to the col between the South Ridge and the Far South Peak. At the col turn R and take the path N up the South Ridge scrambling up its crest to the summit blocks.

Descent: From the summit blocks follow the path down the South Ridge to the col on the north side of the Far South Peak. From the col descend E to the top of Heather Terrace. Follow the terrace as it swings NNE then descends across the base of the east face. At the end of Heather Terrace turn NE and descend steeply to join the Cwm Tryfan Path by Tryfan Bach. Join it and continue NE along it down to Gwern Gof Uchaf. Before the farm turn L and take the track W to the A5.

Cairn at the top of Heather Terrace on the col between Tryfan and Far South Peak GR663592

The first section of Central Buttress

Descending the South Ridge of Tryfan

CWM TRYFAN PATH

Grade: Strenuous
Time: 2.5 hours
Distance: 2.25 miles (3.6km)
Height Gain: 1998ft (609m)
Terrain: Rough pasture, rough open corrie, scree and boulders, high col, rocky ridge and rocky summit
Start: From the A5 opposite Glan Dena, GR668605

Summary: A rough corrie in the shadow of Tryfan's impressive east face provides a lonely route to Bwlch Tryfan at the base of the South Ridge.

Ascent: From the A5 take the track E toward Gwern Gof Uchaf. Before the farm turn R and head SW towards Tryfan Bach. Pass below the slabs of Tryfan Bach and continue generally SW to enter the rough bounds of Cwm Tryfan. Follow the narrow path as it works its way to the corrie head then climbs W to Bwlch Tryfan. At the col turn R and take the path N up the South Ridge (avoiding the Far South Peak on its west side) and scramble up Tryfan's crest to the summit blocks.

Descent: From the summit blocks follow the path down the South Ridge (avoiding the Far South Peak on its west side) to Bwlch Tryfan. From the col descend E to the head of Cwm Tryfan then turn NNE and make the steady descent by the narrow path along the corrie floor to Tryfan Bach. Pass the slabs of Tryfan Bach and head NE towards Gwern Gof Uchaf. Before the farm turn L and take the track W to the A5.

Tryfan's summit

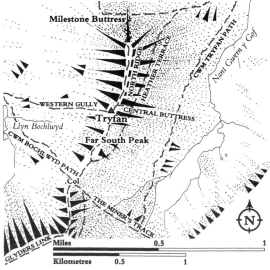

INDEX OF PEAKS AND ROUTES

Anoach Beag, *98*
Allt Daim Path, *101*
An Cul Choire Path, *101*
Aonach Mor Link, *105*
Carn Mor Dearg Link, *105*
Coire Bhealaich Path, *103*
Coire Guibhsachan Path, *100*
Sgurr a' Bhuic Path, *104*
Southwest Ridge, *104*

Aonach Mor, *106*
Allt Daim Path, *109*
An Cul Choire Path, *113*
Aonach an Nid Ridge, *110*
Aonach Beag Link, *112*
Carn Mor Dearg Link, *112*
Coire Guibhsachan Path, *109*
East-Northeast Ridge, *111*
East Ridge, *111*
Lemming Ridge, *110*
Meall Beag Ridge, *109*
Stob an Cul Choire Path, *112*

Ben Macdui, *60*
Coire Cas Track, *68*
Coire Clach nan Taillear
    Path, *63*
Coire Etchachan Path, *69*
Coire Mor Path, *64*
Fiacaill Coire an t-Sneachda, *67*
Garbh Uisge Path, *68*
Loch Etchachan Path, *69*
Lurcher's Crag Path, *66*
March Burn Path, *65*
Sron Riach Path, *62*

Ben Nevis, *48*
Carn Dearg (Southwest) Path, *54*
Carn Mor Dearg Arête, *59*
Coire Leis Route, *58*
Ledge Route, *56*
Pony Track, *55*
South Flank Route, *52*

Braeriach, *70*
Cairn Toul Link, *79*
Coire an Lochain Ridge, *76*
Creag an Loch Ridge, *73*
Duke's Path, *77*
Moine Mhor Path, *73*
Northwest Flank, *75*
South Flank, *78*
Southeast Spur, *78*
Southwest Ridge, *71*
Sron na Lairige Path, *77*
Stalkers' Path, *74*
Broad Crag, *8*

Cairn Gorm, *89*
Ben Macdui Link, *92*
Coire Cas Track, *94*
Coire Domhain Path, *91*
Coire na Ciste Path, *96*

Coire Raibeirt Path, *90*
Fiacaill a' Coire Chais, *94*
Fiacaill Coire an t-Sneachda, *94*
Lurcher's Crag Path, *92*
North Ridge, *97*
Southeast Flank, *90*

Cairn Toul, *80*
Braeriach Link, *87*
Coire Odhar Path, *88*
Creag an Loch Ridge, *83*
Crown Buttress Spur, *87*
East Ridge, *88*
Moine Mhor Path, *83*
Northeast Ridge, *86*
Southwest Ridge, *82*
Stalkers' Path, *85*
Carn Dearg Northwest, *48*

Carn Mor Dearg, *114*
Aonachs Link, *118*
Ben Nevis Link, *119*
Carn Mor Dearg Arête, *115*
East Ridge, *119*
North Flank, *115*
Northeast Ridge, *116*
Northwest Flank, *115*
Pinnacle Ridge, *117*

Carnedd Dafydd, *138*
Braich Ty Du, *140*
Carnedd Llewelyn Link, *141*
Craig-Llugwy Spur, *144*
Cwm Llafar Route, *142*
East Ridge, *142*
Llech Ddu Spur, *141*
Northwest Ridge, *140*
South Ridge, *139*

Carnedd Llewelyn, *130*
Amphitheatre Gully, *137*
Carnedd Dafydd Link, *133*
Craig-fawr Spur, *136*
Cwm Bychan Route, *135*
Cwm Eigiau Path, *137*
Cwm Llafar Route, *134*
Cwm yr Afon Goch Route, *136*
Foel-fras Link, *135*
Northeast Ridge (Yr Elen), *132*
Northwest Ridge (Garnedd
    Uchaf), *135*
Northwest Ridge (Yr Elen), *134*
Southeast Ridge, *132*
Crib Goch, *121*
Crib y Ddysgl, *121*

Einich Cairn, *70*

Elidir Fawr, *167*
Cwm Cywion Route, *172*
Cwm Dudodyn Path, *173*
North Flank Route, *170*
North Ridge, *168*
South Flank, *168*
Y Garn Link, *172*

Foel-fras, *160*
Carnedd Llewelyn Link, *161*
Craig-fawr Spur, *166*
Cwm Anafon Route, *164*
Cwm Eigiau Path, *166*
Cwm Wen Route, *162*
Cwm yr Afon Goch Route, *164*
East Flank Route, *164*
Llwytmor Route, *166*
North Ridge, *165*
Northwest Ridge (Garnedd
    Uchaf), *163*
Foel Grach, *130*

Garnedd Uchaf, *130*
Glyder Fach, *146*

Glyder Fawr, *146*
Bristly Ridge, *150*
Cwm Cneifion Route, *149*
Cwm Tryfan Path, *153*
Cwmffynnon Route, *153*
Devil's Kitchen Path – *see* Twll
    Du Path
Llyn y Cwn Path, *148*
The Miner's Track, *153*
South Ridge, *147*
Tryfan Link, *151*
Twll Du Path, *149*
Y Garn Link, *148*
Y Gribin Ridge, *150*

Helvellyn, *24*
Grisedale Hause Track, *26*
Grisedale Track, *36*
Helvellyn Gill Path, *29*
Kepple Cove Track, *32*
Nethermost Pike – East Ridge, *36*
The Old Pony Route, *29*
Raise Beck Path, *27*
Sticks Pass (from Greenside), *31*
Sticks Pass (from Stanah), *30*
Striding Edge, *35*
Swirral Edge, *33*
Wythburn Path, *29*

Ill Crag, *8*

Lower Man, *24*

North Plateau (Braeriach), *70*
North Top (Ben Macdui), *60*

Pen yr Ole Wen, *138*

Scafell, *16*
Brown Tongue Path, *20*
Cam Spout Route, *23*
Corridor Route, *21*
Green How Path, *20*
Hard Rigg Path, *18*
via Rossett Gill (from
    Langdale), *22*

Slight Side Path, *18*
Scafell Pike, *8*
Brown Tongue Path, *12*
Cam Spout Route, *12*
Corridor Route, *13*
Grains Gill, *15*
Little Narrowcove Path, *10*
via Rossett Gill (from
    Langdale), *15*
Skew Gill and Great End, *14*
Sgor an Lochain Uaine, *80*

Skiddaw, *37*
Bakestall Path, *44*
Barkbethdale Path, *44*
Carl Side Path, *43*
Jenkin Hill Path, *38*
Longside Edge, *43*
Sale How Path, *45*
Slades Gill Path, *40*

Snowdon (yr Wyddfa), *121*
Clogwyn Du'r Arddu – *see*
    Eastern Terrace
Crib Goch, *126*
Eastern Terrace, *125*
Llanberis Path, *125*
The Miners' Track, *128*
Pyg Track, *127*
Rhyd-Ddu Path, *123*
Snowdon Ranger Path, *124*
South Ridge, *123*
Southeast Ridge, *129*
Watkin Path, *129*
Y Gribin, *128*
South Plateau (Braeriach), *70*
Stob Coire Sputan Dearg, *60*
Symonds Knott, *16*

Tryfan, *174*
Bristly Ridge – *see* Glyders Link
Central Buttress, *181*
Cwm Bochlwyd Path, *177*
Cwm Tryfan Path, *182*
Glyders Link, *177*
Heather Terrace, *181*
The Miner's Track, *176*
North Ridge, *180*
Western Gully, *180*

Y Garn, *154*
Cwm Cywion Route, *158*
Cwm Gafr Path, *156*
Devil's Kitchen Path – *see* Twll
    Du Path
Elidir Fawr Link, *156*
Glyder Fawr Link, *159*
Llyn y Cwn Path, *156*
Northeast Ridge, *158*
Southwest Ridge, *157*
Twll Du Path, *159*
Yr Elen, *130*
Yr Wyddfa – *see* Snowdon